<u>Legal</u>

ISBN-13: 978-1515068372
ISBN-10: 1515068374

BOOKS FROM THE GET 800 COLLECTION FOR COLLEGE BOUND STUDENTS

28 SAT Math Lessons to Improve Your Score in One Month
> Beginner Course
> Intermediate Course
> Advanced Course

320 SAT Math Problems Arranged by Topic and Difficulty Level

320 SAT Math Subject Test Problems Arranged by Topic and Difficulty Level
> Level 1 Test
> Level 2 Test

SAT Prep Book of Advanced Math Problems

The 32 Most Effective SAT Math Strategies

SAT Prep Official Study Guide Math Companion

SAT Vocabulary Book

320 ACT Math Problems arranged by Topic and Difficulty Level

320 AP Calculus AB Problems Arranged by Topic and Difficulty Level

320 AP Calculus BC Problems Arranged by Topic and Difficulty Level

555 Math IQ Questions for Middle School Students

555 Geometry Problems for High School Students

Algebra Handbook for Gifted Middle School Students

New SAT Math Problems arranged by Topic and Difficulty Level

New SAT Verbal Prep Book for Reading and Writing Mastery

CONNECT WITH DR. STEVE WARNER

www.facebook.com/SATPrepGet800

www.youtube.com/TheSATMathPrep

www.twitter.com/SATPrepGet800

www.linkedin.com/in/DrSteveWarner

www.pinterest.com/SATPrepGet800

plus.google.com/+SteveWarnerPhD

New AP Calculus BC Problems arranged by Topic and Difficulty Level

320 Level 1, 2, 3, 4, and 5 AP Calculus Problems

Dr. Steve Warner

Table of Contents

Actions to Complete Before You Read This Book   vi

v

ACTIONS TO COMPLETE BEFORE YOU READ THIS BOOK

1. Register for my forum

When you get stuck on any AP Calculus problems you can post your questions in the AP Calculus section of my forum. Sign up for free here:

www.satprepget800.com/forum

2. Sign up for additional AB problems

Visit the following webpage and enter your email address to receive additional AP Calculus AB problems with solutions:

www.thesatmathprep.com/320APCalSup.html

*T*here are many ways that a student can prepare for the AP Calculus BC exam. But not all preparation is created equal. I always teach my students the methods that will give them the maximum result with the minimum amount of effort.

The book you are now reading is self-contained. Each problem was carefully created to ensure that you are making the most effective use of your time while preparing for the AP Calculus exam. By grouping the problems given here by level and topic I have ensured that you can focus on the types of problems that will be most effective to improving your score.

Important: This book was written for the AP Calculus BC exam being given in May 2017. If you are taking the May 2016 exam, visit the following website where you can download the appropriate book at no additional charge:

www.thesatmathprep.com/320APCalSup.html

1. Using this book effectively
- Begin studying at least three months before the AP Calculus exam
- Practice AP Calculus problems twenty to thirty minutes each day
- Choose a consistent study time and location

You will retain much more of what you study if you study in short bursts rather than if you try to tackle everything at once. So try to choose about a thirty minute block of time that you will dedicate to AP Calculus each day. Make it a habit. The results are well worth this small time commitment.

- Every time you get a question wrong, **mark it off, no matter what your mistake**.
- Begin each study session by first redoing problems from previous study sessions that you have marked off.
- If you get a problem wrong again, **keep it marked off**.

2. Overview of the AP Calculus exam

There are four types of questions that you will encounter on the AP Calculus exam:

- Multiple choice questions where calculators are not allowed (Section 1, Part A, 30 Questions, 60 Minutes).
- Multiple choice questions where calculators are allowed (Section 1, Part B, 15 Questions, 45 Minutes).
- Free response questions where calculators are allowed (Section 2, Part A, 2 Questions, 30 Minutes).
- Free response questions where calculators are not allowed (Section 2, Part B, 4 Questions, 60 Minutes).

This book will prepare you for all of these question types. In this book, questions that require a calculator are marked with an asterisk (*).

If a question is not marked with an asterisk, then it could show up on a part where a calculator is or is not allowed. I therefore recommend always trying to solve each of these questions both with and without a calculator. It is especially important that you can solve these without a calculator.

The AP Calculus exam is graded on a scale of 1 through 5, with a score of 3 or above interpreted as "qualified." To get a 3 on the exam you will need to get about 50% of the questions correct.

Approximately 60% of the questions on the BC exam are actually AB questions. You will be given an AB subscore based on your performance on these questions. So it is possible to get a high AB subscore while getting a low overall score. In this case you will most likely get college credit for the AB exam, but not for the BC exam.

3. Structure of this book

This book has been organized in such a way to produce maximum results with the least amount of effort. Every question that is in this book is similar to a question that has appeared on an actual AP Calculus exam. Furthermore, just about every question type that you can expect to encounter is covered in this book.

The organization of this book is by Level and Topic. At first you want to practice each of the four general math topics given on the AP Calculus BC exam and improve in each independently. The four topics are **Differentiation**, **Integration**, **Limits and Continuity**, and **Series**.

The first 2 Levels are broken into these four topics. Levels 3 and 4 are broken into just three of these topics, differentiation, integration, and series. And Level 5 mixes all the topics together in the form of free response questions just like the ones you will encounter in Section 2 of the exam.

Speaking of Level, you will want to progress through the 5 Levels of difficulty at your own pace. Stay at each Level as long as you need to. Keep redoing each problem you get wrong over and over again until you can get each one right on your own.

I strongly recommend that for each topic you *do not* move on to the next level until you are getting most of the questions from the previous level correct. This will reduce your frustration and keep you from burning out.

There are two parts to this book. The first part contains 160 problems, and the solution to each problem appears right after the problem is given. The second part contains 160 supplemental problems with an answer key at the very end. Full solutions to the supplemental problems are not given in this book. Most of these additional problems are similar to problems from the first section, but the limits, derivatives, integrals, and series tend to be a bit more challenging.

Any student that can successfully answer all 160 questions from *either* part of this book should be able to get a 5 on the BC exam.

Additional AP Calculus AB questions organized by Level and Topic are available as a free digital download at

<u>www.thesatmathprep.com/320APCalSup.html</u>

4. Practice in small amounts over a long period of time
Ideally you want to practice doing AP Calculus problems twenty to thirty minutes each day beginning at least three months before the exam. You will retain much more of what you study if you study in short bursts than if you try to tackle everything at once.

So try to choose about a thirty minute block of time that you will dedicate to AP Calculus every night. Make it a habit. The results are well worth this small time commitment.

5. Redo the problems you get wrong over and over and over until you get them right

If you get a problem wrong, and never attempt the problem again, then it is extremely unlikely that you will get a similar problem correct if it appears on the AP exam.

Most students will read an explanation of the solution, or have someone explain it to them, and then never look at the problem again. This is *not* how you optimize your score on a standardized test. To be sure that you will get a similar problem correct on the actual exam, you must get the problem correct before the exam—and without actually remembering the problem.

This means that after getting a problem incorrect, you should go over and understand why you got it wrong, wait at least a few days, then attempt the same problem again. If you get it right you can cross it off your list of problems to review. If you get it wrong, keep revisiting it every few days until you get it right. Your score *does not* improve by getting problems correct. **Your score improves when you learn from your mistakes.**

6. Check your answers properly

When you are taking the exam and you go back to check your earlier answers for careless errors *do not* simply look over your work to try to catch a mistake. This is usually a waste of time. Always redo the problem without looking at any of your previous work. If possible, use a different method than you used the first time.

7. Take a guess whenever you cannot solve a problem

There is no guessing penalty on the AP Calculus BC exam. Whenever you do not know how to solve a problem take a guess. Ideally you should eliminate as many answer choices as possible before taking your guess, but if you have no idea whatsoever do not waste time overthinking. Simply put down an answer and move on. You should certainly mark it off and come back to it later if you have time.

Try not to leave free response questions completely blank. Begin writing anything you can related to the problem. The act of writing can often spark some insight into how to solve the problem, and even if it does not, you may still get some partial credit.

8. Pace yourself

Do not waste your time on a question that is too hard or will take too long. After you've been working on a question for about a minute you need to make a decision. If you understand the question and think that you can get the answer in a reasonable amount of time, continue to work on the problem. If you still do not know how to do the problem or you are using a technique that is going to take a very long time, mark it off and come back to it later.

If you do not know the correct answer to a multiple choice question, eliminate as many answer choices as you can and take a guess. But you still want to leave open the possibility of coming back to it later. Remember that every multiple choice question is worth the same amount. Do not sacrifice problems that you may be able to do by getting hung up on a problem that is too hard for you.

LEVEL 1: DIFFERENTIATION

1. If $f(x) = 7x^4 + x + 3\pi - \sec x$, then $f'(x) =$

   (A) $28x^3 + 1 - \sec x \tan x$

   (B) $28x^3 + 1 + \sec x \tan x$

   (C) $28x^3 + 3 - \sec x \tan x$

   (D) $\frac{7}{5}x^5 + \frac{x^2}{2} + 3\pi x - \ln|\sec x + \tan x|$

Solution: $f'(x) = 28x^3 + 1 - \sec x \tan x$. This is choice (A).

Notes: (1) If n is any real number, then the derivative of x^n is nx^{n-1}.

Symbolically, $\frac{d}{dx}[x^n] = nx^{n-1}$.

For example, $\frac{d}{dx}[x^4] = 4x^3$.

As another example, $\frac{d}{dx}[x] = \frac{d}{dx}[x^1] = 1x^0 = 1(1) = 1$.

(2) Of course it is worth just remembering that $\frac{d}{dx}[x] = 1$.

(3) The derivative of a constant is 0. A **constant** is just a real number.

For example, 3π is a constant. So $\frac{d}{dx}[3\pi] = 0$.

(4) The derivative of a constant times a function is the constant times the derivative of the function.

Symbolically, $\frac{d}{dx}[cg(x)] = c\frac{d}{dx}[g(x)]$.

For example, $\frac{d}{dx}[7x^4] = 7\frac{d}{dx}[x^4] = 7 \cdot 4x^3 = 28x^3$.

(5) You should know the derivatives of the six basic trig functions:

$$\frac{d}{dx}[\sin x] = \cos x \qquad \frac{d}{dx}[\csc x] = -\csc x \cot x$$

$$\frac{d}{dx}[\cos x] = -\sin x \qquad \frac{d}{dx}[\sec x] = \sec x \tan x$$

$$\frac{d}{dx}[\tan x] = \sec^2 x \qquad \frac{d}{dx}[\cot x] = -\csc^2 x$$

(6) If g and h are functions, then $(g + h)'(x) = g'(x) + h'(x)$.

In other words, when differentiating a sum we can simply differentiate term by term.

Similarly, $(g - h)'(x) = g'(x) - h'(x)$.

(7) In the given problem we differentiate each of x^4, x, 3π and $\sec x$ separately and then use notes (4) and (6) to write the final answer.

    2.   If $g(x) = \frac{e^{4x-4}}{4} - \ln(x^2) + (2x - 1)^{\frac{5}{2}}$, then $g'(1) =$

        (A) 1

        (B) 2

        (C) 3

        (D) 4

Solution: $g'(x) = e^{4x-4} - \frac{2}{x} + 5(2x - 1)^{\frac{3}{2}}$.

Therefore $g'(1) = 1 - 2 + 5 = 4$, choice (D).

Notes: (1) The derivative of e^x is e^x.

Symbolically, $\frac{d}{dx}[e^x] = e^x$.

(2) The derivative of $\ln x$ is $\frac{1}{x}$.

Symbolically, $\frac{d}{dx}[\ln x] = \frac{1}{x}$.

(3) In this problem we need the **chain rule** which says the following:

If $f(x) = (g \circ h)(x) = g(h(x))$, then

$$f'(x) = g'(h(x)) \cdot h'(x)$$

13

For example, if $f(x) = \ln(x^2)$, then $f(x) = g(h(x))$ where $g(x) = \ln x$ and $h(x) = x^2$. So $f'(x) = g'(h(x)) \cdot h'(x) = \frac{1}{x^2} \cdot 2x = \frac{2}{x}$.

Similarly, we have $\frac{d}{dx}[\frac{e^{4x-4}}{4}] = \frac{1}{4} \cdot \frac{d}{dx}[e^{4x-4}] = \frac{1}{4}e^{4x-4} \cdot 4 = e^{4x-4}$, and

$\frac{d}{dx}[(2x-1)^{\frac{5}{2}}] = \frac{5}{2}(2x-1)^{\frac{3}{2}}(2) = 5(2x-1)^{\frac{3}{2}}$.

(4) As an alternative to using the chain rule to differentiate $\ln(x^2)$, we can rewrite $\ln(x^2)$ as $2\ln x$. Then $\frac{d}{dx}[2\ln x] = 2\frac{d}{dx}[\ln x] = 2 \cdot \frac{1}{x} = \frac{2}{x}$. See the first table in problem 3 for the rule of logarithms used here.

(5) In the given problem we differentiate each of $\frac{e^{4x-4}}{4}$, $\ln(x^2)$, and $(2x-1)^{\frac{5}{2}}$ separately and then use note (6) from problem 1 to write the final answer.

(6) If we could use a calculator for this problem, we can compute $g'(x)$ at $x = 1$ using our TI-84 calculator by first selecting nDeriv((or pressing 8) under the MATH menu, then typing the following:

$$e^\wedge(4X-4)/4 - \ln(X^\wedge 2) + (2X-1)^\wedge(5/2), X, 1),$$

and pressing ENTER. The display will show approximately 4.

3. $\frac{d}{dx}\left[\frac{x\ln e^{x^5}}{6}\right] =$

    (A) $6x^5$

    (B) x^5

    (C) $6x^5 + x^6$

    (D) $x^5 + x^6$

Solution: $\ln e^{x^5} = x^5$, so that $\frac{x\ln e^{x^5}}{6} = \frac{x \cdot x^5}{6} = \frac{1}{6}x^6$. Therefore we have

$\frac{d}{dx}\left[\frac{x\ln e^{x^5}}{6}\right] = \frac{d}{dx}\left[\frac{1}{6}x^6\right] = \frac{1}{6} \cdot 6x^5 = x^5$, choice (B).

Notes: (1) $f(x) = \log_e x$ is called the *natural logarithmic function* and is usually abbreviated as $f(x) = \ln x$.

(2) Here are two ways to simplify $\ln e^{x^5}$.

Method 1: Recall that $\ln e = 1$. We have $\ln e^{x^5} = x^5 \ln e = x^5(1) = x^5$. Here we have used the last law in the following table:

Laws of Logarithms: Here is a review of the basic laws of logarithms.

Law	Example
$\log_b 1 = 0$	$\log_2 1 = 0$
$\log_b b = 1$	$\log_6 6 = 1$
$\log_b x + \log_b y = \log_b(xy)$	$\log_5 7 + \log_5 2 = \log_5 14$
$\log_b x - \log_b y = \log_b(\frac{x}{y})$	$\log_3 21 - \log_3 7 = \log_3 3 = 1$
$\log_b x^n = n\log_b x$	$\log_8 3^5 = 5\log_8 3$

Method 2: Recall that the functions e^x and $\ln x$ are inverses of each other. This means that $e^{\ln x} = x$ and $\ln e^x = x$. Replacing x by x^5 in the second equation gives $\ln e^{x^5} = x^5$.

(3) Geometrically inverse functions have graphs that are mirror images across the line $y = x$. Here is a picture of the graphs of $y = e^x$ and $y = \ln x$ together with the line $y = x$. Notice how the line $y = x$ acts as a mirror for the two functions.

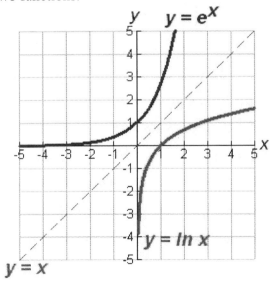

(4) $x \cdot x^5 = x^1 \cdot x^5 = x^{1+5} = x^6$.

15

Here is a complete review of the laws of exponents:

Law	Example
$x^0 = 1$	$3^0 = 1$
$x^1 = x$	$9^1 = 9$
$x^a x^b = x^{a+b}$	$x^3 x^5 = x^8$
$x^a/x^b = x^{a-b}$	$x^{11}/x^4 = x^7$
$(x^a)^b = x^{ab}$	$(x^5)^3 = x^{15}$
$(xy)^a = x^a y^a$	$(xy)^4 = x^4 y^4$
$(x/y)^a = x^a/y^a$	$(x/y)^6 = x^6/y^6$
$x^{-1} = 1/x$	$3^{-1} = 1/3$
$x^{-a} = 1/x^a$	$9^{-2} = 1/81$
$x^{1/n} = \sqrt[n]{x}$	$x^{1/3} = \sqrt[3]{x}$
$x^{m/n} = \sqrt[n]{x^m} = \left(\sqrt[n]{x}\right)^m$	$x^{9/2} = \sqrt{x^9} = \left(\sqrt{x}\right)^9$

4. The slope of the tangent line to the graph of $y = xe^{2x}$ at $x = \ln 3$ is

   (A) 9
   (B) 18
   (C) $18 \ln 3$
   (D) $18 \ln 3 + 9$

Solution: $y' = xe^{2x} \cdot 2 + e^{2x} \cdot 1 = 2xe^{2x} + e^{2x} = e^{2x}(2x + 1)$. When $x = \ln 3$, we have that the slope of the tangent line is

$$y'|_{x=\ln 3} = e^{2\ln 3}(2\ln 3 + 1) = e^{\ln 3^2}(2\ln 3 + 1)$$

$$= 3^2(2\ln 3 + 1) = 9(2\ln 3 + 1) = 18\ln 3 + 9.$$

This is choice (D).

Notes: (1) To find the slope of a tangent line to the graph of a function, we simply take the derivative of that function. If we want the slope of the tangent line at a specified x-value, we substitute that x-value into the derivative of the function.

(2) The derivative of $f(x) = e^x$ is $f'(x) = e^x$

(3) In this problem we used the **product rule** which says the following:

If $f(x) = u(x)v(x)$, then

$$f'(x) = u(x)v'(x) + v(x)u'(x)$$

16

(4) When differentiating e^{2x} we needed to use the chain rule. See problem 2 for details.

(5) See problem 3 for information on logarithms.

(6) The functions e^x and $\ln x$ are inverses of each other. This means that $e^{\ln x} = x$ and $\ln e^x = x$. In particular, $e^{\ln 3^2} = 3^2$.

(7) $n \ln x = \ln x^n$. In particular, $2 \ln 3 = \ln 3^2$. See the first table in problem 3 for the rule of logarithms used here.

(8) Using notes (6) and (7) together we get $e^{2 \ln 3} = e^{\ln 3^2} = e^{\ln 9} = 9$.

(9) As an alternative to using the rule of logarithms as was done in note (8), we can use a law of exponents instead to write $e^{2 \ln 3} = \left(e^{\ln 3} \right)^2$. Since $e^{\ln 3} = 3$, we have $e^{2 \ln 3} = \left(e^{\ln 3} \right)^2 = 3^2 = 9$.

The rule that we used here is $(x^a)^b = x^{ab}$ with $a = \ln 3$ and $b = 2$.

(9) If we could use a calculator for this problem, we can compute y' at $x = \ln 2$ using our TI-84 calculator by first selecting nDeriv((or pressing 8) under the MATH menu, then typing the following: Xe^(2X), X, ln 3), and pressing ENTER. The display will show approximately 28.775.

When we put choice (D) in our calculator we also get approximately 28.775.

5. If $x = \ln(t^2 + 1)$ and $y = \cos 3t$, then $\dfrac{dy}{dx} =$

   (A) $-\dfrac{3 \sin 3t}{t^2 + 1}$

   (B) $-\dfrac{3 \sin 3t}{2t(t^2 + 1)}$

   (C) $-\dfrac{3(t^2 + 1) \sin 3t}{2t}$

   (D) $-\dfrac{3 \sin 3t}{2t}$

Solution: $\dfrac{dy}{dt} = -3 \sin 3t$ and $\dfrac{dx}{dt} = \dfrac{2t}{t^2 + 1}$. Therefore

$$\frac{dy}{dx} = \frac{\frac{dy}{dt}}{\frac{dx}{dt}} = (-3 \sin 3t) \div \frac{2t}{t^2 + 1} = (-3 \sin 3t) \cdot \frac{t^2 + 1}{2t} = -\frac{3(t^2 + 1) \sin 3t}{2t}.$$

This is choice (C).

17

Notes: (1) In this problem we are given a parametrically defined curve. The variable t is called the **parameter**, and the two given equations are called **parametric equations**.

For example, when $t = 0$, we have that $x = \ln(0^2 + 1) = \ln 1 = 0$ and $y = \cos(3 \cdot 0) = 1$. So the point $(0,1)$ is on the given parametrically defined curve, and this point corresponds to the parameter value $t = 0$.

Each value for t corresponds to a point (x, y) in the xy-plane.

(2) The derivative $\frac{dy}{dx}$ is equal to $\frac{\frac{dy}{dt}}{\frac{dx}{dt}}$.

(3) The derivative of $\ln x$ is $\frac{1}{x}$.

Symbolically, $\frac{d}{dx}[\ln x] = \frac{1}{x}$.

(4) The derivatives $\frac{dy}{dt}$ and $\frac{dx}{dt}$ both required the chain rule. See problem 2 for a detailed explanation of this rule.

6.   If $g(x) = \pi e^3 + \frac{1}{\sqrt[3]{x^2}} + \left(\frac{x+2}{x-2}\right)^2 - 11^x$, then $g'(x) =$

Solution: We first rewrite g as $g(x) = \pi e^3 + x^{-\frac{2}{3}} + \left(\frac{x+2}{x-2}\right)^2 - 11^x$.

$$g'(x) = 0 - \frac{2}{3}x^{-\frac{5}{3}} + 2\left(\frac{x+2}{x-2}\right)\frac{(x-2)(1) - (x+2)(1)}{(x-2)^2} - 11^x(\ln 11)$$

$$= -\frac{2}{3\sqrt[3]{x^5}} - 8\frac{x+2}{(x-2)^3} - (\ln 11)11^x.$$

Notes: (1) πe^3 is a constant. Therefore $\frac{d}{dx}[\pi e^3] = 0$.

(2) $\frac{1}{\sqrt[3]{x^2}} = \frac{1}{x^{\frac{2}{3}}} = x^{-\frac{2}{3}}$. So $\frac{d}{dx}\left[\frac{1}{\sqrt[3]{x^2}}\right] = \frac{d}{dx}\left[x^{-\frac{2}{3}}\right] = -\frac{2}{3}x^{-\frac{2}{3}-1} = -\frac{2}{3}x^{-\frac{5}{3}}$.

(3) $-\frac{2}{3}x^{-\frac{5}{3}} = -\frac{2}{3x^{\frac{5}{3}}} = -\frac{2}{3\sqrt[3]{x^5}}$.

(4) The **quotient rule** says the following:

If $f(x) = \frac{N(x)}{D(x)}$, then

18

$$f'(x) = \frac{D(x)N'(x) - N(x)D'(x)}{[D(x)]^2}$$

I like to use the letters N for "numerator" and D for "denominator."

(5) The derivative of $x + 2$ is 1 because the derivative of x is 1, and the derivative of any constant is 0.

Similarly, the derivative of $x - 2$ is also 1.

Now using the quotient rule we see that the derivative of $\frac{x+2}{x-2}$ is $\frac{(x-2)(1)-(x+2)(1)}{(x-2)^2} = \frac{x-2-x-2}{(x-2)^2} = \frac{-4}{(x-2)^2}$.

(6) Differentiating $\left(\frac{x+2}{x-2}\right)^2$ requires the chain rule. Using note (5) we see that this derivative is $2\left(\frac{x+2}{x-2}\right)\left(\frac{-4}{(x-2)^2}\right) = -8\frac{x+2}{(x-2)^3}$.

(7) If $b > 0$, then $\frac{d}{dx}[b^x] = b^x(\ln b)$.

In particular, $\frac{d}{dx}[11^x] = 11^x(\ln 11)$.

(8) For $b > 0$, $b^x = e^{x \ln b}$.

To see this, first observe that $e^{x \ln b} = e^{\ln b^x}$ by the power rule for logarithms (see problem 3 for the laws of logarithms).

Second, recall that the functions e^x and $\ln x$ are inverses of each other. This means that $e^{\ln x} = x$ and $\ln e^x = x$. Replacing x by b^x in the first formula yields $e^{\ln b^x} = b^x$.

(9) The formula in note (8) gives an alternate method for differentiating 11^x. We can rewrite 11^x as $e^{x \ln 11}$ and use the chain rule. Here are the details:

$$\frac{d}{dx}[11^x] = \frac{d}{dx}[e^{x \ln 11}] = e^{x \ln 11}(\ln 11) = 11^x(\ln 11).$$

Note that in the last step we rewrote $e^{x \ln 11}$ as 11^x.

(10) There is one more method we can use to differentiate 11^x. We can use **logarithmic differentiation**.

We start by writing $y = 11^x$.

We then take the natural log of each side of this equation: $\ln y = \ln 11^x$.

19

We now use the power rule for logarithms to bring the x out of the exponent: $\ln y = x \ln 11$.

Now we differentiate implicitly to get $\frac{1}{y} \cdot \frac{dy}{dx} = \ln 11$.

Solve for $\frac{dy}{dx}$ by multiplying each side of the last equation by y to get $\frac{dy}{dx} = y \ln 11$.

Finally, replacing y by 11^x gives us $\frac{dy}{dx} = 11^x(\ln 11)$.

(11) **Logarithmic differentiation** is a general method that can often be used to handle expressions that have exponents with variables.

(12) See problem 35 for more information on implicit differentiation.

7. Differentiate $f(x) = \dfrac{e^{\cot 3x}}{\sqrt{x}}$ and express your answer as a simple fraction.

Solution:

$$f'(x) = \frac{\sqrt{x}(e^{\cot 3x})(-\csc^2 3x)(3) - e^{\cot 3x}(\frac{1}{2\sqrt{x}})}{x} = \frac{-6x(\csc^2 3x)e^{\cot 3x} - e^{\cot 3x}}{2x\sqrt{x}}.$$

Notes: (1) $\frac{d}{dx}[e^x] = e^x$

$\frac{d}{dx}[\cot x] = -\csc^2 x$

$\frac{d}{dx}[3x] = 3$

$\frac{d}{dx}[\sqrt{x}] = \frac{d}{dx}[x^{\frac{1}{2}}] = \frac{1}{2}x^{-\frac{1}{2}} = \frac{1}{2} \cdot \frac{1}{x^{\frac{1}{2}}} = \frac{1}{2} \cdot \frac{1}{\sqrt{x}} = \frac{1}{2\sqrt{x}}$

(2) We start off using the quotient rule (see problem 6 for a detailed explanation of the quotient rule). Here we get

$$\frac{\sqrt{x} \cdot \frac{d}{dx}[e^{\cot 3x}] - e^{\cot 3x} \cdot \frac{d}{dx}[\sqrt{x}]}{(\sqrt{x})^2}$$

(3) $\frac{d}{dx}[e^{\cot 3x}]$ requires two applications of the chain rule. See problem 2 for a detailed explanation of the chain rule. Here we get

$$\frac{d}{dx}[e^{\cot 3x}] = e^{\cot 3x}(-\csc^2 3x)(3).$$

20

(4) After differentiating we wind up with a complex fraction:

$$\frac{\sqrt{x}(e^{\cot 3x})(-\csc^2 3x)(3)-e^{\cot 3x}(\frac{1}{2\sqrt{x}})}{x}$$

We simplify this complex fraction by multiplying the numerator and denominator by $2\sqrt{x}$.

Note the following:

$x(2\sqrt{x}) = 2x\sqrt{x}$ (this is where the final denominator comes from).

$\sqrt{x}(e^{\cot 3x})(-\csc^2 3x)(3)(2\sqrt{x}) = -6\sqrt{x}\sqrt{x}\,(\csc^2 3x)e^{\cot 3x} = -6x\,(\csc^2 3x)e^{\cot 3x}$

$e^{\cot 3x}\left(\frac{1}{2\sqrt{x}}\right)(2\sqrt{x}) = e^{\cot 3x}$

The last two results give the final numerator.

8.　If $\boldsymbol{F}$ is the vector-valued function defined by $\boldsymbol{F}(t) = \langle\frac{\ln t}{t}, \cos^2 t\rangle$, then $\boldsymbol{F}''(t) =$

Solution:

$\boldsymbol{F}'(t) = \langle\frac{t(\frac{1}{t})-(\ln t)(1)}{t^2}, 2\,(\cos t)(-\sin t)\rangle = \langle\frac{1-\ln t}{t^2}, -2\cos t\sin t\rangle,$　and

so $\boldsymbol{F}''(t) = \langle\frac{t^2(\frac{-1}{t})-(1-\ln t)(2t)}{t^4}, -2\cos t\cos t - 2(\sin t)(-\sin t)\rangle$

$= \langle\frac{-t-2t+2t\ln t}{t^4}, -2\,(\cos^2 t - \sin^2 t)\rangle = \langle\frac{2\ln t-3}{t^3}, -2\cos 2t\rangle.$

Notes: (1) A 2-dimensional **vector-valued function** $\boldsymbol{F}$ has the form $\boldsymbol{F}(t) = \langle x(t), y(t)\rangle$ where x and y are ordinary functions of the variable t.

A vector-valued function is just a convenient way to give a parametrically defined curve with a single function.

The vector-valued function given in the problem is equivalent to the parametric equations

$$x = \frac{\ln t}{t}, y = \cos^2 t$$

Can you express the parametric equations given in problem 5 as a vector-valued function?

(2) The derivative of the vector-valued function $\boldsymbol{F}$ which is defined by $\boldsymbol{F}(t) = \langle x(t), y(t)\rangle$ is the vector-valued function $\boldsymbol{F}'$ which is defined by

$F'(t) = \langle x'(t), y'(t) \rangle$. In other words, we simply differentiate each component.

In this problem we have $x(t) = \frac{\ln t}{t}$ and $y(t) = \cos^2 t$.

Note also that $F''(t) = \langle x''(t), y''(t) \rangle$.

(3) Recall from problem 5 that $\frac{d}{dx}[\ln x] = \frac{1}{x}$.

(4) We used the quotient rule to differentiate x and x'. See problem 6 for a detailed explanation of the quotient rule.

(5) $\cos^2 t$ is an abbreviation for $(\cos t)^2$. To differentiate y therefore required the chain rule.

(6) To differentiate y' we used the product rule.

(7) The following two identities can be useful:

$$\sin 2t = 2 \sin t \cos t \qquad \cos 2t = \cos^2 t - \sin^2 t$$

The second identity was used when simplifying $y''(t)$.

We could have used the first identity to write

$$y'(t) = -2 \cos t \sin t = -2 \sin t \cos t = -\sin 2t.$$

Differentiating this last expression then gives

$$y''(t) = -2 \cos 2t.$$

LEVEL 1: INTEGRATION

9. $\int (3x^2 - 6\sqrt{x} + e^x)\, dx =$

   (A) $6x - \frac{3}{\sqrt{x}} + e^x + C$

   (B) $x^3 - 4\sqrt{x^3} + e^x + C$

   (C) $x^3 - 3x + e^x + C$

   (D) $x^3 - 3x + xe^{x-1} + C$

Solution:

$$\int (3x^2 - 6\sqrt{x} + e^x)\, dx = 3 \cdot \frac{x^3}{3} - \frac{6x^{\frac{3}{2}}}{\frac{3}{2}} + e^x + C = x^3 - 4\sqrt{x^3} + e^x + C$$

22

This is choice (B).

Notes: (1) If n is any real number, then an antiderivative of x^n is $\frac{x^{n+1}}{n+1}$.

Symbolically, $\int x^n dx = \frac{x^{n+1}}{n+1} + C$, where C is an arbitrary constant.

For example, $\int x^2 dx = \frac{x^3}{3} + C$.

As another example,

$$\int \sqrt{x}\,dx = \int x^{\frac{1}{2}} dx = \frac{x^{\frac{3}{2}}}{\frac{3}{2}} + C = x^{\frac{3}{2}} \div \frac{3}{2} + C = x^{\frac{3}{2}} \cdot \frac{2}{3} + C = \frac{2}{3}x^{\frac{3}{2}} + C.$$

(2) Since $\frac{d}{dx}[e^x] = e^x$, it follows that $\int e^x dx = e^x + C$

(3) If g and h are functions, then

$$\int [g(x) + h(x)]dx = \int g(x)dx + \int h(x)dx.$$

In other words, when integrating a sum we can simply integrate term by term.

Similarly, $\int [g(x) - h(x)]dx = \int g(x)dx - \int h(x)dx$.

(4) If g is a function and k is a constant, then

$$\int kg(x)dx = k \int g(x)dx$$

For example, $\int 3x^2 dx = 3 \int x^2 dx = 3\left(\frac{x^3}{3}\right) + C = x^3 + C$.

(5) In the given problem we integrate each of x^2, $\sqrt{x}$, and e^x separately and then use notes (3) and (4) to write the final answer.

(6) We do not need to include a constant C for each individual integration since if we add or subtract two or more constants we simply get a new constant. This is why we simply add one constant C at the end of the integration.

(7) It is also possible to solve this problem by differentiating the answer choices. For example, if we start with choice (C), then we have that $\frac{d}{dx}(x^3 - 3x + e^x + C) = 3x^2 - 3 + e^x$. So we can immediately see that choice (C) is incorrect.

When we differentiate choice (B) however, we get

$$\frac{d}{dx}\left[x^3 - 4\sqrt{x^3} + e^x + C\right] = \frac{d}{dx}\left[x^3 - 4x^{\frac{3}{2}} + e^x + C\right]$$

$$= 3x^2 - 4\left(\frac{3}{2}x^{\frac{1}{2}}\right) + e^x + 0 = 3x^2 - 6\sqrt{x} + e^x.$$

This is the **integrand** (the expression between the integral symbol and dx) that we started with. So the answer is choice (B).

(8) Note that the derivative of any constant is always 0, ie. $\frac{d}{dx}[C] = 0$.

10. $\int_0^2 (x^2 - 4x)e^{6x^2-x^3} dx =$

    (A) $-\frac{e^{16}}{3}$

    (B)   0

    (C) $\frac{e^{16}}{3}$

    (D) $\frac{1-e^{16}}{3}$

Solution:

$$\int_0^2 (x^2 - 4x)e^{6x^2-x^3} dx = -\frac{1}{3}e^{6x^2-x^3}\Big|_0^2 = -\frac{1}{3}e^{16} - \left(-\frac{1}{3}e^0\right) = \frac{-e^{16}+1}{3}$$

This is equivalent to choice (D).

Notes: (1) To evaluate $\int (x^2 - 4x)e^{6x^2-x^3} dx$, we can formally make the substitution $u = 6x^2 - x^3$. It then follows that

$$du = (12x - 3x^2)dx = 3(4x - x^2)dx = -3(x^2 - 4x)dx$$

Uh oh! There is no factor of -3 inside the integral. But constants never pose a problem. We simply multiply by -3 and $-\frac{1}{3}$ at the same time. We place the -3 inside the integral where it is needed, and we leave the $-\frac{1}{3}$ outside of the integral sign as follows:

$$\int (x^2 - 4x)e^{6x^2-x^3} dx = -\frac{1}{3}\int (-3)(x^2 - 4x)e^{6x^2-x^3} dx$$

We have this flexibility to place the -3 and $-\frac{1}{3}$ where we like because multiplication is commutative, and constants can be pulled outside of the integral sign freely.

24

We now have

$$\int (x^2 - 4x)e^{6x^2-x^3} dx = -\frac{1}{3}\int (-3)(x^2 - 4x)e^{6x^2-x^3} dx$$

$$= -\frac{1}{3}\int e^u du = -\frac{1}{3}e^u + C = -\frac{1}{3}e^{6x^2-x^3} + C$$

(2) $\int_a^b f(x)dx = F(b) - F(a)$ where F is any antiderivative of f.

In this example, $F(x) = -\frac{1}{3}e^{6x^2-x^3}$ is an antiderivative of the function $f(x) = (x^2 - 4x)e^{6x^2-x^3}$. So

$$\int_0^2 f(x)dx = F(2) - F(0) = -\frac{1}{3}e^{6\cdot2^2-2^3} - (-\frac{1}{3}e^0).$$

(3) We sometimes write $F(b) - F(a)$ as $F(x)\Big|_a^b$.

This is just a convenient way of focusing on finding an antiderivative before worrying about plugging in the **upper** and **lower limits of integration** (these are the numbers b and a, respectively).

(4) If we are doing the substitution formally, we can save some time by changing the limits of integration. We do this as follows:

$$\int_0^2 (x^2 - 4x)e^{6x^2-x^3} dx = -\frac{1}{3}\int_0^2 (-3)(x^2 - 4x)e^{6x^2-x^3} dx$$

$$= -\frac{1}{3}\int_0^{16} e^u du = -\frac{1}{3}e^u\Big|_0^{16} = -\frac{1}{3}(e^{16} - e^0) = \frac{-e^{16}+1}{3}$$

Notice that the limits 0 and 2 were changed to the limits 0 and 16, respectively. We made this change using the formula that we chose for the substitution: $u = 6x^2 - x^3$. When $x = 0$, we have $u = 0$ and when $x = 2$, we have $u = 6(2)^2 - 2^3 = 6 \cdot 4 - 8 = 24 - 8 = 16$.

11. $\int \frac{1}{x \ln x} dx =$

Solution: $\int \frac{1}{x \ln x} dx = \ln|\ln x| + C.$

Notes: (1) To evaluate $\int \frac{1}{x \ln x} dx$, we can formally make the substitution $u = \ln x$. It then follows that $du = \frac{1}{x}dx$. So we have

$$\int \frac{1}{x \ln x} dx = \int \frac{1}{\ln x} \cdot \frac{1}{x} dx = \int \frac{1}{u} du = \ln|u| + C = \ln|\ln x| + C.$$

25

To get the first equality we simply rewrote $\frac{1}{x \ln x}$ as $\frac{1}{x} \cdot \frac{1}{\ln x} = \frac{1}{\ln x} \cdot \frac{1}{x}$. This way it is easier to see exactly where u and du are.

To get the second equality we simply replaced $\ln x$ by u, and $\frac{1}{x} dx$ by du.

To get the third equality we used the basic integration formula

$$\int \frac{1}{x} dx = \ln|x| + C.$$

To get the last equality we replaced u by $\ln x$ (since we set $u = \ln x$ in the beginning).

(2) Recall from problem 5 that $\frac{d}{dx}[\ln x] = \frac{1}{x}$. It therefore seems like it should follow that $\int \frac{1}{x} dx = \ln x + C$. But this is *not* completely accurate.

Observe that we also have $\frac{d}{dx}[\ln(-x)] = \frac{1}{-x}(-1) = \frac{1}{x}$ (the chain rule was used here). So it appears that we also have $\int \frac{1}{x} dx = \ln(-x) + C$.

How can the same integral lead to two different answers? Well it doesn't. Note that $\ln x$ is only defined for $x > 0$, and $\ln(-x)$ is only defined for $x < 0$.

Furthermore, observe that $\ln|x| = \begin{cases} \ln x & \text{if } x > 0 \\ \ln(-x) & \text{if } x < 0 \end{cases}$.

It follows that

$$\int \frac{1}{x} dx = \ln|x| + C.$$

12. $\int 5^{\cot x} \csc^2 x \, dx =$

Solution: $\int 5^{\cot x} \csc^2 x \, dx = -\frac{5^{\cot x}}{\ln 5} + C.$

Notes: (1) Recall from problem 6 that $\frac{d}{dx}[5^x] = 5^x(\ln 5)$. It follows that $\int 5^x \, dx = \frac{5^x}{\ln 5} + C.$

To verify this, note that

$$\frac{d}{dx}\left[\frac{5^x}{\ln 5} + C\right] = \frac{1}{\ln 5}\frac{d}{dx}[5^x] + \frac{d}{dx}[C] = \frac{1}{\ln 5} \cdot 5^x(\ln 5) + 0 = 5^x.$$

More generally, we have that for any $b > 0$, $b \neq 1$, $\int b^x \, dx = \frac{b^x}{\ln b} + C.$

26

(2) As an alternative way to evaluate $\int 5^x \, dx$, we can rewrite 5^x as $e^{x \ln 5}$ and perform the substitution $u = x \ln 5$, so that $du = (\ln 5) \, dx$. So we have

$$\int 5^x \, dx = \int e^{x \ln 5} \, dx = \frac{1}{\ln 5} \int e^{x \ln 5} (\ln 5) \, dx = \frac{1}{\ln 5} \int e^u \, du$$

$$= \frac{1}{\ln 5} e^u + C = \frac{1}{\ln 5} e^{x \ln 5} + C = \frac{1}{\ln 5} 5^x + C = \frac{5^x}{\ln 5} + C.$$

(3) To evaluate $\int 5^{\cot x} \csc^2 x \, dx$, we can formally make the substitution $u = \cot x$. It then follows that $du = - \csc^2 x \, dx$. So we have

$$\int 5^{\cot x} \csc^2 x \, dx = - \int 5^{\cot x} (-\csc^2 x) dx = - \int 5^u \, du = - \frac{5^u}{\ln 5} + C$$

$$= - \frac{5^{\cot x}}{\ln 5} + C.$$

(4) As an alternative, we can combine notes (2) and (3) to evaluate the integral in a single step by rewriting $5^{\cot x} \csc^2 x$ as $e^{(\cot x)(\ln 5)} \csc^2 x$, and then letting $u = (\cot x)(\ln 5)$, so that $du = (- \csc^2 x)(\ln 5) dx$. I leave the details of this solution to the reader.

13. If f is a continuous function for all real x, and g is an antiderivative of f, then $\lim_{h \to 0} \frac{1}{h} \int_c^{c+h} f(x) \, dx$ is

(A) $g(0)$
(B) $g'(0)$
(C) $g(c)$
(D) $g'(c)$

Solution: $\lim_{h \to 0} \frac{1}{h} \int_c^{c+h} f(x) \, dx = \lim_{h \to 0} \frac{1}{h} [g(x)]_c^{c+h}$

$$= \lim_{h \to 0} \frac{g(c+h) - g(c)}{h} = g'(c).$$

This is choice (D).

Notes: (1) The second Fundamental Theorem of Calculus says that if f is a Riemann integrable function on $[a, b]$, then $\int_a^b f(x) \, dx = F(b) - F(a)$ where F is any antiderivative of f.

In this problem, since g is an antiderivative of f, we have $\int_c^{c+h} f(x) \, dx = g(c + h) - g(c)$.

(2) We sometimes use the notation $[F(x)]_a^b$ as an abbreviation for $F(b) - F(a)$.

This is just a convenient way of focusing on finding an antiderivative before worrying about plugging in the **upper** and **lower limits of integration** (these are the numbers b and a, respectively).

In the problem above we have

$$\int_c^{c+h} f(x)\,dx = [g(x)]_c^{c+h} = g(c+h) - g(c)$$

(3) If a function f is continuous on $[a, b]$, then f is Riemann integrable on $[a, b]$.

(4) Recall the definition of the derivative:

$$g'(x) = \lim_{h \to 0} \frac{g(x+h) - g(x)}{h}$$

So we have $g'(c) = \lim_{h \to 0} \frac{g(c+h) - g(c)}{h}$

14. If the function g given by $g(x) = \sqrt{x^3}$ has an average value of 2 on the interval $[0, b]$, then $b =$

(A) $5^{\frac{3}{2}}$

(B) 5

(C) $5^{\frac{2}{3}}$

(D) $5^{\frac{1}{2}}$

Solution: The average value of g on $[0, b]$ is

$$\frac{1}{b-0} \int_0^b x^{\frac{3}{2}}\,dx = \frac{2}{5b} x^{\frac{5}{2}} \Big|_0^b = \frac{2}{5b} \cdot b^{\frac{5}{2}} = \frac{2}{5} b^{\frac{3}{2}}.$$

So we have $\frac{2}{5} b^{\frac{3}{2}} = 2$. Therefore $b^{\frac{3}{2}} = 5$, and so $b = 5^{\frac{2}{3}}$, choice (C).

Notes: (1) The **average value** of the function f over the interval $[a, b]$ is

$$\frac{1}{b-a} \int_a^b f(x)\,dx.$$

(2) Recall from problem 9 that for any real number n, we have $\int x^n dx = \frac{x^{n+1}}{n+1} + C$, where C is an arbitrary constant.

For example, $\int x^{\frac{3}{2}}dx = \frac{x^{\frac{5}{2}}}{\frac{5}{2}} + C = x^{\frac{5}{2}} \div \frac{5}{2} + C = x^{\frac{5}{2}} \cdot \frac{2}{5} + C = \frac{2}{5}x^{\frac{5}{2}} + C.$

(3) $\int_a^b f(x)dx = F(b) - F(a)$ where F is any antiderivative of f.

Here, $G(x) = \frac{2}{5}x^{\frac{5}{2}}$ is an antiderivative of the function $g(x) = x^{\frac{3}{2}}$. So $\int_0^b g(x)dx = G(b) - G(0) = \frac{2}{5}b^{\frac{5}{2}} - 0 = \frac{2}{5}b^{\frac{5}{2}}.$

(4) $\frac{1}{b} \cdot b^{\frac{5}{2}} = b^{-1} \cdot b^{\frac{5}{2}} = b^{-1+\frac{5}{2}} = b^{-\frac{2}{2}+\frac{5}{2}} = b^{\frac{3}{2}}.$

It follows that $\frac{2}{5b} \cdot b^{\frac{5}{2}} = \frac{2}{5} \cdot \frac{1}{b} \cdot b^{\frac{5}{2}} = \frac{2}{5}b^{\frac{3}{2}}.$

(5) We solve the equation $\frac{2}{5}b^{\frac{3}{2}} = 2$ by first multiplying each side of the equation by $\frac{5}{2}$. Since $\frac{5}{2} \cdot \frac{2}{5} = 1$, we get $b^{\frac{3}{2}} = 2\left(\frac{5}{2}\right) = 5.$

We then raise each side of this last equation to the power $\frac{2}{3}$. Since $(b^{\frac{3}{2}})^{\frac{2}{3}} = b^{\frac{3}{2}\cdot\frac{2}{3}} = b^1 = b$, we get $b = 5^{\frac{2}{3}}.$

(6) See problem 3 for a review of the laws of exponents used in notes (4) and (5).

15. $\int_0^\infty 2xe^{-x^2}\, dx$ is

(A) divergent

(B) -1

(C) $\frac{1}{2}$

(D) 1

Solution: $\int_0^\infty 2xe^{-x^2}\, dx = -e^{-x^2}\,|_0^\infty = 0 - (-1) = 1$, choice (D).

Notes: (1) The given integral is an **improper integral** because one of the limits of integration is ∞. This is actually a **Type II improper integral**. For an example of a Type I improper integral, see problem 45.

(2) $\int_0^\infty f(x)\, dx$ is an abbreviation for $\lim\limits_{b\to\infty} \int_0^b f(x)\, dx$, and $F(x)\,|_0^\infty$ is an abbreviation for $\lim\limits_{b\to\infty} F(x)\,|_0^b$.

In this problem, $f(x) = 2xe^{-x^2}$ and $F(x) = -e^{-x^2}$.

29

(3) To evaluate the integral $\int 2xe^{-x^2}\, dx$, we can formally make the substitution $u = -x^2$. It then follows that $du = -2xdx$.

Uh oh! There is no minus sign inside the integral. But constants never pose a problem. We simply multiply by -1 inside the integral where it is needed, and also outside of the integral sign as follows:

$$\int 2xe^{-x^2}dx = -\int -2xe^{-x^2}dx$$

We have this flexibility to do this because constants can be pulled outside of the integral sign freely, and $(-1)(-1) = 1$, so that the two integrals are equal in value.

We now have

$$-\int -2xe^{-x^2}dx = -\int e^u du = -e^u + C = -e^{-x^2} + C.$$

We get the leftmost equality by replacing $-x^2$ by u, and $-2xdx$ by du.

We get the second equality by the basic integration formula

$$\int e^u du = e^u + C.$$

And we get the rightmost equality by replacing u with $-x^2$.

(4) Note that the function $f(x) = e^{-x^2}$ can be written as the composition $f(x) = g(h(x))$ where $g(x) = e^x$ and $h(x) = -x^2$.

Since $h(x) = -x^2$ is the inner part of the composition, it is natural to try the substitution $u = -x^2$.

Note that the derivative of $-x^2$ is $-2x$, so that $du = -2xdx$.

(5) With a little practice, we can evaluate an integral like this very quickly with the following reasoning: The derivative of $-x^2$ is $-2x$. So to integrate $-2xe^{-x^2}$ we simply pretend we are integrating e^x but as we do it we leave the $-x^2$ where it is. This is essentially what was done in the above solution.

Note that the $-2x$ "goes away" because it is the derivative of $-x^2$. We need it there for everything to work.

(6) If we are doing the substitution formally, we can save some time by changing the limits of integration. We do this as follows:

$$\int_0^\infty 2xe^{-x^2}\, dx = -\int_0^\infty -2xe^{-x^2}\, dx$$

$$= -\int_0^{-\infty} e^u\, du = -e^u \Big|_0^{-\infty} = -(0 - e^0) = -(-1) = 1.$$

Notice that the limits 0 and ∞ were changed to the limits 0 and $-\infty$, respectively. We made this change using the formula that we chose for the substitution: $u = -x^2$. When $x = 0$, we have that $u = 0$ and when $x = \infty$, we have "$u = -\infty^2 = -\infty \cdot \infty = -\infty$."

I used quotation marks in that last computation because the computation $\infty \cdot \infty$ is not really well-defined. What we really mean is that if we have two expressions that are approaching ∞, then their product is approaching ∞ as well. For all practical purposes, the following computations are valid:

$$\infty \cdot \infty = \infty \qquad \infty + \infty = \infty \qquad -\infty - \infty = -\infty$$

For example, if $\lim_{x\to\infty} f(x) = \infty$ and $\lim_{x\to\infty} g(x) = \infty$, then $\lim_{x\to\infty}[f(x) \cdot g(x)] = \infty$ and $\lim_{x\to\infty}[f(x) + g(x)] = \infty$.

Note that the following forms are **indeterminate**:

$$\frac{\infty}{\infty} \qquad \frac{0}{0} \qquad 0 \cdot \infty \qquad \infty - \infty \qquad 0^0 \qquad 1^\infty \qquad \infty^0$$

For example, if $\lim_{x\to\infty} f(x) = \infty$ and $\lim_{x\to\infty} g(x) = \infty$, then in general we cannot say anything about $\lim_{x\to\infty} \frac{f(x)}{g(x)}$. The value of this limit depends on the specific functions f and g.

16. Let $y = f(x)$ be the solution to the differential equation $\frac{dy}{dx} = \arctan(xy)$ with the initial condition $f(0) = 2$. What is the approximation of $f(1)$ if Euler's method is used, starting at $x = 0$ with a step size of 0.5?

   (A) 1

   (B) 2

   (C) $2 + \frac{\pi}{8}$

   (D) $2 + \frac{\pi}{4}$

31

Solution: Let's make a table:

(x, y)	dx	$\frac{dy}{dx}$	$dx\left(\frac{dy}{dx}\right) = dy$	$(x + dx, y + dy)$
$(0,2)$	$.5$	0	0	$(.5,2)$
$(.5,2)$	$.5$	$\dfrac{\pi}{4}$	$\dfrac{\pi}{8}$	$(1,2 + \frac{\pi}{8})$

From the last entry of the table we see that $f(1) \approx 2 + \frac{\pi}{8}$, choice (C).

Notes: (1) **Euler's method** is a procedure for approximating the solution of a differential equation.

(2) To use Euler's method we must be given a differential equation $\frac{dy}{dx} = f(x, y)$, an initial condition $f(x_0) = y_0$, and a step size dx.

In this problem, we have $\frac{dy}{dx} = \arctan(xy)$, $f(0) = 2$, and $dx = 0.5$.

(3) The initial condition $f(x_0) = y_0$ is equivalent to saying that the point (x_0, y_0) is on the solution curve.

So in this problem we are given that $(0,2)$ is on the solution curve.

(4) We can get an approximation to $f(x_0 + dx)$ by using a table (as shown in the above solution) as follows:

In the first column we put the point (x_0, y_0) as given by the initial condition.

In the second column we put the step size dx.

In the third column we plug the point (x_0, y_0) into the differential equation to get $\frac{dy}{dx}$.

In the fourth column we multiply the numbers in the previous two columns to get dy.

In the fifth column we add dx to x_0 and dy to y_0 to get the point $(x_0 + dx, y_0 + dy)$. This is equivalent to $f(x_0 + dx) = y_0 + dy$.

(5) We can now copy the point from the fifth column into the first column of the next row, and repeat this procedure to approximate $f(x_0 + 2dx)$.

In this problem, since $x_0 = 0$ and $dx = 0.5$, we have $x_0 + 2dx = 1$, and so we are finished after the second iteration of the procedure.

17. The area of the region bounded by the lines $x = 1$, $x = 4$, and $y = 0$ and the curve $y = e^{3x}$ is

(A) $\frac{1}{3}e^3(e^9 - 1)$

(B) $e^3(e^9 - 1)$

(C) $e^{12} - 1$

(D) $3e^3(e^9 - 1)$

Solution: $\int_1^4 e^{3x}\, dx = \frac{1}{3}e^{3x}\Big|_1^4 = \frac{1}{3}e^{12} - \frac{1}{3}e^3 = \frac{1}{3}e^3(e^9 - 1)$.

This is choice (A).

Notes: (1) To compute the area under the graph of a function that lies entirely above the x-axis (the line $y = 0$) from $x = a$ to $x = b$, we simply integrate the function from a to b.

In this problem, the function is $y = e^{3x}$, $a = 1$, and $b = 4$.

Note that $e^x > 0$ for all x. So $e^{3x} > 0$ for all x. It follows that the graph of $y = e^{3x}$ lies entirely above the x-axis.

(2) Although it is not needed in this problem, here is a sketch of the area we are being asked to find.

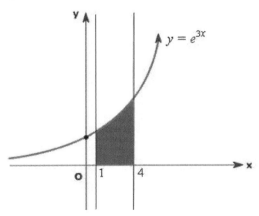

(3) To evaluate $\int e^{3x}\, dx$, we can formally make the substitution $u = 3x$. It then follows that $du = 3dx$.

We place the 3 next to dx where it is needed, and we leave the $\frac{1}{3}$ outside of the integral sign as follows:

$$\int e^{3x}\,dx = \frac{1}{3}\int e^{3x} \cdot 3\,dx$$

We now have

$$\int e^{3x}\,dx = \frac{1}{3}\int e^{3x} \cdot 3\,dx = \frac{1}{3}\int e^{u}\,du = \frac{1}{3}e^{u} + C = \frac{1}{3}e^{3x} + C.$$

We get the second equality by replacing $3x$ by u, and $3dx$ by du.

We get the third equality by the basic integration formula

$$\int e^{u}\,du = e^{u} + C.$$

And we get the rightmost equality by replacing u with $3x$.

(4) With a little practice, we can evaluate an integral like this very quickly with the following reasoning: The derivative of $3x$ is 3. So we artificially insert a factor of 3 next to dx, and $\frac{1}{3}$ outside the integral sign. Now to integrate $3e^{3x}$ we simply pretend we are integrating e^{x} but as we do it we leave the $3x$ where it is. This is essentially what was done in the above solution.

Note that the 3 "goes away" because it is the derivative of $3x$. We need it to be there for everything to work.

(5) If we are doing the substitution formally, we can save some time by changing the limits of integration. We do this as follows:

$$\int_{1}^{4} e^{3x}\,dx = \frac{1}{3}\int_{1}^{4} e^{3x} \cdot 3\,dx = \frac{1}{3}\int_{3}^{12} e^{u}\,du = \frac{1}{3}e^{u}\Big|_{3}^{12} = \frac{1}{3}e^{12} - \frac{1}{3}e^{3}.$$

Notice that the limits 1 and 4 were changed to the limits 3 and 12. We made this change using the formula that we chose for the substitution: $u = 3x$. When $x = 1$, we have $u = 3(1) = 3$. And when $x = 4$, we have $u = 3(4) = 12$.

Note that this method has the advantage that we do not have to change back to a function of x at the end.

18. Which of the following integrals gives the length of the graph of $y = e^{3x}$ between $x = 1$ and $x = 2$?

(A) $\int_1^2 \sqrt{e^{6x} + e^{3x}}\, dx$

(B) $\int_1^2 \sqrt{x + 3e^{3x}}\, dx$

(C) $\int_1^2 \sqrt{1 + 3e^{3x}}\, dx$

(D) $\int_1^2 \sqrt{1 + 9e^{6x}}\, dx$

Solution: $\frac{dy}{dx} = 3e^{3x}$, so that $1 + \left(\frac{dy}{dx}\right)^2 = 1 + 9e^{6x}$. It follows that the desired length is $\int_1^2 \sqrt{1 + 9e^{6x}}\, dx$, choice (D).

Notes: (1) The **arc length** of the differentiable curve with equation $y = f(x)$ from $x = a$ to $x = b$ is

$$\text{Arc length} = \int_a^b \sqrt{1 + \left(\frac{dy}{dx}\right)^2}\, dx$$

(2) By the chain rule, we have $\frac{dy}{dx} = e^{3x}(3) = 3e^{3x}$. See problem 2 for details.

(3) $\left(\frac{dy}{dx}\right)^2 = (3e^{3x})^2 = 3^2(e^{3x})^2 = 9e^{3x \cdot 2} = 9e^{6x}$. See problem 3 for a review of the laws of exponents used here.

LEVEL 1: LIMITS AND CONTINUITY

19. $\lim_{x \to 7} \frac{2x^2 - 13x - 7}{x - 7} =$

(A) ∞
(B) 0
(C) 2
(D) 15

Solution 1: $\lim_{x \to 7} \frac{2x^2 - 13x - 7}{x - 7} = \lim_{x \to 7} \frac{(x-7)(2x+1)}{x-7} = \lim_{x \to 7}(2x + 1)$

$$= 2(7) + 1 = 15.$$

This is choice (D).

Notes: (1) When we try to substitute 7 in for x we get the **indeterminate form** $\frac{0}{0}$. Here is the computation:

$$\frac{2(7)^2-13(7)-7}{7-7} = \frac{98-91-7}{7-7} = \frac{0}{0}.$$

This means that we cannot use the method of "plugging in the number" to get the answer. So we have to use some other method.

(2) One algebraic "trick" that works in this case is to factor the numerator as $2x^2 - 13x - 7 = (x - 7)(2x + 1)$. Note that one of the factors is $(x - 7)$ which is identical to the factor in the denominator. This will *always* happen when using this "trick." This makes factoring pretty easy in these problems.

(3) **Most important limit theorem:** If $f(x) = g(x)$ for all x in some interval containing $x = c$ *except* possibly at c itself, then we have $\lim_{x \to c} f(x) = \lim_{x \to c} g(x)$.

In this problem, our two functions are

$$f(x) = \frac{2x^2-13x-7}{x-7} \text{ and } g(x) = 2x + 1.$$

Note that f and g agree everywhere *except* at $x = 7$. Also note that $f(7)$ is undefined, whereas $g(7) = 15$.

(4) To compute a limit, first try to simply plug in the number. This will only fail when the result is an indeterminate form. The two **basic** indeterminate forms are $\frac{0}{0}$ and $\frac{\infty}{\infty}$ (the more **advanced** ones are $0 \cdot \infty$, $\infty - \infty$, 0^0, 1^∞, and ∞^0, but these can always be manipulated into one of the two basic forms).

If an indeterminate form results from plugging in the number, then there are two possible options:

Option 1: Use some algebraic manipulations to create a new function that agrees with the original except at the value that is being approached, and then use the limit theorem mentioned in note (3).

This is how we solved the problem above.

Option 2: Try L'Hôpital's rule (see solution 2 below).

Solution 2: We use L'Hôpital's rule to get

$$\lim_{x \to 7} \frac{2x^2 - 13x - 7}{x - 7} = \lim_{x \to 7} \frac{4x - 13}{1} = 4(7) - 13 = 15, \text{ choice (D).}$$

Notes: (1) L'Hôpital's rule says the following: Suppose that

(i) g and k are differentiable on some interval containing c (except possibly at c itself).

(ii) $\lim_{x \to c} g(x) = \lim_{x \to c} k(x) = 0$ or $\lim_{x \to c} g(x) = \lim_{x \to c} k(x) = \pm\infty$

(iii) $\lim_{x \to c} \frac{g'(x)}{k'(x)}$ exists, and

(iv) $k'(x) \neq 0$ for all x in the interval (except possibly at c itself).

Then $\lim_{x \to c} \frac{g(x)}{k(x)} = \lim_{x \to c} \frac{g'(x)}{k'(x)}$.

In this problem $g(x) = 2x^2 - 13x - 7$ and $k(x) = x - 7$.

(2) It is very important that we first check that the expression has the correct form before applying L'Hôpital's rule.

In this problem, note that when we substitute 7 in for x in the given expression we get $\frac{0}{0}$ (see note 1 above). So in this case L'Hôpital's rule can be applied.

37

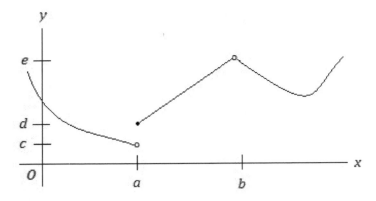

20. The graph of the function h is shown in the figure above. Which of the following statements about h is true?

(A) $\lim_{x \to a} h(x) = c$

(B) $\lim_{x \to a} h(x) = d$

(C) $\lim_{x \to b} h(x) = e$

(D) $\lim_{x \to b} h(x) = h(b)$

Solution: From the graph we see that $\lim_{x \to b} h(x) = e$, choice (C).

Notes: (1) The open circles on the graph at a and b indicate that there is *no* point at that location. The darkened circle at a indicates $h(a) = d$.

(2) $\lim_{x \to a^-} h(x) = c$ and $\lim_{x \to a^+} h(x) = d$. Therefore $\lim_{x \to a} h(x)$ does not exist.

(3) h is not defined at $x = b$, ie. $h(b)$ does not exist. In particular, h is not continuous at b. So $\lim_{x \to b} h(x) \ne h(b)$.

21. What is $\lim_{h \to 0} \dfrac{\tan\left(\frac{\pi}{4}+h\right)-\tan\left(\frac{\pi}{4}\right)}{h}$?

(A) 0

(B) 1

(C) 2

(D) The limit does not exist.

Solution 1: If we let $f(x) = \tan x$, then $f'(x) = \lim_{h \to 0} \dfrac{\tan(x+h)-\tan(x)}{h}$.

So $f'\left(\frac{\pi}{4}\right) = \lim_{h \to 0} \dfrac{\tan\left(\frac{\pi}{4}+h\right)-\tan\left(\frac{\pi}{4}\right)}{h}$.

Now, the derivative of $\tan x$ is $\sec^2 x$. So we have

$$\lim_{h\to 0}\frac{\tan\left(\frac{\pi}{4}+h\right)-\tan\left(\frac{\pi}{4}\right)}{h} = f'\left(\frac{\pi}{4}\right) = \sec^2\left(\frac{\pi}{4}\right) = \left(\sqrt{2}\right)^2 = 2.$$

This is choice (C).

Notes: (1) The derivative of the function f is defined by

$$f'(x) = \lim_{h\to 0}\frac{f(x+h)-f(x)}{h}$$

In this problem $f(x) = \tan x$, so that $f'(x) = \lim_{h\to 0}\frac{\tan(x+h)-\tan(x)}{h}$

(2) See problem 1 for the basic trig derivatives. In particular,

$$\frac{d}{dx}[\tan x] = \sec^2 x.$$

(3) $\cos\left(\frac{\pi}{4}\right) = \frac{1}{\sqrt{2}}$. Therefore $\sec\left(\frac{\pi}{4}\right) = \frac{1}{\cos\left(\frac{\pi}{4}\right)} = 1 \div \frac{1}{\sqrt{2}} = 1 \cdot \sqrt{2} = \sqrt{2}.$

(4) $\sec^2\left(\frac{\pi}{4}\right) = \left(\sec\frac{\pi}{4}\right)^2 = \left(\sqrt{2}\right)^2 = 2.$

Solution 2: We use L'Hôpital's rule to get

$$\lim_{h\to 0}\frac{\tan\left(\frac{\pi}{4}+h\right)-\tan\left(\frac{\pi}{4}\right)}{h} = \lim_{h\to 0}\frac{\sec^2\left(\frac{\pi}{4}+h\right)}{1} = \sec^2\left(\frac{\pi}{4}\right) = \left(\sqrt{2}\right)^2 = 2.$$

This is choice (C).

Note: See problem 19 for a detailed description of L'Hôpital's rule.

22. What is $\lim_{x\to\infty}\frac{5-x^2+3x^3}{x^3-2x+3}$?

    (A) 1

    (B) $\frac{5}{3}$

    (C) 3

    (D) The limit does not exist.

Solution: $\lim_{x\to\infty}\frac{5-x^2+3x^3}{x^3-2x+3} = \lim_{x\to\infty}\frac{3x^3}{x^3} = 3$, choice (C).

Notes: (1) If p and q are polynomials, then $\lim_{x\to\infty}\frac{p(x)}{q(x)} = \lim_{x\to\infty}\frac{a_nx^n}{b_mx^m}$ where we have $p(x) = a_nx^n + a_{n-1}x^{n-1} + \cdots + a_1x + a_0$ and $q(x) = a_mx^m + a_{m-1}x^{m-1} + \cdots + a_1x + a_0.$

(2) If $n = m$, then $\lim_{x \to \infty} \frac{a_n x^n}{b_m x^m} = \frac{a_n}{b_m}$.

(3) Combining notes (1) and (2), we could have gotten the answer to this problem immediately by simply taking the coefficients of x^3 in the numerator and denominator and dividing.

The coefficient of x^3 in the numerator is 3, and the coefficient of x^3 in the denominator is 1. So the final answer is $\frac{3}{1} = 3$.

(4) If $n > 0$, then $\lim_{x \to \infty} \frac{1}{x^n} = 0$.

(5) For a more rigorous solution, we can multiply both the numerator and denominator of the fraction by $\frac{1}{x^3}$ to get

$$\frac{5-x^2+3x^3}{x^3-2x+3} = \frac{\left(\frac{1}{x^3}\right)}{\left(\frac{1}{x^3}\right)} \cdot \frac{(5-x^2+3x^3)}{(x^3-2x+3)} = \frac{\frac{5}{x^3}-\frac{1}{x}+3}{1-\frac{2}{x^2}+\frac{3}{x^3}}.$$

It follows that $\lim_{x \to \infty} \frac{5-x^2+3x^3}{x^3-2x+3} = \frac{5 \lim_{x \to \infty}\left(\frac{1}{x^3}\right) - \lim_{x \to \infty}\left(\frac{1}{x}\right) + \lim_{x \to \infty} 3}{\lim_{x \to \infty} 1 - 2\lim_{x \to \infty}\left(\frac{1}{x^2}\right) + 3\lim_{x \to \infty}\left(\frac{1}{x^3}\right)} = \frac{5 \cdot 0 - 0 + 3}{1 - 2 \cdot 0 + 3 \cdot 0} = 3.$

(6) L'Hôpital's rule can also be used to solve this problem since the limit has the form $\frac{\infty}{\infty}$:

$$\lim_{x \to \infty} \frac{5-x^2+3x^3}{x^3-2x+3} = \lim_{x \to \infty} \frac{-2x+9x^2}{3x^2-2} = \lim_{x \to \infty} \frac{-2+18x}{6x} = \lim_{x \to \infty} \frac{18}{6} = 3.$$

Observe that we applied L'Hôpital's rule three times. Each time we differentiated the numerator and denominator with respect to x to get another expression of the form $\frac{\infty}{\infty}$.

See problem 19 for a detailed description of L'Hôpital's rule.

23. $\lim_{h \to 0} \frac{1}{h} \ln\left(\frac{10+h}{10}\right)$ is equal to

(A) $\frac{1}{10}$

(B) 10

(C) e^{10}

(D) The limit does not exist.

Solution 1: If we let $f(x) = \ln x$, then

$$f'(x) = \lim_{h\to 0} \frac{\ln(x+h)-\ln(x)}{h} = \lim_{h\to 0} \frac{1}{h} \ln\left(\frac{x+h}{x}\right).$$

So $f'(10) = \lim_{h\to 0} \frac{1}{h} \ln\left(\frac{10+h}{10}\right)$.

Now, the derivative of $\ln x$ is $\frac{1}{x}$. So we have

$$\lim_{h\to 0} \frac{1}{h} \ln\left(\frac{10+h}{10}\right) = f'(10) = \frac{1}{10}, \text{ choice (A)}.$$

Notes: (1) The derivative of the function f is defined by

$$f'(x) = \lim_{h\to 0} \frac{f(x+h)-f(x)}{h}$$

In this problem $f(x) = \ln x$, so that $f'(x) = \lim_{h\to 0} \frac{\ln(x+h)-\ln(x)}{h}$.

(2) Recall that $\ln a - \ln b = \ln\left(\frac{a}{b}\right)$. So $\ln(x+h) - \ln(x) = \ln\left(\frac{x+h}{x}\right)$, and therefore $\frac{\ln(x+h)-\ln(x)}{h} = \frac{1}{h}[\ln(x+h) - \ln(x)] = \frac{1}{h}\ln\left(\frac{x+h}{x}\right)$.

(3) See the notes at the end of problem 3 for a review of the laws of logarithms.

Solution 2: We use L'Hôpital's rule to get

$$\lim_{h\to 0} \frac{1}{h} \ln\left(\frac{10+h}{10}\right) = \lim_{h\to 0} \frac{\ln\left(\frac{10+h}{10}\right)}{h} = \lim_{h\to 0} \frac{\left(\frac{1}{\frac{10+h}{10}}\right)\left(\frac{1}{10}\right)}{1} = \frac{1}{10}, \text{ choice (A)}.$$

Note: (1) See problem 19 for more information on L'Hôpital's rule.

(2) To apply L'Hôpital's rule we separately took the derivative of $g(x) = \ln\left(\frac{10+h}{10}\right)$ and $k(x) = h$.

(3) $g(x) = \ln\left(\frac{10+h}{10}\right)$ is a composition of the functions $\ln x$ and $\frac{10+h}{10}$. We therefore need to use the Chain Rule to differentiate it.

The first part of the Chain Rule gives us $\frac{1}{\frac{10+h}{10}}$.

For the second part, it may help to rewrite $\frac{10+h}{10}$ as $\frac{1}{10}(10 + h)$. It is now easy to see that the derivative of this expression with respect to h is $\frac{1}{10}(0 + 1) = \frac{1}{10}$.

41

24. $\lim_{x \to 0} \frac{\sin 7x}{\sin 4x} =$

Solution: $\lim_{x \to 0} \frac{\sin 7x}{\sin 4x} = \lim_{x \to 0} \frac{7 \cdot 4x \sin 7x}{4 \cdot 7x \sin 4x} = \frac{7}{4} \lim_{x \to 0} \frac{\sin 7x}{7x} \cdot \frac{4x}{\sin 4x}$

$= \frac{7}{4} \left(\lim_{7x \to 0} \frac{\sin 7x}{7x} \right) \left(\lim_{4x \to 0} \frac{4x}{\sin 4x} \right) = \frac{7}{4} \left(\lim_{u \to 0} \frac{\sin u}{u} \right) \frac{1}{\left(\lim_{v \to 0} \frac{\sin v}{v} \right)} = \frac{7}{4} \cdot 1 \cdot \frac{1}{1} = \frac{7}{4}.$

Notes: (1) A basic limit worth memorizing is

$$\lim_{x \to 0} \frac{\sin x}{x} = 1.$$

(2) The limit in note (1) is actually very easy to compute using L'Hôpital's rule:

$$\lim_{x \to 0} \frac{\sin x}{x} = \lim_{x \to 0} \frac{\cos x}{1} = \cos 0 = 1$$

(3) It is not hard to see that $x \to 0$ if and only if $4x \to 0$ if and only if $7x \to 0$. This is why we can replace x by $4x$ and $7x$ in the subscripts of the limits above.

(4) $\frac{\sin 7x}{\sin 4x}$ can be rewritten as $\frac{7 \cdot 4x \sin 7x}{4 \cdot 7x \sin 4x}$.

It follows that we can rewrite $\frac{\sin 7x}{\sin 4x}$ as $\frac{7}{4} \cdot \frac{\sin 7x}{7x} \cdot \frac{4x}{\sin 4x}$.

(5) Using the substitution $u = 7x$, we have

$$\lim_{7x \to 0} \frac{\sin 7x}{7x} = \lim_{u \to 0} \frac{\sin u}{u}.$$

Using the substitution $v = 4x$, we have

$$\lim_{4x \to 0} \frac{4x}{\sin 4x} = \frac{1}{\lim_{4x \to 0} \frac{\sin 4x}{4x}} = \frac{1}{\lim_{v \to 0} \frac{\sin v}{v}}$$

(6) We can also solve this problem using L'Hôpital's rule as follows:

$$\lim_{x \to 0} \frac{\sin 7x}{\sin 4x} = \lim_{x \to 0} \frac{7 \cos 7x}{4 \cos 4x} = \frac{7(1)}{4(1)} = \frac{7}{4}.$$

25. $\lim_{x \to 11} \frac{x}{(x-11)^2} =$

Solution: The function $f(x) = \frac{x}{(x-11)^2}$ has a vertical asymptote of $x = 11$.

If x is "near" 11, then $\frac{x}{(x-11)^2}$ is positive. It follows that $\lim_{x \to 11} \frac{x}{(x-11)^2} = +\infty$.

Notes: (1) When we substitute 11 in for x into $f(x) = \frac{x}{(x-11)^2}$, we get $\frac{11}{0}$. This is *not* an indeterminate form.

For a rational function, the form $\frac{a}{0}$ where a is a nonzero real number *always* indicates that $x = a$ is a vertical asymptote. This means that at least one of $\lim_{x \to a^-} f(x)$ or $\lim_{x \to a^+} f(x)$ is $+$ or $-\infty$. If both limits agree, then $\lim_{x \to a} f(x)$ is the common value. If the two limits disagree, then $\lim_{x \to a} f(x)$ does not exist.

(2) A nice visual way to find the left hand and right hand limits is by creating a **sign chart**. We split up the real line into intervals using the x-values where the numerator and the denominator of the fraction are zero, and then check the sign of the function in each subinterval formed.

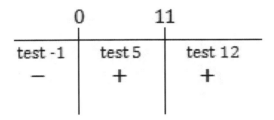

In this case we split up the real line into three pieces. Notice that the cutoff points are 0 and 11 because the numerator of the function is zero when $x = 0$, and the denominator of the function is zero when $x = 11$.

We then plug a real number from each of these three intervals into the function to see if the answer is positive or negative. For example, $f(5) = \frac{5}{(5-11)^2} > 0$. Note that we do not need to finish the computation. We only need to know if the answer is positive or negative. Since there are $+$ signs on both sides of $x = 11$, we have that $\lim_{x \to 11} \frac{x}{(x-11)^2} = +\infty$.

(3) We actually do not care about the minus sign to the left of 0. We could have left that part out of the sign chart. It is however important that we include the zero as a cutoff point. This tells us that we can test any value between 0 and 11 to find $\lim_{x \to a^-} f(x)$.

26. Let f be the function defined by

$$f(x) = \begin{cases} \dfrac{5e^{x-7}}{1 + \ln|x - 8|}, & x \le 7 \\ \dfrac{15\cos(x - 7)}{\sin(7 - x) + 3}, & x > 7 \end{cases}$$

Show that f is continuous at $x = 7$.

Solution:

$$\lim_{x \to 7^-} f(x) = \frac{5e^{7-7}}{1 + \ln|7-8|} = \frac{5e^0}{1 + \ln 1} = \frac{5}{1+0} = 5.$$

$$\lim_{x \to 7^+} f(x) = \frac{15\cos(7-7)}{\sin(7-7)+3} = \frac{15\cos 0}{\sin 0 + 3} = \frac{15(1)}{0+3} = \frac{15}{3} = 5.$$

So $\lim_{x \to 7} f(x) = 5$.

Also, $f(7) = \dfrac{5e^{7-7}}{1 + \ln|7-8|} = 5$. So, $\lim_{x \to 7} f(x) = f(7)$.

It follows that f is continuous at $x = 7$.

LEVEL 1: SERIES

27. The sum of the infinite geometric series $\dfrac{5}{7} + \dfrac{15}{28} + \dfrac{45}{112} + \cdots$ is

Solution: The first term of the geometric series is $a = \dfrac{5}{7}$, and the common

ratio is $r = \dfrac{15}{28} \div \dfrac{5}{7} = \dfrac{15}{28} \cdot \dfrac{7}{5} = \dfrac{3}{4}$. It follows that the sum is

$$\frac{a}{1-r} = \frac{\frac{5}{7}}{1 - \frac{3}{4}} = \frac{5}{7} \div \frac{1}{4} = \frac{5}{7} \cdot \frac{4}{1} = \frac{20}{7}.$$

Notes: (1) A **geometric sequence** is a sequence of numbers such that the quotient r between consecutive terms is constant. The number r is called the **common ratio** of the geometric sequence.

For example, consider the sequence

$$\frac{5}{7}, \frac{15}{28}, \frac{45}{112}, \dots$$

We have $\dfrac{15}{28} \div \dfrac{5}{7} = \dfrac{15}{28} \cdot \dfrac{7}{5} = \dfrac{3}{4}$ and $\dfrac{45}{112} \div \dfrac{15}{28} = \dfrac{45}{112} \cdot \dfrac{28}{15} = \dfrac{3}{4}$. It follows that the sequence is geometric with common ratio $r = \frac{3}{4}$.

(2) A **geometric series** is the sum of the terms of a geometric sequence. The series in this problem is an **infinite** geometric series.

(3) The sum G of an infinite geometric series with first term a and common ratio r with $-1 < r < 1$ is

$$G = \frac{a}{1 - r}$$

Note that if the common ratio r is greater than 1 or less than -1, then the geometric series has no sum.

(4) As we saw in note (1), we can get the common ratio r of a geometric series, by dividing any term by the term which precedes it.

    28. Which of the following series converge?

      I. $\sum_{n=1}^{\infty} \frac{1}{n}$

      II. $\sum_{n=1}^{\infty} \frac{n^3}{2n^3+5}$

      III. $\sum_{n=1}^{\infty} \frac{\cos(n\pi)}{n}$

      (A) I only
      (B) II only
      (C) III only
      (D) I and III only

Solution: The first series is the harmonic series which diverges.

$\lim_{n \to \infty} \frac{n^3}{2n^3+5} = \frac{1}{2}$ and so $\sum_{n=1}^{\infty} \frac{n^3}{2n^3+5}$ diverges by the divergence test.

$$\sum_{n=1}^{\infty} \frac{\cos(n\pi)}{n} = \sum_{n=1}^{\infty} \frac{(-1)^n}{n}$$

Since $\left(\frac{1}{n}\right)$ is a decreasing sequence with $\lim_{n \to \infty} \frac{1}{n} = 0$, the series $\sum_{n=1}^{\infty} \frac{(-1)^n}{n}$ converges by the alternating series test.

So the answer is choice (C).

Notes: (1) $\sum_{n=1}^{\infty} \frac{1}{n} = 1 + \frac{1}{2} + \frac{1}{3} + \frac{1}{4} + \cdots$ is called the **harmonic series**. This series **diverges**.

It is not at all obvious that this series diverges, and one of the reasons that it is not obvious is because it diverges so slowly.

The advanced student might want to show that given any $M > 0$, there is a positive integer k such that $1 + \frac{1}{2} + \frac{1}{3} + \cdots + \frac{1}{k} > M$. This would give a proof that the harmonic series diverges.

(2) The **divergence test** or **nth term test** says:

(i) if $\sum_{n=1}^{\infty} a_n$ converges, then $\lim_{n\to\infty} a_n = 0$, or equivalently

(ii) if $\lim_{n\to\infty} a_n \neq 0$, then $\sum_{n=1}^{\infty} a_n$ diverges.

Note that statements (i) and (ii) are **contrapositives** of each other, and are therefore **logically equivalent**.

It is usually easier to apply the divergence test by using statement (ii).

In other words, simply check the limit of the underlying *sequence* of the series. If this limit is not zero, then the *series* diverges.

In this problem, the limit of the underlying sequence is $\frac{1}{2}$. Since this is not zero, the given series diverges.

A common mistake is to infer from $\lim_{n\to\infty} \frac{n^3}{2n^3+5} = \frac{1}{2}$ that the series converges to $\frac{1}{2}$. This is of course not true: the *sequence* $\left(\frac{n^3}{2n^3+5}\right)$ converges to $\frac{1}{2}$, but the corresponding *series* diverges by the divergence test.

(3) The **converse** of the divergence test is *false*. In other words, if $\lim_{n\to\infty} a_n = 0$, it does not necessarily follow that $\sum_{n=1}^{\infty} a_n$ converges.

Students make this mistake all the time! It is absolutely necessary for $\lim_{n\to\infty} a_n = 0$ for the series to have any chance of converging. But it is not enough! A simple counterexample is the harmonic series.

To summarize: (a) if $\lim_{n\to\infty} a_n \neq 0$, then $\sum_{n=1}^{\infty} a_n$ diverges.

(b) if $\lim_{n\to\infty} a_n = 0$, then $\sum_{n=1}^{\infty} a_n$ may converge or diverge.

(4) To see that $\cos(n\pi) = (-1)^n$, first note that $\cos(0\pi) = \cos 0 = 1$. It follows that $\cos(2k\pi) = \cos(0 + 2k\pi) = 1$ for all integers n, or equivalently, $\cos(n\pi) = 1$ whenever n is even.

Next note that $\cos(1\pi) = \cos \pi = -1$. It then follows that $\cos((2k + 1)\pi) = \cos(\pi + 2k\pi) = \cos \pi = -1$ for all integers n, or equivalently, $\cos(n\pi) = -1$ whenever n is odd.

Finally note that $(-1)^n = \begin{cases} 1 & \text{if } n \text{ is even} \\ -1 & \text{if } n \text{ is odd} \end{cases}$

(5) An **alternating series** has one of the forms $\sum_{n=1}^{\infty}(-1)^n a_n$ or $\sum_{n=1}^{\infty}(-1)^{n+1} a_n$ where $a_n > 0$ for each positive integer n.

For example, the series given in III is an alternating series since it is equal to $\sum_{n=1}^{\infty}\frac{(-1)^n}{n} = \sum_{n=1}^{\infty}(-1)^n\left(\frac{1}{n}\right)$, and $a_n = \frac{1}{n} > 0$ for all positive integers n.

(6) The **alternating series test** says that if (a_n) is a decreasing sequence with $\lim_{n\to\infty} a_n = 0$, then the alternating series $\sum_{n=1}^{\infty}(-1)^n a_n$ or $\sum_{n=1}^{\infty}(-1)^{n+1} a_n$ converges.

Since for all positive integers n, $n < n + 1$, it follows that $\frac{1}{n} > \frac{1}{n+1}$, and the sequence $\left(\frac{1}{n}\right)$ is decreasing. Also it is clear that $\lim_{n\to\infty}\frac{1}{n} = 0$. It follows that $\sum_{n=1}^{\infty}\frac{(-1)^n}{n}$ converges by the alternating series test.

(7) Another way to check that the sequence $\left(\frac{1}{n}\right)$ is decreasing is to note that $\frac{d}{dn}\left[\frac{1}{x}\right] = \frac{d}{dn}[x^{-1}] = -1x^{-2} = -\frac{1}{x^2} < 0$. So the function $f(x) = \frac{1}{x}$ is a decreasing function, and therefore the sequence $\left(\frac{1}{n}\right)$ is also decreasing.

29. Let f be a decreasing function with $f(x) \geq 0$ for all positive real numbers x. If $\lim_{b\to\infty}\int_1^b f(x)\, dx$ is finite, then which of the following must be true?

    (A) $\sum_{n=1}^{\infty} f(n)$ converges

    (B) $\sum_{n=1}^{\infty} f(n)$ diverges

    (C) $\sum_{n=1}^{\infty}\frac{1}{f(n)}$ converges

    (D) $\sum_{n=1}^{\infty}\frac{1}{f(n)}$ diverges

Solution: By the integral test, $\sum_{n=1}^{\infty} f(n)$ converges, choice (A).

Notes: (1) The **integral test** says the following:

47

Let f be a continuous, positive, decreasing function on $[c, \infty)$. Then $\sum_{n=c}^{\infty} f(n)$ converges if and only if $\int_c^{\infty} f(x)\, dx$ converges.

(2) $\int_1^{\infty} f(x)\, dx = \lim_{b \to \infty} \int_1^{b} f(x)\, dx$.

(3) The integral test cannot be used to evaluate $\sum_{n=1}^{\infty} f(n)$. In general $\sum_{n=1}^{\infty} f(n) \neq \int_1^{\infty} f(x)\, dx$.

(4) The condition of f decreasing can actually be weakened to f "eventually decreasing." For example, $f(x) = \frac{\ln x}{x}$ is not decreasing on $[1, \infty)$, but is decreasing eventually. This can be verified by using the first derivative test. See problem 37 for details on how to apply this test. I leave the details to the reader.

Now, $\int_1^{\infty} \frac{\ln x}{x}\, dx = \frac{1}{2}(\ln x)^2 \big|_1^{\infty} = \lim_{b \to \infty}(\ln b)^2 = \infty$. It follows that $\int_1^{\infty} \frac{\ln x}{x}\, dx$ diverges. By the integral test $\sum_{n=1}^{\infty} \frac{\ln n}{n}$ diverges.

(5) For details on how to integrate $\int \frac{\ln x}{x}\, dx$, see the solution to problem 5.

30. Which of the following series converge to -1 ?

I. $\sum_{n=1}^{\infty} \frac{3}{(-2)^n}$

II. $\sum_{n=1}^{\infty} \frac{1-3n^2}{3n^2+2}$

III. $\sum_{n=1}^{\infty} \frac{1}{n(n+1)}$

(A) I only
(B) II only
(C) III only
(D) I and III only

Solution: The first series is geometric with first term $a = -\frac{3}{2}$ and common ratio $r = -\frac{1}{2}$. So the sum is $\sum_{n=1}^{\infty} \frac{3}{(-2)^n} = \frac{-\frac{3}{2}}{1+\frac{1}{2}} = -1$.

$\lim_{n \to \infty} \frac{1-3n^2}{3n^2+2} = -1$ and so $\sum_{n=1}^{\infty} \frac{1-3n^2}{3n^2+2}$ diverges by the divergence test.

$$\sum_{n=1}^{\infty} \frac{1}{n(n+1)} = \sum_{n=1}^{\infty} \left(\frac{1}{n} - \frac{1}{n+1}\right)$$

48

$$= \lim_{n\to\infty} \left[\left(1 - \tfrac{1}{2}\right) + \left(\tfrac{1}{2} - \tfrac{1}{3}\right) + \cdots + \left(\tfrac{1}{n} - \tfrac{1}{n+1}\right)\right] = \lim_{n\to\infty}\left(1 - \tfrac{1}{n+1}\right) = 1.$$

So the answer is choice (A).

Notes: (1) See problem 27 for more information on infinite geometric series.

(2) For the first series it might help to write out the first few terms:

$$\sum_{n=1}^{\infty} \frac{3}{(-2)^n} = -\frac{3}{2} + \frac{3}{4} - \frac{3}{8} + \cdots + \frac{3}{(-2)^n} + \cdots$$

It is now easy to check that the series is geometric by checking the first two quotients: $\frac{3}{4} \div \left(-\frac{3}{2}\right) = \frac{3}{4}\cdot\left(-\frac{2}{3}\right) = -\frac{1}{2}$, $-\frac{3}{8} \div \frac{3}{4} = -\frac{3}{8}\cdot\frac{4}{3} = -\frac{1}{2}$.

So we see that the series is geometric with common ratio $r = -\frac{1}{2}$. It is also quite clear that the first term is $a = -\frac{3}{2}$.

(3) A geometric series has the form $\sum_{n=0}^{\infty} ar^n$. In this form, the first term is a and the common ratio is r. I wouldn't get too hung up on this form though. Once you recognize that a series is geometric, it's easy enough to just write out the first few terms and find the first term and common ratio as we did in note (2) above.

If we were to put the given series in this precise form it would look like this: $\sum_{n=0}^{\infty} \left(-\frac{3}{2}\right)\left(-\frac{1}{2}\right)^n$. But again, this is unnecessary (and confusing).

(4) See problem 28 for more information on the divergence test.

(5) The third series is a **telescoping sum**. We can formally do a partial fraction decomposition to see that $\sum_{n=1}^{\infty} \frac{1}{n(n+1)} = \sum_{n=1}^{\infty}\left(\frac{1}{n} - \frac{1}{n+1}\right)$. We start by writing $\frac{1}{n(n+1)} = \frac{A}{n} + \frac{B}{n+1}$. Now multiply each side of this equation by $n(n+1)$ to get $1 = A(n+1) + Bn = An + A + Bn$.

So we have $0n + 1 = (A + B)n + A$. Equating coefficients gives us $A + B = 0$ and $A = 1$, from which we also get $B = -1$.

So $\frac{1}{n(n+1)} = \frac{A}{n} + \frac{B}{n+1} = \frac{1}{n} + \frac{(-1)}{n+1} = \frac{1}{n} - \frac{1}{n+1}$.

(6) Another way to find A and B in the equation $1 = A(n + 1) + Bn$ is to substitute in specific values for n. Two good choices are $n = 0$ and $n = -1$.

$n = 0$: $1 = A(0 + 1) + B(0) = A$. So $A = 1$.

$n = -1$: $1 = A(-1 + 1) + B(-1)$. So $1 = -B$, and $B = -1$.

31. Which of the following series diverge?

I. $\sum_{n=1}^{\infty} \frac{e^n}{n^2+1}$

II. $\sum_{n=1}^{\infty} (\frac{99}{100})^n$

III. $\sum_{n=1}^{\infty} \frac{2^n}{n!}$

(A) I only
(B) II only
(C) III only
(D) I and III only

Solution: $\lim_{n \to \infty} \frac{e^n}{n^2+1} = \infty$ and so $\sum_{n=1}^{\infty} \frac{e^n}{n^2+1}$ diverges by the divergence test.

$\sum_{n=1}^{\infty} (\frac{99}{100})^n$ is geometric with common ratio $r = \frac{99}{100} < 1$, and so $\sum_{n=1}^{\infty} (\frac{99}{100})^n$ converges.

$\lim_{n \to \infty} \left| \frac{\frac{2^{n+1}}{(n+1)!}}{\frac{2^n}{n!}} \right| = \lim_{n \to \infty} \left| \frac{2^{n+1}}{(n+1)!} \cdot \frac{n!}{2^n} \right| = \lim_{n \to \infty} \frac{2}{n+1} = 0 < 1$, and so $\sum_{n=1}^{\infty} \frac{2^n}{n!}$ converges by the ratio test.

Therefore the answer is choice (A).

Notes: (1) See problems 27 and 30 for more information on infinite geometric series, and see problem 28 for more information on the divergence test.

(2) We say that the series $\sum_{n=0}^{\infty} a_n$ **converges absolutely** if $\sum_{n=0}^{\infty} |a_n|$ converges. If a series converges absolutely, then it converges.

A series which is convergent, but not absolutely convergent is said to **converge conditionally**.

(3) **The Ratio Test:** For the series $\sum_{n=0}^{\infty} a_n$, define $L = \lim_{n \to \infty} \left| \frac{a_{n+1}}{a_n} \right|$.

If $L < 1$, then the series converges absolutely, and therefore converges. If $L > 1$, then the series diverges. If $L = 1$, then the ratio test fails.

For the series $\sum_{n=1}^{\infty} \frac{2^n}{n!}$ given in this problem, we have $a_n = \frac{2^n}{n!}$, and so $a_{n+1} = \frac{2^{n+1}}{(n+1)!}$.

32. What are all values of x for which the series $\sum_{n=1}^{\infty} \frac{5^n x^n}{n}$ converges?

(A) All x except $x = 0$

(B) $|x| < \frac{1}{5}$

(C) $-\frac{1}{5} \leq x < \frac{1}{5}$

(D) $-\frac{1}{5} \leq x \leq \frac{1}{5}$

Solution: $\lim_{n \to \infty} \left| \frac{\frac{5^{n+1} x^{n+1}}{(n+1)}}{\frac{5^n x^n}{n}} \right| = \lim_{n \to \infty} \left| \frac{5^{n+1} x^{n+1}}{n+1} \cdot \frac{n}{5^n x^n} \right| = 5|x|$. So by the ratio test, the series converges for all x such that $5|x| < 1$, or equivalently $|x| < \frac{1}{5}$. Removing the absolute values gives $-\frac{1}{5} < x < \frac{1}{5}$.

We still need to check the endpoints. When $x = \frac{1}{5}$, we get the divergent harmonic series $\sum_{n=1}^{\infty} \frac{1}{n}$, and when $x = -\frac{1}{5}$ we get the convergent alternating series $\sum_{n=1}^{\infty} (-1)^n \frac{1}{n}$. So the series diverges at $x = \frac{1}{5}$ and converges at $x = -\frac{1}{5}$.

The answer is therefore choice (C).

Notes: (1) A **power series** about $x = 0$ is a series of the form $\sum_{n=1}^{\infty} a_n x^n$. To determine where a power series converges we use the ratio test. In other words we compute

$$L = \lim_{n \to \infty} \left| \frac{a_{n+1} x^{n+1}}{a_n x^n} \right| = \lim_{n \to \infty} \left| \frac{a_{n+1}}{a_n} \right| |x|.$$

If $L = 0$, then the series converges only for $x = 0$.

If $L = \infty$, then the series converges absolutely for all x (and therefore converges for all x – see problem 31, note 2).

Otherwise we solve the equation $L < 1$ for $|x|$ to get an inequality of the form $|x| < R$. In this case the series converges absolutely for $|x| < R$ and diverges for $|x| > R$. The positive number R is called the **radius of convergence** of the power series.

As always the ratio test fails when $L = 1$. So the endpoints $x = -R$ and $x = R$ have to be checked separately.

(2) In this problem we have

$$L = \lim_{n\to\infty} \left| \frac{\frac{5^{n+1}x^{n+1}}{(n+1)}}{\frac{5^n x^n}{n}} \right| = \lim_{n\to\infty} \left| \frac{5^{n+1}x^{n+1}}{n+1} \cdot \frac{n}{5^n x^n} \right| = \lim_{n\to\infty} \frac{n}{n+1} \cdot 5|x| = 5|x|$$

Setting $L < 1$ gives $5|x| < 1$, or equivalently $|x| < \frac{1}{5}$. So the radius of convergence is $R = \frac{1}{5}$.

Note that we needed to check the endpoints $x = -\frac{1}{5}$ and $x = \frac{1}{5}$ separately.

LEVEL 2: DIFFERENTIATION

33. Write an equation of the normal line to the curve $y = \sqrt{25 - x}$ at the point $(0,5)$.

Solution: $y' = -\frac{1}{2\sqrt{25-x}}$, so that the slope of the tangent line to y at $(0,5)$ is $y'|_{x=0} = -\frac{1}{2\sqrt{25}} = -\frac{1}{2\cdot5} = -\frac{1}{10}$. So the slope of the normal line is 10.

An equation of the normal line is then $y = 10x + 5$.

Notes: (1) To find the slope of the tangent line to a curve y at $x = x_0$ we take the derivative y', and substitute in x_0 for x.

In this problem, we used the chain rule to find y', and then substituted 0 in for x. See problem 2 for more information on the chain rule.

(2) The **normal line** to a curve is perpendicular to the tangent line. Therefore the slope of the normal line is the negative reciprocal of the slope of the tangent line.

(3) We wrote an equation of the line in **slope-intercept** form. We have $y = mx + b$, where m is the slope of the line and the point $(0, b)$ is the y-intercept of the line.

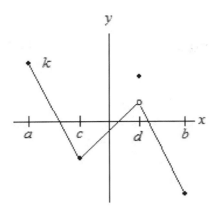

34. The function k, whose graph consists of three line segments, is shown above. Which of the following are true for k on the open interval (a, b) ?

    I. $\lim_{x \to c} k(x)$ exists.
    II. The domain of the derivative of k is the open interval (c, d).
    III. The derivative of k is negative on the interval (d, b).

    (A) I only
    (B) II only
    (C) III only
    (D) I and III only

Solution: Since $\lim_{x \to c^-} k(x) = \lim_{x \to c^+} k(x)$, $\lim_{x \to c} k(x)$ exists. So I is true.

On (a, b), the function k fails to be differentiable at $x = c$ and $x = d$ only. So the domain of the derivative of k contains points that are not in (c, d). So II is false.

The function k is decreasing on (d, b). Therefore the derivative of k is negative on (d, b). So III is true.

It follows that the answer is choice (D).

Notes: (1) $\lim_{x \to c} k(x)$ exists because as we approach c from both the left and the right, we are heading toward the same point.

In this case it is actually true that the function k is continuous at $x = c$ because the value that we are approaching is actually attained.

Note however that k is *not* differentiable at $x = c$ because there is a "sharp edge" there. More specifically, the slope of the tangent line from the left is negative because the function is decreasing to the left of c, and the slope of the tangent line from the right is positive because the function is increasing to the right of c.

Let's compare this to the situation at $x = d$. $\lim_{x \to d} k(x)$ exists because as we approach d from both the left and the right, we are heading toward the same point.

In this case however the function k is *not* continuous at $x = d$ because the value that we are approaching is *not* the same as $k(d)$ which is a larger number (because it is *higher* on the graph).

Of course k is not differentiable at $x = d$ since continuity is required for differentiability.

(2) The domain of the derivative of k is $(a, c) \cup (c, d) \cup (d, b)$. In other words, the derivative of k exists at all x values between a and b *except* for $x = c$ and $x = d$.

The derivative of k does not exist at $x = c$ because there is a "sharp edge" there, and the derivative of k does not exist at $x = d$ because k is discontinuous at $x = d$.

(3) If f is differentiable, then the derivative of f is positive if and only if f is increasing, and the derivative of f is negative if and only if f is decreasing.

In this problem, the function k is differentiable and increasing on (c, d). Therefore $k'(x) > 0$ for all x in (c, d).

The function k is decreasing on the intervals (a, c) and (d, b). Therefore $k'(x) < 0$ for all x in (a, c) and for all x in (d, b).

35. The slope of the tangent line to the curve $xy^5 - x^3y^4 = 10$ at $(-2, -1)$ is

    (A)   0

    (B) $-\dfrac{2}{7}$

    (C) $-\dfrac{13}{42}$

    (D) $-\dfrac{1}{3}$

Solution: We have

$$x\left(5y^4 \cdot \frac{dy}{dx}\right) + y^5(1) - x^3\left(4y^3 \cdot \frac{dy}{dx}\right) + y^4(-3x^2) = 0.$$

We now substitute -2 for x and -1 for y to get

$$(-2)\left(5(-1)^4 \cdot \frac{dy}{dx}\right) + (-1)^5(1) - (-2)^3\left(4(-1)^3 \cdot \frac{dy}{dx}\right) + (-1)^4(-3(-2)^2) = 0$$

$$(-2)\left(5 \cdot 1 \cdot \frac{dy}{dx}\right) + (-1)(1) - (-8)\left(4(-1) \cdot \frac{dy}{dx}\right) + (1)(-3 \cdot 4) = 0$$

$$-10\frac{dy}{dx} - 1 - 32\frac{dy}{dx} - 12 = 0$$

$$-42\frac{dy}{dx} - 13 = 0$$

So we have $-42\frac{dy}{dx} = 13$, and therefore $\frac{dy}{dx} = -\frac{13}{42}$, choice (C).

Notes: (1) The given equation defines the dependent variable y **implicitly** as a function of x.

This just means that the variable y is *not* by itself on one side of the equation.

An example of an **explicitly** defined function is $y = 2x$.

This same function can be defined implicitly as $2x - y = 0$.

(2) When the dependent variable y is defined implicitly as a function of x, we can use **implicit differentiation** to find the derivative $\frac{dy}{dx}$.

This is just an application of the chain rule. Since y is a function of x, we can write $y = f(x)$ for some function f. So if we want to differentiate $g(y)$, simply note that this is $g(f(x))$, and so the derivative is $g'(f(x)) \cdot f'(x) = g'(y) \cdot \frac{dy}{dx}$.

For example, the derivative of y^5 is $5y^4\frac{dy}{dx}$, and the derivative of y^4 is $4y^3\frac{dy}{dx}$.

(3) To get the derivative in this problem we needed to use the product rule twice: once for the product xy^5, and once for the product $-x^3y^4$.

(4) Remember that the derivative of a constant is 0. So once we differentiate, we get 0 on the right hand side of the equation. A common mistake is to leave this as 10.

(5) In the solution above after differentiating we plugged in -2 for x and -1 for y first, *and then* solved for $\frac{dy}{dx}$. This is generally much faster than solving for $\frac{dy}{dx}$ first and then plugging in the point.

(6) If we were not given a point in the question, and were simply asked to find $\frac{dy}{dx}$, then we would do the following:

$$x\left(5y^4 \cdot \frac{dy}{dx}\right) + y^5(1) - x^3\left(4y^3 \cdot \frac{dy}{dx}\right) + y^4(-3x^2) = 0$$

$$5xy^4\frac{dy}{dx} + y^5 - 4x^3y^3\frac{dy}{dx} - 3x^2y^4 = 0$$

$$5xy^4\frac{dy}{dx} - 4x^3y^3\frac{dy}{dx} = 3x^2y^4 - y^5$$

$$(5xy^4 - 4x^3y^3)\frac{dy}{dx} = 3x^2y^4 - y^5$$

$$\frac{dy}{dx} = \frac{3x^2y^4 - y^5}{5xy^4 - 4x^3y^3} = \frac{y^4(3x^2-y)}{xy^3(5y-4x^2)} = \frac{y(3x^2-y)}{x(5y-4x^2)}$$

(7) As an alternative solution to this problem (although not recommended), after differentiating, we can first solve for $\frac{dy}{dx}$ as in note (6), and then plug in -2 for x and -1 for y as follows:

$$\frac{dy}{dx} = \frac{y(3x^2-y)}{x(5y-4x^2)} = \frac{(-1)(3(-2)^2-(-1))}{(-2)(5(-1)-4(-2)^2)} = \frac{(-1)(3(4)+1)}{(-2)(-5-4(4))} = \frac{(-1)(12+1)}{(-2)(-5-16)} = \frac{-13}{42}$$

36. Let $f(x) = x \ln x$. A value of c that satisfies the conclusion of the Mean Value Theorem for f on the interval $[e, e^2]$ is

Solution: $f'(x) = x \cdot \frac{1}{x} + (\ln x) \cdot 1 = 1 + \ln x$. So $f'(c) = 1 + \ln c$.

$f(e) = e \ln e = e \cdot 1 = e$.

$f(e^2) = e^2 \ln e^2 = e^2 \cdot 2 = 2e^2$.

We now solve the equation $f'(c) = \frac{f(e^2)-f(e)}{e^2-e}$ to get

$$1 + \ln c = \frac{2e^2-e}{e^2-e} = \frac{e(2e-1)}{e(e-1)} = \frac{2e-1}{e-1}.$$

56

So $\ln c = \frac{2e-1}{e-1} - 1 = \frac{2e-1}{e-1} - \frac{e-1}{e-1} = \frac{2e-1-e+1}{e-1} = \frac{e}{e-1}$, and so we have $c = e^{\frac{e}{e-1}}$.

Notes: (1) The **Mean Value Theorem** says that if f is a function that is continuous on the closed interval $[a, b]$ and differentiable on the open interval (a, b), then there is a real number c with $a < c < b$ such that $f'(c) = \frac{f(b)-f(a)}{b-a}$.

In this problem $a = e$, $b = e^2$, and $f(x) = x \ln x$.

(2) Note that the function $g(x) = x$ is a polynomial. It is therefore continuous and differentiable everywhere. In particular, it is continuous on $[e, e^2]$ and differentiable on (e, e^2).

The function $h(x) = \ln x$ is continuous and differentiable on its domain which is $(0, \infty)$. It is therefore continuous on $[e, e^2]$ and differentiable on (e, e^2).

It follows that the product $f(x) = g(x) \cdot h(x) = x \ln x$ is continuous on $[e, e^2]$ and differentiable on (e, e^2).

Therefore by the Mean Value Theorem, there is a c between e and e^2 such that

$$f'(c) = \frac{f(e^2)-f(e)}{e^2-e}.$$

(3) Geometrically, $f'(c)$ is the slope of the tangent line to the graph of the function f at c, and $\frac{f(b)-f(a)}{b-a}$ is the slope of the secant line passing through the points $A(a, f(a))$, and $B(b, f(b))$.

The Mean Value Theorem says that the slopes of these two lines are the same. In other words, they are parallel.

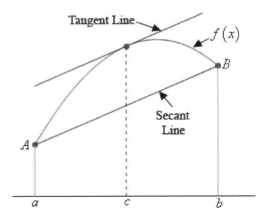

37. The *derivative* of $g(x) = \frac{x^7}{7} - \frac{x^6}{5}$ attains its minimum value at $x =$

    (A) $\frac{7}{5}$

    (B) $\frac{6}{5}$

    (C) 1

    (D) 0

Solution: $g'(x) = x^6 - \frac{6}{5}x^5$.

To minimize $g'(x)$ we first take its derivative

$$g''(x) = 6x^5 - 6x^4 = 6x^4(x - 1).$$

We then check when $g''(x)$ is equal to 0 to find the **critical numbers** of g'. The critical numbers of g' are $x = 0$ and $x = 1$.

Now note that for $x < 1$, $g''(x) < 0$, and for $x > 1$, $g''(x) > 0$. So g' is decreasing for $x < 1$ and increasing for $x > 1$. So g' attains its minimum value at $x = 1$, choice (C).

Notes: (1) A **critical number** of a function f is a real number c in the domain of f such that $f'(c) = 0$ or $f'(c)$ is undefined.

(2) A function f attains a **relative minimum** (or **local minimum**) at a real number $x = c$ if there is an interval (a, b) containing c such that $f(c) < f(x)$ for all x in the interval.

If a function is decreasing to the left of c, and increasing to the right of c, then f attains a relative minimum at c.

In terms of derivatives, if $f'(x) < 0$ for $x < c$, and $f'(x) > 0$ for $x > c$, then f attains a relative minimum at c.

This method of finding the relative extrema of a function is called the **first derivative test**.

(3) Take careful note that in this problem we are trying to minimize the *derivative* of g. So we need to be checking $g''(x)$ near $x = c$.

(4) A nice visual way to apply the first derivative test is by creating a **sign chart**. We split up the real line into intervals using the critical numbers of the function (and we also include any points of discontinuity if they exist), and then check the sign of the derivative in each subinterval formed.

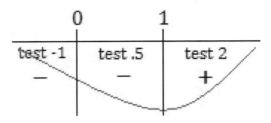

In this case we split up the real line into three pieces. Notice that the cutoff points are 0 and 1, the critical numbers of g'. We then plug a real number from each of these three intervals into g'' to see if the answer is positive or negative. For example, $g''(2) = 6(2)^4(2 - 1) > 0$. Note that we do not need to finish the computation. We only need to know if the answer is positive or negative. Finally we make a quick sketch that decreases across the intervals where there is a minus sign, and increases across the intervals where there is a plus sign. We can then clearly see that there is a minimum at $x = 1$.

(5) The sketch of the graph in the sign chart is not meant to be completely accurate (and it is not). It is only being used to demonstrate where the function is increasing and decreasing, so we can determine if there is a minimum or maximum (or neither) at each critical number.

(6) Let's take a look at the expression $g''(x) = 6x^4(x - 1)$.

We see that $g'(x) = 0$ when $x = 0$ and $x = 1$. Note that $x = 0$ is a zero of the equation of multiplicity 4. In particular, it has even multiplicity. It follows that the graph of g'' *does not* pass through the x-axis at $x = 0$. In other words, g'' does not change sign there, and so a maximum or minimum *cannot* occur at $x = 0$.

On the other hand, $x = 1$ is a zero of multiplicity 1. In particular, it has odd multiplicity. It follows that the graph of g' *does* pass through the x-axis at $x = 1$. In other words, g'' does change sign there, and so a maximum or minimum *does* occur at $x = 1$.

(7) Based on the reasoning of note (6) we can get the answer to this question just by looking at the factored form of g''. Since $x = 1$ is the only zero with odd multiplicity, it is the only possible place where a minimum can occur. So the answer must be choice (C).

In other words, in this problem we do not actually need to perform the first derivative test (and in particular, we do not need to draw a sign chart). But it's not a bad idea to do so just to check your work.

38. A curve is described by the parametric equations $x = 3t^2 - 4t$ and $y = \sqrt{4t + 1}$. An equation of the line tangent to the curve at the point where $t = 2$ is

(A) $3x - y = 0$
(B) $12y - x = 32$
(C) $12x - y = 32$
(D) $x - 12y = 32$

Solution: When $t = 2$, $x = 3(2)^2 - 4 \cdot 2 = 4$ and $y = \sqrt{4(2) + 1} = 3$. So the point $(4, 3)$ is on the tangent line.

$\dfrac{dy}{dt} = \dfrac{2}{\sqrt{4t+1}}$ and $\dfrac{dx}{dt} = 6t - 4$, and so $\dfrac{dy}{dt}\Big|_{t=2} = \dfrac{2}{\sqrt{4(2)+1}} = \dfrac{2}{3}$ and $\dfrac{dx}{dt}\Big|_{t=2} = 6(2) - 4 = 8$.

It follows that the slope of the tangent line when $t = 2$ is

$$m = \frac{dy}{dx}\Big|_{t=2} = \frac{\frac{dy}{dt}\big|_{t=2}}{\frac{dx}{dt}\big|_{t=2}} = \frac{2}{3} \div 8 = \frac{2}{3} \cdot \frac{1}{8} = \frac{1}{12}.$$

So an equation of the tangent line in point–slope form is

$$y - 3 = \frac{1}{12}(x - 4).$$

Multiplying each side of this equation by 12 yields $12y - 36 = x - 4$. So we get the equation $12y - x = 32$, choice (B).

Notes: (1) See problem 5 for more information on parametric equations.

(2) As usual, the slope of the tangent line to the curve is $\dfrac{dy}{dx}$. In this case we have $\dfrac{dy}{dx} = \dfrac{\frac{dy}{dt}}{\frac{dx}{dt}}$.

(3) The **point-slope form of an equation of a line** is

$$y - y_0 = m(x - x_0)$$

where m is the slope of the line and (x_0, y_0) is any point on the line.

It is generally easiest to write an equation of a line in point-slope form once the slope of the line and a point on the line are known. In this problem, the slope is $\frac{1}{12}$ and the point is $(4,3)$.

39. The line perpendicular to the tangent line to the curve represented by the equation $y = x^2 + 3x + 2$ at the point $(-3,2)$ also intersects the curve at $x =$

    (A) $\frac{1}{3}$

    (B) 2

    (C) 3

    (D) $\frac{7}{2}$

Solution: $y' = 2x + 3$, so that $y'|_{x=-3} = 2(-3) + 3 = -6 + 3 = -3$. So the slope of the line perpendicular to the tangent line is $m = \frac{1}{3}$. An equation of this line is $y - 2 = \frac{1}{3}(x + 3)$, or equivalently $y = \frac{1}{3}x + 3$.

We now solve the equation $\frac{1}{3}x + 3 = x^2 + 3x + 2$ for x to get

$$x + 9 = 3x^2 + 9x + 6$$
$$0 = 3x^2 + 8x - 3$$
$$0 = (3x - 1)(x + 3)$$

So $3x - 1 = 0$, and therefore $x = \frac{1}{3}$, choice (A).

40. If $\frac{d}{dx}[k(x)] = h(x)$ and   if $g(x) = 2x^3 - 5$,   then $\frac{d}{dx}[k(g(x))] =$

    (A) $(2x^3 - 5)h(2x^3 - 5)$
    (B) $6x^2 h(2x^3 - 5)$
    (C) $h'(x)$
    (D) $6x^2 h(x)$

Solution: $\frac{d}{dx}[k(g(x))] = k'(g(x)) \cdot g'(x) = h(2x^3 - 5) \cdot 6x^2$. So the answer is choice (B).

Note: We used the chain rule here. See problem 2 for more information.

LEVEL 2: INTEGRATION

41. Each of the following is an antiderivative of $\frac{(\ln x)^2 - 2}{x}$ EXCEPT

(A) $\frac{(\ln x)^3}{3} - \ln x^2$

(B) $\ln x - \ln x^2$

(C) $\frac{(\ln x)^3}{3} - 2\ln|x|$

(D) $1 - \ln x^2 + \frac{(\ln x)^3}{3}$

Solution: $\int \frac{(\ln x)^2 - 2}{x} dx = \frac{(\ln x)^3}{3} - 2\ln|x| + C = \frac{(\ln x)^3}{3} - \ln x^2 + C$

All answer choices have one of the two forms above except choice (B).

Notes: (1) $\frac{(\ln x)^2 - 2}{x} = \frac{(\ln x)^2}{x} - \frac{2}{x}$. So we integrate each of the two terms separately.

(2) To evaluate $\int \frac{(\ln x)^2}{x} dx$, we can formally make the substitution $u = \ln x$. It then follows that $du = \frac{1}{x} dx$. So we have

$$\int \frac{(\ln x)^2}{x} dx = \int (\ln x)^2 \cdot \frac{1}{x} dx = \int u^2 du = \frac{u^3}{3} + C = \frac{(\ln x)^3}{3} + C.$$

(3) With a little practice, we can evaluate an integral like this very quickly with the following reasoning: The derivative of $\ln x$ is $\frac{1}{x}$. So to integrate $\frac{(\ln x)^2}{x}$ we simply pretend we are integrating x^2 but as we do it we leave the $\ln x$ where it is. This is essentially what was done in the above solution.

Note that the $\frac{1}{x}$ "goes away" because it is the derivative of $\ln x$. We need it there for everything to work.

(4) You should know $\int \frac{1}{x} dx = \ln|x| + C$ (See problem 5 for details.)

It follows that $\int \frac{2}{x} dx = 2 \int \frac{1}{x} dx = 2 \ln|x| + C$.

(5) Putting notes (1) through (4) together gives us

$$\int \frac{(\ln x)^2 - 2}{x} dx = \int \frac{(\ln x)^2}{x} dx - \int \frac{2}{x} dx = \frac{(\ln x)^3}{3} - 2 \ln|x| + C.$$

(6) $n \ln x = \ln x^n$. So we have $2 \ln|x| = \ln|x|^2 = \ln x^2$

(7) $|x|^2 = x^2$ because x^2 is always nonnegative.

(8) We can also solve this problem by differentiating the answer choices.

For example, looking at choice (A), we have

$$\frac{d}{dx}\left[\frac{(\ln x)^3}{3} - \ln x^2\right] = \frac{3(\ln x)^2}{3} \cdot \frac{1}{x} - \frac{1}{x^2} \cdot 2x = \frac{(\ln x)^2}{x} - \frac{2}{x} = \frac{(\ln x)^2 - 2}{x}.$$

This shows that we can eliminate choice (A), and a moment's thought allows us to eliminate choice (D) as well.

Let's look at choice (C) next. We have

$$\frac{d}{dx}\left[\frac{(\ln x)^3}{3} - 2\ln|x|\right] = \frac{3(\ln x)^2}{3} \cdot \frac{1}{x} - 2 \cdot \frac{1}{x} = \frac{(\ln x)^2}{x} - \frac{2}{x} = \frac{(\ln x)^2 - 2}{x}.$$

So we can eliminate choice (C) and the answer must be choice (B).

(Note that $\frac{d}{dx}[\ln|x|] = \frac{1}{x}$.)

For completeness, let's differentiate the expression in choice (B).

$$\frac{d}{dx}[\ln x - \ln x^2] = \frac{1}{x} - \frac{1}{x^2} \cdot 2x = \frac{1}{x} - \frac{2}{x} = -\frac{1}{x}.$$

Since $-\frac{1}{x} \neq \frac{(\ln x)^2 - 2}{x}$, the answer is definitely choice (B).

42. $\int \frac{8}{1+x^2} dx =$

      (A) $8 \ln(1 + x^2) + C$

      (B) $8x - \frac{8}{x} + C$

      (C) $8 \tan^{-1} x + C$

      (D) $-\frac{16x}{(1+x^2)^2}$

Solution: $\int \frac{8}{1+x^2} dx = 8 \int \frac{1}{1+x^2} dx = 8 \tan^{-1} x + C$, choice (C).

Notes: (1) You should know the following basic inverse trig integrals:

$$\int \frac{1}{\sqrt{1-x^2}}dx = \sin^{-1}x + C$$

$$\int \frac{1}{1+x^2}dx = \tan^{-1}x + C$$

$$\int \frac{1}{|x|\sqrt{x^2-1}}dx = \sec^{-1}x + C$$

(2) If you already know the derivatives corresponding to each of the integrals given in note (1), then there is no need to memorize anything new. See problem 71 for the six inverse trig derivatives.

43. The solution to the differential equation $\frac{dy}{dx} = \frac{x^2}{y^4}$, where $y(3) = 0$, is

(A) $y = \sqrt[5]{\frac{5}{3}x^3 - 45}$

(B) $y = \sqrt[5]{\frac{5}{3}x^3 - 9}$

(C) $y = \sqrt[5]{\frac{5}{3}x^3} - 45$

(D) $y = \sqrt[5]{\frac{5}{3}x^3} - \sqrt[5]{45}$

Solution: We separate variables to get $y^4 dy = x^2 dx$. We then integrate both sides of this equation to get $\frac{y^5}{5} = \frac{x^3}{3} + C$.

Now we substitute in $x = 3$ and $y = 0$ to get $\frac{0^5}{5} = \frac{3^3}{3} + C$. So $C = -9$, and we have $\frac{y^5}{5} = \frac{x^3}{3} - 9$. We multiply each side of this equation by 5 to get $y^5 = \frac{5}{3}x^3 - 45$, and then we take the fifth root of each side of this last equation to get $y = \sqrt[5]{\frac{5}{3}x^3 - 45}$, choice (A).

Notes: (1) A **separable differential equation** (or separable **DE**) has the form $\frac{dy}{dx} = f(x)g(y)$. We can solve this type of differential equation by rewriting it in the form $\frac{1}{g(y)}dy = f(x)dx$. This is called **separating variables**. We then integrate each side to get $\int \frac{1}{g(y)}dy = \int f(x)dx + C$.

In this problem we have $f(x) = x^2$ and $g(y) = \frac{1}{y^4}$.

(2) The condition $y(3) = 0$ is called an **initial condition**. We can use the initial condition to find the constant C.

In this case we substitute in $x = 3$ and $y = 0$, and then solve for C.

(3) It is usually more efficient to find the constant C before solving for the dependent variable y.

(4) Note that when we substitute 3 in for x into the answer choices, only choices (A) and (D) yield $y = 0$. We can use this reasoning to eliminate choices (B) and (C).

44. What is the area of the closed region bounded by the curve $y = \ln \sqrt[3]{x}$, and the lines $x = 1$ and $y = -2$?

(A) $\dfrac{e^{-6}+5}{3}$

(B) $\dfrac{e^{-6}+3}{3}$

(C) $\dfrac{e^{-6}+1}{3}$

(D) $\dfrac{e^{-6}-1}{3}$

Solution: First note that $y = \frac{1}{3}\ln x$, so that $3y = \ln x$ and therefore $x = e^{3y}$. So we have

$$\text{Area} = \int_{-2}^{0}(1 - e^{3y})dy = y - \frac{1}{3}e^{3y}\Big|_{-2}^{0} = -\frac{1}{3} - \left(-2 - \frac{1}{3}e^{-6}\right) = \frac{e^{-6}+5}{3}.$$

This is choice (A).

Notes: (1) Let's draw a picture of the region.

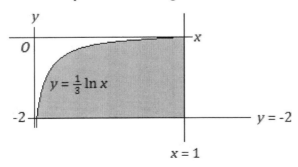

65

(2) The area between the curves $y = f(x)$ and $y = g(x)$ from $x = a$ to $x = b$ is $\int_a^b |f(x) - g(x)|\, dx$. The x-values a and b are usually the x-coordinates of points of intersection of the two graphs.

In this problem we can let $a = e^{-6}$, $b = 1$, $f(x) = \frac{1}{3}\ln x$, $g(x) = -2$. We then have Area $= \int_{e^{-6}}^{1}(\frac{1}{3}\ln x - (-2))dx = \int_{e^{-6}}^{1}(\frac{1}{3}\ln x + 2)dx$. This is a fairly difficult integral that requires integration by parts. We will see how to evaluate this integral in notes (4) and (5) below.

(3) Observe that in the solution above we are thinking of the shaded region as $-2 \le y \le 0$ and $e^{3y} \le x \le 1$ (we already showed that $y = \ln \sqrt[3]{x} = \frac{1}{3}\ln x$ is equivalent to $x = e^{3y}$).

So instead of subtracting the upper curve minus the lower curve inside the integrand, we subtract the rightmost curve minus the leftmost curve. This leads to a much easier integral than the integral we wound up with in note (2). Be aware that a simple substitution is required to integrate e^{3y}. I leave the details to the reader.

(4) Note that $\frac{d}{dx}[x \ln x - x] = x\left(\frac{1}{x}\right) + \ln x - 1 = 1 + \ln x - 1 = \ln x$. It follows that $\int \ln x \, dx = x \ln x - x$.

So we can now evaluate the integral given in note (2):

$$\int_{e^{-6}}^{1}(\tfrac{1}{3}\ln x - (-2))dx = \int_{e^{-6}}^{1}(\tfrac{1}{3}\ln x + 2)dx$$

$$= \left[\tfrac{1}{3}(x \ln x - x) + 2x\right]\Big|_{e^{-6}}^{1} = \tfrac{1}{3}[x \ln x + 5x]\Big|_{e^{-6}}^{1}$$

$$= \tfrac{1}{3}([0 + 5] - [e^{-6}(-6) + 5e^{-6}]) = \tfrac{1}{3}(5 + e^{-6}) = \frac{e^{-6}+5}{3}.$$

This is choice (A).

(5) To integrate $\ln x$ formally requires **Integration by Parts**.

Integration by parts is a technique for integrating products of functions. It is quite a bit more complicated than the product rule for derivatives. The integration by parts formula is

$$\int u \, dv = uv - \int v \, du$$

To compute $\int \ln x \, dx$, we can let $u = \ln x$, and $dv = dx$. It then follows that $du = \frac{1}{x} dx$ and $v = x$. So we have

$$\int \ln x \, dx = (\ln x)(x) - \int x \frac{1}{x} dx = x \ln x - \int dx = x \ln x - x + C$$

See problem 47 for more information on integration by parts.

45. $\int_1^3 \frac{dx}{(2-x)^3} \, dx$ is

     (A) divergent

     (B) -1

     (C) $\frac{1}{2}$

     (D) 1

Solution: $\int_1^3 \frac{dx}{(2-x)^3} \, dx = \int_1^2 \frac{dx}{(2-x)^3} \, dx + \int_2^3 \frac{dx}{(2-x)^3} \, dx.$

Now, $\int_1^2 \frac{dx}{(2-x)^3} = \lim_{t \to 2^-} \frac{1}{2(2-x)^2} \Big|_1^t.$

Since $\lim_{t \to 2^-} \frac{1}{2(2-t)^2} = +\infty$, it follows that the improper integral is divergent, choice (A).

Notes: (1) The given integral is an **improper integral** because the function $\frac{1}{(2-x)^3}$ has a discontinuity at $x = 2$, and 2 is in the interval $[1,3]$. In other words the integrand has a discontinuity inside the interval of integration. This is a **Type I improper integral**. For an example of a Type II improper integral, see problem 15.

(2) If f has a discontinuity at $x = a$, then

$$\int_a^b f(x) \, dx = \lim_{t \to a^+} \int_t^b f(x) \, dx$$

If f has a discontinuity at $x = b$, then

$$\int_a^b f(x) \, dx = \lim_{t \to b^-} \int_a^t f(x) \, dx$$

If f has a discontinuity at $x = c$, and $a < c < b$, then

$$\int_a^b f(x)\,dx = \int_a^c f(x)\,dx + \int_c^b f(x)\,dx$$

In this last case, $\int_a^b f(x)\,dx$ only converges if both $\int_a^c f(x)\,dx$ and $\int_c^b f(x)\,dx$ converge.

(3) To evaluate the integral $\int \frac{dx}{(2-x)^3}$, we can formally make the substitution $u = 2 - x$. It then follows that $du = -dx$.

So we have $\int \frac{dx}{(2-x)^3} = -\int \frac{-dx}{(2-x)^3} = -\int \frac{du}{u^3} = -\int u^{-3}\,du = -\frac{u^{-2}}{-2} + C$

$$= \frac{1}{2u^2} + C = \frac{1}{2(2-x)^2} + C.$$

(4) By note (2) above we have $\int_1^2 \frac{dx}{(2-x)^3}\,dx = \lim_{t\to 2^-} \int_1^t \frac{dx}{(2-x)^3}$. Then using note (3) we have $\lim_{t\to 2^-} \int_1^t \frac{dx}{(2-x)^3} = \lim_{t\to 2^-} \frac{1}{2(2-x)^2} \big|_1^t$.

$$\lim_{t\to 2^-} \frac{1}{2(2-x)^2} \big|_1^t = \lim_{t\to 2^-} \left(\frac{1}{2(2-t)^2} - \frac{1}{2}\right) = \left(\lim_{t\to 2^-} \frac{1}{2(2-t)^2}\right) - \frac{1}{2}.$$

(5) Since $\int_1^2 \frac{dx}{(2-x)^3} = \infty$, we say that $\int_1^2 \frac{dx}{(2-x)^3}$ diverges. By note (2) above it follows that $\int_1^3 \frac{dx}{(2-x)^3}$ diverges.

(6) It is not necessary to compute the second integral, but it can be shown in the same way that $\int_2^3 \frac{dx}{(2-x)^3} = \infty$ as well.

46. Which of the following integrals gives the length of the graph $y = e^{\sqrt{x}}$ between $x = a$ and $x = b$?

(A) $\int_a^b \sqrt{\frac{1+e^{2\sqrt{x}}}{4x}}\,dx$

(B) $\int_a^b \sqrt{1 + \frac{1}{4x}e^{2\sqrt{x}}}\,dx$

(C) $\int_a^b \sqrt{e^{\sqrt{x}} + \frac{1}{4x}e^{2\sqrt{x}}}\,dx$

(D) $\int_a^b \sqrt{1 + e^{2\sqrt{x}}}\,dx$

Solution: $\frac{dy}{dx} = \frac{1}{2\sqrt{x}} e^{\sqrt{x}}$, and so $\left(\frac{dy}{dx}\right)^2 = \frac{1}{4x}\left(e^{\sqrt{x}}\right)^2 = \frac{1}{4x}e^{2\sqrt{x}}$. So the desired length is $\int_a^b \sqrt{1 + \frac{1}{4x}e^{2\sqrt{x}}}\, dx$, choice (B).

Note: See problem 18 for more information on computing arc length.

47. $\int x \cos 3x\, dx =$

    (A) $\frac{x^2}{2}\sin 3x + C$

    (B) $\frac{x^2}{6}\sin 3x + C$

    (C) $\frac{x}{3}\sin 3x + \frac{1}{3}\cos 3x + C$

    (D) $\frac{x}{3}\sin 3x + \frac{1}{9}\cos 3x + C$

Solution: We use integration by parts.

+	x	$\cos 3x$
$-$	1	$\frac{1}{3}\sin 3x$
+	0	$-\frac{1}{9}\cos 3x$

The answer is $\frac{x}{3}\sin 3x + \frac{1}{9}\cos 3x + C$, choice (D).

Notes: (1) **Integration by parts** is a technique for integrating products of functions. It is especially useful for integrating products of "different types" of functions. In this problem we are multiplying the polynomial x with the trigonometric function $\cos 3x$. The standard method of integration by parts is by the formula

$$\int u\, dv = uv - \int v\, du$$

To compute $\int x \cos 3x\, dx$, we can let $u = x$, and $dv = \cos 3x\, dx$. It then follows that $du = dx$ and $v = \frac{1}{3}\sin 3x$. So we have

$$\int x \cos 3x\, dx = (x)\left(\frac{1}{3}\sin 3x\right) - \int \frac{1}{3}\sin 3x\, dx = \frac{x}{3}\sin 3x + \frac{1}{9}\cos 3x + C$$

(2) In the original solution above, we actually used a shortcut which is sometimes called **tabular integration by parts**.

In the first column we simply alternate signs starting with a plus sign.

In the middle column we put our choice for u, and we differentiate as we go down the column.

In the third column we put our choice for dv, and we integrate as we go down the column.

In this particular example we stop at the third row since we get a 0 in the middle column.

Finally we follow the arrow pattern as seen in the solution above to write down the final answer. As we follow each arrow we multiply, and we add up individual arrows.

(3) How do we figure out how to choose u and dv? There are no absolute rules, but as a general guideline, it is helpful to memorize the mnemonic LIATE.

L stands for Logarithmic, I stands for Inverse Trigonometric, A stands for Algebraic, T stands for Trigonometric, and E stands for exponential.

As a first attempt choose the "leftmost" letter for u and the "rightmost" letter for dv.

In this problem we chose the algebraic function x for u, and the trigonometric function $\cos 3x$ for dv.

(4) For those of you unfamiliar with the term "algebraic function," this class of functions includes polynomials and rational functions, but is more general in the sense that roots can appear in the functions as well. For example, $\sqrt{x}$ and $\dfrac{\left(\sqrt[5]{x}+3x^2\right)}{x^{\frac{2}{7}}-5}$ are algebraic, but not polynomial or rational.

(5) The notes at the end of problem 44 show how to integrate $\ln x$ using integration by parts.

(6) The T and E in "LIATE" are generally interchangeable.

48. The area enclosed by the graph of the polar equation $r = 3\sin(2\theta)$ is given by

(A) $9 \int_0^{\frac{\pi}{2}} \sin^2(2\theta)\, d\theta$

(B) $18 \int_0^{\frac{\pi}{2}} \sin^2(2\theta)\, d\theta$

(C) $18 \int_0^{\pi} \sin^2(2\theta)\, d\theta$

(D) $\frac{9}{2} \int_0^{2\pi} \sin^2(2\theta)\, d\theta$

Solution: One loop of the graph of $r = 3\sin(2\theta)$ can be graphed from $\theta = 0$ to $\theta = \frac{\pi}{2}$. So the area of one loop of the polar graph is given by

$$A = \frac{1}{2}\int_0^{\frac{\pi}{2}} r^2\, d\theta = \frac{1}{2}\int_0^{\frac{\pi}{2}}[3\sin(2\theta)]^2\, d\theta = \frac{9}{2}\int_0^{\frac{\pi}{2}} \sin^2(2\theta)\, d\theta.$$

The entire graph contains 4 such loops, and so we multiply this area by 4 to get $18 \int_0^{\frac{\pi}{2}} \sin^2(2\theta)\, d\theta$, choice (B).

Notes: (1) Let's sketch the graph. The usual "key points" for $r = \sin\theta$ are $\theta = 0, \frac{\pi}{2}, \pi, \frac{3\pi}{2}, 2\pi$. In other words for $r = \sin\theta$ we would substitute multiples of $\frac{\pi}{2}$ in for θ, and connect these points with smooth curves.

But in place of θ we have 2θ. Therefore our first few key points should satisfy $2\theta = 0, \frac{\pi}{2}, \pi, \frac{3\pi}{2}, 2\pi$. Dividing by 2 yields $\theta = 0, \frac{\pi}{4}, \frac{\pi}{2}, \frac{3\pi}{4}, \pi$. In other words for $r = 3\sin 2\theta$ we would substitute multiples of $\frac{\pi}{4}$ in for θ, and connect these points with smooth curves.

So for example, when $\theta = 0$, we have $r = 3\sin 2(0) = 3(0) = 0$. So the point $(0,0)$ is on the graph. As another example, when $\theta = \frac{\pi}{4}$, we have $r = 3\sin 2(\frac{\pi}{4}) = 3\sin\frac{\pi}{2} = 3(1) = 3$. So the point $(\frac{\pi}{4}, 3)$ is on the graph. Note that these are polar points (*not* rectangular). So to plot the point $(\frac{\pi}{4}, 3)$ we form an angle of $\frac{\pi}{4}$ (or 45°) with the positive x-axis, and move outwards 3 units along the terminal ray.

We continue in this fashion as illustrated in the following step-by-step diagram:

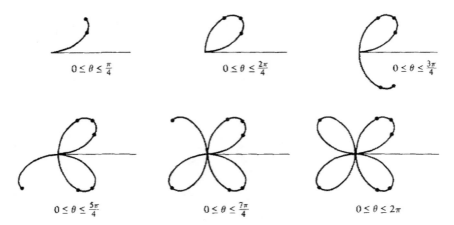

$0 \leq \theta \leq \frac{\pi}{4}$ $0 \leq \theta \leq \frac{2\pi}{4}$ $0 \leq \theta \leq \frac{3\pi}{4}$

$0 \leq \theta \leq \frac{5\pi}{4}$ $0 \leq \theta \leq \frac{7\pi}{4}$ $0 \leq \theta \leq 2\pi$

(2) From the second picture above we see that one complete loop is graphed from $\theta = 0$ to $\theta = \frac{2\pi}{4} = \frac{\pi}{2}$, and from the last picture we see that there are a total of 4 loops.

(3) The area of the polar curve $r(\theta)$ from $\theta = a$ to $\theta = b$ is $A = \frac{1}{2}\int_a^b r^2 \, d\theta$.

In this problem $r = 3\sin(2\theta)$, $a = 0$ and $b = \frac{\pi}{2}$.

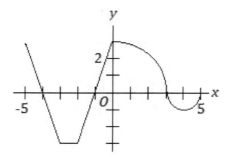

49. Let g be the continuous function defined on $[-5,5]$ whose graph, consisting of three line segments, a quarter circle centered at the origin, and a semicircle centered at $(4,0)$, is shown above. If $G(x) = \int_0^x g(t)\,dt$, where is $G(x)$ nonnegative?

(A) $[0,5]$ only
(B) $[-5,-4] \cup [0,5]$ only
(C) $[-5,-4] \cup [-1,3]$ only
(D) $[-5,-2] \cup [0,5]$ only

Solution: If $0 \leq x \leq 5$, then $G(x) = \int_0^x g(t)\,dt$ is positive because the area of the quarter circle is greater than the area of the semicircle.

If $x < 0$, then $G(x) = \int_0^x g(t)\,dt = -\int_x^0 g(t)\,dt$. For this expression to be nonnegative, we need $\int_x^0 g(t)\,dt$ to be nonpositive, and this happens when there is more area below the x-axis than above the x-axis from x to 0. This occurs for $-5 \leq x \leq -2$.

So the answer is choice (D).

Notes: (1) $\int_a^b f(t)\,dt = -\int_b^a f(t)\,dt$.

We used this theorem in the second paragraph to get

$$\int_0^x g(t)\,dt = -\int_x^0 g(t)\,dt.$$

(2) If $a < c < b$, then $\int_a^b f(x)\,dx = \int_a^c f(x)\,dx + \int_c^b f(x)\,dx$.

For example, if $x > 3$, then

$$\int_0^x g(t)\,dt = \int_0^3 g(t)\,dt + \int_3^x g(t)\,dt.$$

(3) Geometrically, if the graph of f lies above the x-axis between a and b, then $\int_a^b f(x)\,dx$ is the area under the graph of f between $x = a$ and $x = b$.

For example, $\int_0^3 g(t)\,dt$ is the area of the quarter circle centered at the origin with radius 3. So $\int_0^3 g(t)\,dt = \frac{\pi}{4}(3^2) = \frac{9\pi}{4}$

If the graph of f lies below the x-axis between a and b, then $\int_a^b f(x)\,dx$ is the negative of the area above the graph of f between a and b.

For example, $\int_3^5 g(t)\,dt$ is the negative of the area of the semicircle centered at $(4,0)$ with radius 1. So $\int_3^5 g(t)\,dt = -\frac{\pi}{2}(1^2) = -\frac{\pi}{2}$.

50. Find the length of the arc of the curve defined by $x(t) = \frac{1}{12}(8t + 16)^{\frac{3}{2}}$ and $y(t) = \frac{t^2}{2}$, from $t = 0$ to $t = 4$.

Solution: $\frac{dx}{dt} = \left(\frac{1}{12}\right)\left(\frac{3}{2}\right)(8t + 16)^{\frac{1}{2}}(8) = \sqrt{8t + 16}$ and $\frac{dy}{dt} = t$. So $\left(\frac{dx}{dt}\right)^2 = 8t + 16$ and $\left(\frac{dy}{dt}\right)^2 = t^2$. So the desired length is

$$\int_0^4 \sqrt{8t + 16 + t^2}\, dt = \int_0^4 \sqrt{t^2 + 8t + 16}\, dt = \int_0^4 \sqrt{(t+4)^2}\, dt$$

$$= \int_0^4 (t + 4)\, dt = \left(\frac{t^2}{2} + 4t\right) \Big|_0^4 = \frac{4^2}{2} + 4(4) = 8 + 16 = \mathbf{24}.$$

Notes: (1) The **arc length** of the differentiable curve with parametric equations $x = x(t)$ and $y = y(t)$ from $t = a$ to $t = b$ is

$$\text{Arc length} = \int_a^b \sqrt{\left(\frac{dx}{dt}\right)^2 + \left(\frac{dy}{dt}\right)^2}\, dt$$

(2) We used the chain rule to compute $\frac{dx}{dt}$ and a simple power rule to compute $\frac{dy}{dt}$. See problem 2 for more information on the chain rule.

LEVEL 2: LIMITS AND CONTINUITY

51. Let the function f be defined by $f(x) = \begin{cases} \frac{\tan x}{x}, & \text{for } x \neq 0. \\ 0, & \text{for } x = 0. \end{cases}$
Which of the following are true about f?

   I. $\lim_{x \to 0} f(x)$ exists.
   II. $f(0)$ exists.
   III. f is continuous at $x = 0$.

   (A) None
   (B) I only
   (C) 1I only
   (D) I and II only

Solution: $\lim_{x \to 0} f(x) = \lim_{x \to 0} \frac{\tan x}{x} = 1$. In particular, $\lim_{x \to 0} f(x)$ exists. So I is true.

$f(0) = 0$ by the definition of f. So II is true.

Since $\lim_{x \to 0} \frac{\tan x}{x} = 1 \neq 0 = f(0)$, f is *not* continuous at $x = 0$. So III is false.

The answer is therefore choice (D).

Notes: (1) f is a **piecewise defined function**. It is equal to $\frac{\tan x}{x}$ for nonzero values of x, and it is equal to 0 for $x = 0$.

(2) Two basic limits worth memorizing are

$$\lim_{x \to 0} \frac{\sin x}{x} = 1 \text{ and } \lim_{x \to 0} \frac{\tan x}{x} = 1.$$

(3) Each of the limits in note (2) is actually very easy to compute using L'Hôpital's rule (see problem 24).

(4) A function f is continuous at $x = a$ if and only if

$$\lim_{x \to a} f(x) = f(a).$$

In this problem $\lim_{x \to 0} f(x) = 1$ and $f(0) = 0$. Since these two numbers disagree, f is not continuous at $x = 0$.

52. Let the function k satisfy $\lim_{h \to 0} \frac{k(7+h)-k(7)}{h} = 12$. Which of the following must be true ?

    I. k is continuous at $x = 7$
   II. $k'(7)$ exists
  III. k' is continuous at $x = 7$

    (A) I only
    (B) 1I only
    (C) I and II only
    (D) I, II, and III

Solution: The equation $\lim_{h \to 0} \frac{k(7+h)-k(7)}{h} = 12$ can be rewritten as $k'(7) = 12$. In particular $k'(7)$ exists so that II is true.

Since k is differentiable at $x = 7$, it must also be continuous at $x = 7$. So I is true.

There is nothing here to suggest that k' is continuous at $x = 7$. So III does not need to be true (coming up with a specific counterexample is difficult, but one is given in note (3) below).

Therefore the answer is choice (C).

Notes: (1) Differentiability of a function always implies continuity of the function.

75

More precisely, if f is differentiable at $x = c$, then f must be continuous at $x = c$.

(2) By definition, $f'(x) = \lim_{h \to 0} \frac{f(x+h) - f(x)}{h}$.

So $k'(7) = \lim_{h \to 0} \frac{k(7+h) - k(7)}{h}$.

(3) **[Advanced Material]:** Let $k(x) = \begin{cases} (x-7)^2 \sin \frac{1}{x-7}, & x \neq 7 \\ 0, & x = 7 \end{cases}$

Then $k'(x) = \begin{cases} 2(x-7) \sin \frac{1}{x-7} - \cos \frac{1}{x-7}, & x \neq 7 \\ 0, & x = 7 \end{cases}$

Observe that $k'(7) = 0$ (see note (4) below) so that $k'(7)$ exists.

Also observe that $\lim_{x \to 7} k'(x)$ does not exist, because as x approaches 7, $\frac{1}{x-7}$ tends toward $+$ or $-\infty$, and so $\cos \frac{1}{x-7}$ oscillates between -1 and 1. So k' is not continuous at $x = 7$.

(4) $k'(7) = \lim_{h \to 0} \frac{k(7+h) - k(7)}{h} = \lim_{h \to 0} \frac{h^2 \sin \frac{1}{h} - 0}{h} = \lim_{h \to 0} h \sin \frac{1}{h} = 0$

because $\lim_{h \to 0} h = 0$ and $\sin \frac{1}{h}$ is bounded (this can be proved using the squeeze theorem – details are left to the interested reader).

53. If $\lim_{x \to c} f(x) = f(\lim_{x \to c} x)$ for all c in the interval (a, b), which of the following *must* be true?

   (A) f is continuous on (a, b).
   (B) f is differentiable on (a, b).
   (C) f is a polynomial.
   (D) $f'(x) = 0$ for some $x \in (a, b)$.

Solution: $\lim_{x \to c} x = c$. Therefore $f(\lim_{x \to c} x) = f(c)$. So the given condition can be rewritten as $\lim_{x \to c} f(x) = f(c)$. This is precisely the definition for f to be continuous at $x = c$.

Since we are given that this condition is true for all c in (a, b), the answer is choice (A).

54. Let f be defined by $f(x) = \frac{1}{\sqrt{17-x^2}} + \sqrt{x-3}$ for $-2 \le x \le 10$.

Let g be defined by $g(x) = \begin{cases} f(x)+2 & \text{for } -2 \le x \le 4 \\ |x-8| & \text{for } \quad 4 < x \le 10 \end{cases}$

Is g continuous at $x = 4$? Use the definition of continuity to explain your answer.

Solution:

$$\lim_{x \to 4^-} g(x) = f(4) + 2 = \frac{1}{\sqrt{17-4^2}} + \sqrt{4-3} + 2 = 1 + 1 + 2 = 4.$$

$$\lim_{x \to 4^+} g(x) = |4-8| = |-4| = 4$$

So $\lim_{x \to 4} g(x) = 4$.

Also, $g(4) = f(4) + 2 = 4$. So, $\lim_{x \to 4} g(x) = g(4)$.

It follows that g is continuous at $x = 4$.

55. A 5000 gallon tank is filled to capacity with water. At time $t = 0$, water begins to leak out of the tank at a rate modeled by $R(t)$, measured in gallons per hour, where

$$R(t) = \begin{cases} \dfrac{300t}{t+1}, & 0 \le t \le 4 \\ 500e^{-0.5t}, & t > 4 \end{cases}$$

Is R continuous at $t = 4$? Show the work that leads to your answer.

Solution:

$$\lim_{t \to 4^-} R(t) = \frac{300(4)}{4+1} = 240.$$

$$\lim_{t \to 4^+} R(t) = 500e^{-0.5(4)} = 500e^{-2}$$

Since $\lim_{t \to 4^-} R(t) \ne \lim_{t \to 4^+} r(t)$, $\lim_{t \to 4} R(t)$ does not exist.

It follows that R is *not* continuous at $t = 4$.

56. The function $g(x) = \frac{x^2+4x-12}{x^2+3x-10}$ has a removable discontinuity at $x = c$. Find c, and define a function G such that G is continuous at $x = c$ and $G(x) = g(x)$ for all x in the domain of g.

Solution: $g(x) = \frac{x^2+4x-12}{x^2+3x-10} = \frac{(x-2)(x+6)}{(x-2)(x+5)} = \frac{x+6}{x+5}$, $x \ne 2$.

So $\lim_{x \to 2} g(x) = \frac{2+6}{2+5} = \frac{8}{7}$.

It follows that g has a removable discontinuity at $x = 2$. So $c = 2$.

Define G by $G(x) = \begin{cases} \frac{x^2+4x-12}{x^2+3x-10}, & x \neq 2 \\ \frac{8}{7}, & x = 2 \end{cases}$.

Notes: (1) If f is not continuous at $x = c$, then the discontinuity is **removable** if $\lim_{x \to c} f(x)$ exists (and is a finite number). Otherwise the discontinuity is **nonremovable**.

In this problem $x = 2$ is a removable discontinuity of g because $\lim_{x \to 2} g(x) = \frac{8}{7}$. On the other hand, $x = -5$ is a nonremovable discontinuity of g because $\lim_{x \to -5} g(x)$ does not exist (see problem 25 for more information on how to compute this limit).

(2) If $x = c$ is a removable discontinuity of f, then we can **extend** f to a function F such that F is continuous at $x = c$, and $F(x) = f(x)$ for all x in the domain of f. We simply set $F(c) = \lim_{x \to c} f(x)$, and we let $F(x) = f(x)$ for all $x \neq c$.

LEVEL 2: SERIES

57. $\sum_{n=2}^{\infty} \frac{1}{n \ln n} =$

    (A) $\frac{1}{\ln(\ln 2)}$

    (B) $\ln(\ln 2)$

    (C) $\frac{1}{\ln 2}$

    (D) The series diverges.

Solution: $\int_2^{\infty} \frac{1}{x \ln x} dx = \ln(\ln x) \Big|_2^{\infty} = \lim_{b \to \infty} \ln(\ln x) \Big|_2^b$

$$= \lim_{b \to \infty} (\ln(\ln b) - \ln(\ln 2)) = \infty.$$

By the integral test $\sum_{n=2}^{\infty} \frac{1}{n \ln n}$ diverges, choice (D).

Notes: (1) Since $f(x) = \frac{1}{x \ln x}$ is a continuous, positive, decreasing function for $x \geq 2$, we can use the integral test to determine if the given sum converges. See problem 29 for more information on the integral test, and see problem 15 for more information on computing the type of improper integral given in this problem.

(2) You should know $\int \frac{1}{x} dx = \ln|x| + C$ (see problem 5 for details.)

(3) To evaluate $\int \frac{1}{x \ln x} dx$, we can formally make the substitution $u = \ln x$. It then follows that $du = \frac{1}{x} dx$. So we have

$$\int \frac{1}{x \ln x} dx = \int \frac{1}{\ln x} \cdot \frac{1}{x} dx = \int \frac{1}{u} du = \ln|u| + C = \ln|\ln x| + C.$$

Since we are considering only $x \geq 2$, it follows that $\ln x > 0$. So we can replace $\ln|\ln x|$ by $\ln(\ln x)$.

(4) With a little practice, we can evaluate an integral like this very quickly with the following reasoning: The derivative of $\ln x$ is $\frac{1}{x}$. So to integrate $\frac{1}{x \ln x}$ we simply pretend we are integrating $\frac{1}{x}$ but as we do it we leave the $\ln x$ where it is. This is essentially what was done in the above solution.

Note that the $\frac{1}{x}$ "goes away" because it is the derivative of $\ln x$. We need it there for everything to work.

58. If $g(x) = \sum_{n=1}^{\infty}(\sin^2 x)^n$, then $g\left(\frac{\pi}{3}\right) =$

    (A) 3

    (B) 1

    (C) $\frac{3}{4}$

    (D) $\frac{1}{2}$

Solution: $g\left(\frac{\pi}{3}\right) = \sum_{n=1}^{\infty}\left(\sin^2\left(\frac{\pi}{3}\right)\right)^n = \sum_{n=1}^{\infty}\left(\left(\frac{\sqrt{3}}{2}\right)^2\right)^n = \sum_{n=1}^{\infty}\left(\frac{3}{4}\right)^n$

$$= \frac{\frac{3}{4}}{1 - \frac{3}{4}} = \frac{3}{4} \div \frac{1}{4} = \frac{3}{4} \cdot 4 = 3.$$

This is choice (A).

Note: $\sum_{n=1}^{\infty} \left(\frac{3}{4}\right)^n$ is a geometric series with first term $a = \frac{3}{4}$ and common ratio $r = \frac{3}{4}$. See problems 27 and 30 for more information on geometric series.

59. $\sum_{n=1}^{\infty} \left(\frac{3^n}{(7+n^2)^{50}}\right) \left(\frac{(6+n^2)^{50}}{3^{n+1}}\right) =$

    (A) $\frac{1}{6}$

    (B) $\frac{1}{3}$

    (C) $\frac{3}{7}$

    (D) The series diverges.

Solution: $\lim_{n\to\infty} \left(\frac{3^n}{(7+n^2)^{50}}\right) \left(\frac{(6+n^2)^{50}}{3^{n+1}}\right) = \lim_{n\to\infty} \left(\frac{3^n}{3^{n+1}}\right) \left(\frac{6+n^2}{7+n^2}\right)^{50} = \frac{1}{3}$

By the divergence test, the given series diverges, choice (D).

Notes: (1) See problem 28 for more information on the divergence test.

(2) $\lim_{n\to\infty} \left(\frac{3^n}{3^{n+1}}\right) \left(\frac{6+n^2}{7+n^2}\right)^{50} = \lim_{n\to\infty} \left(\frac{1}{3}\right) \left(\frac{6+n^2}{7+n^2}\right)^{50} = \frac{1}{3} \lim_{n\to\infty} \left(\frac{6+n^2}{7+n^2}\right)^{50}$

$\qquad = \frac{1}{3} \left(\lim_{n\to\infty} \frac{6+n^2}{7+n^2}\right)^{50} = \frac{1}{3}(1)^{50} = \frac{1}{3}(1) = \frac{1}{3}.$

(3) Be careful! The sequence $\left(\left(\frac{3^n}{(7+n^2)^{50}}\right) \left(\frac{(6+n^2)^{50}}{3^{n+1}}\right)\right)$ converges to $\frac{1}{3}$. The corresponding series however diverges by the divergence test (because the limit of the sequence is not 0).

60. Which of the following statements about the series $\sum_{n=1}^{\infty} \frac{(-1)^n}{5+\sqrt{n}}$ is true?

    (A) The series converges absolutely.
    (B) The series converges conditionally.
    (C) The series converges but neither conditionally nor absolutely.
    (D) The series diverges.

Solution: The series $\sum_{n=1}^{\infty}\frac{1}{\sqrt{n}} = \sum_{n=1}^{\infty}\frac{1}{n^{\frac{1}{2}}}$ is a divergent p-series. Since

$$\lim_{n\to\infty}\frac{\frac{1}{\sqrt{n}}}{\frac{1}{5+\sqrt{n}}} = \lim_{n\to\infty}\frac{1}{\sqrt{n}}\cdot\frac{5+\sqrt{n}}{1} = 1, \quad \text{it} \quad \text{follows} \quad \text{from} \quad \text{the} \quad \text{limit}$$

comparison test that $\sum_{n=1}^{\infty}\frac{1}{5+\sqrt{n}}$ also diverges. So $\sum_{n=1}^{\infty}\frac{(-1)^n}{5+\sqrt{n}}$ does not converge absolutely.

Since $(\frac{1}{5+\sqrt{n}})$ is a decreasing sequence and $\lim_{n\to\infty}\frac{1}{5+\sqrt{n}} = 0$, by the alternating series test, $\sum_{n=1}^{\infty}\frac{(-1)^n}{5+\sqrt{n}}$ converges.

It follows that $\sum_{n=1}^{\infty}\frac{(-1)^n}{5+\sqrt{n}}$ converges conditionally, choice (B).

Notes: (1) See problem 31 for the definitions of absolute and conditional convergence.

(2) A **p-series** is a series of the form $\sum_{n=1}^{\infty}\frac{1}{n^p} = \frac{1}{1^p} + \frac{1}{2^p} + \frac{1}{3^p} + \cdots$

A p-series converges if $p > 1$ and diverges if $p \le 1$. Note that a 1-series is simply the divergent harmonic series.

For the series $\sum_{n=1}^{\infty}\frac{1}{\sqrt{n}} = \sum_{n=1}^{\infty}\frac{1}{n^{\frac{1}{2}}}$, $p = \frac{1}{2} \le 1$, so that $\sum_{n=1}^{\infty}\frac{1}{\sqrt{n}}$ diverges.

(3) The **limit comparison test** says that if $\sum_{n=1}^{\infty} a_n$ and $\sum_{n=1}^{\infty} b_n$ are series with nonnegative terms and $\lim_{n\to\infty}\frac{a_n}{b_n} > 0$ is finite, then $\sum_{n=1}^{\infty} a_n$ and $\sum_{n=1}^{\infty} b_n$ either both converge or both diverge.

In this problem $a_n = \frac{1}{\sqrt{n}}$ and $b_n = \frac{1}{5+\sqrt{n}}$ and $\lim_{n\to\infty}\frac{a_n}{b_n} = 1$. Since we had already seen that $\sum_{n=1}^{\infty}\frac{1}{\sqrt{n}}$ diverges, it follows from the limit comparison test that $\sum_{n=1}^{\infty}\frac{1}{5+\sqrt{n}}$ also diverges.

(4) See problem 28 for more information on the alternating series test.

61. Find the interval of convergence for the series $\sum_{n=1}^{\infty}\frac{(x-2)^n}{n^3(3^n)}$.

Solution: $\lim_{n\to\infty}\left|\dfrac{\frac{(x-2)^{n+1}}{(n+1)^3(3^{n+1})}}{\frac{(x-2)^n}{n^3(3^n)}}\right| = \lim_{n\to\infty}\left|\dfrac{(x-2)^{n+1}}{(n+1)^3(3^{n+1})}\cdot\dfrac{n^3(3^n)}{(x-2)^n}\right| = \dfrac{|x-2|}{3}$. So

by the ratio test, the series converges for all x such that $\dfrac{|x-2|}{3} < 1$, or equivalently $|x-2| < 3$. Removing the absolute values, we have $-3 < x - 2 < 3$, or equivalently $-1 < x < 5$.

We still need to check the endpoints. When $x = 5$, we get the convergent p-series $\sum_{n=1}^{\infty}\frac{1}{n^3}$, and when $x = -1$ we get the absolutely convergent series $\sum_{n=1}^{\infty}(-1)^n\frac{1}{n^3}$ .So the series converges for $-1 \le x \le 5$.

Therefore the interval of convergence is $[-1, 5]$.

Notes: (1) See problems 31 and 32 for more information on the ratio test, power series, radius of convergence, and interval of convergence. In problem 32 we looked at a power series about $x = 0$.

(2) A **power series** about $x = a$ is a series of the form $\sum_{n=1}^{\infty} a_n(x - a)^n$. To determine where this power series converges we use the ratio test. In other words we compute

$$L = \lim_{n\to\infty}\left|\dfrac{a_{n+1}(x-a)^{n+1}}{a_n(x-a)^n}\right| = \lim_{n\to\infty}\left|\dfrac{a_{n+1}}{a_n}\right||x - a|.$$

If $L = 0$, then the series converges only for $x = a$.

If $L = \infty$, then the series converges absolutely for all x (and therefore converges for all x – see problem 31, note 2).

Otherwise we solve the equation $L < 1$ for $|x - a|$ to get an inequality of the form $|x - a| < R$. In this case the series converges absolutely for $|x - a| < R$ and diverges for $|x - a| > R$. The positive number R is called the **radius of convergence** of the power series.

As always the ratio test fails when $L = 1$. So the endpoints $x - a = -R$ and $x - a = R$, or equivalently $x = a - R$ and $x = a + R$ have to be checked separately.

(2) In this problem we have

$$L = \lim_{n\to\infty}\left|\dfrac{\frac{(x-2)^{n+1}}{(n+1)^3(3^{n+1})}}{\frac{(x-2)^n}{n^3(3^n)}}\right| = \lim_{n\to\infty}\left|\dfrac{(x-2)^{n+1}}{(n+1)^3(3^{n+1})}\cdot\dfrac{n^3(3^n)}{(x-2)^n}\right|$$

$$= \lim_{n \to \infty} \frac{n^3}{(n+1)^3} \cdot \frac{1}{3}|x - 2| = \frac{1}{3}|x - 2|$$

Setting $L < 1$ gives $\frac{1}{3}|x - 2| < 1$, or equivalently $|x - 2| < 3$. So the radius of convergence is $R = 3$.

(3) We can use the formulas $x = a - R$ and $x = a + R$ to see that the endpoints of the interval are $x = 2 - 3 = -1$ and $x = 2 + 3 = 5$. These need to be checked separately.

Alternatively, we can remove the absolute values and solve for x as was done in the solution above.

(4) See problem 60 for detailed information on p-series.

In this problem, when $x = 5$ we get a 3-series which converges because $3 > 1$.

When $x = -1$ we get the series $\sum_{n=1}^{\infty}(-1)^n \frac{1}{n^3}$. Since $\left|(-1)^n \frac{1}{n^3}\right| = \frac{1}{n^3}$ and $\sum_{n=1}^{\infty} \frac{1}{n^3}$ converges, the series $\sum_{n=1}^{\infty}(-1)^n \frac{1}{n^3}$ is absolutely convergent, and therefore convergent.

(5) See problem 31 for more information on absolute convergence.

62. The second-degree Taylor polynomial about $x = 0$ of $\ln(2 - 2x)$ is

(A) $-x - \frac{x^2}{2}$

(B) $-x - x^2$

(C) $\ln 2 - x - x^2$

(D) $\ln 2 - x - \frac{x^2}{2}$

Solution: Let $f(x) = \ln(2 - 2x)$. Then $f'(x) = -\frac{1}{1-x} = -(1 - x)^{-1}$ and $f''(x) = -(1 - x)^{-2}$. So we have $f(0) = \ln 2$, $f'(0) = -1$, and $f''(0) = -1$.

The second-degree Taylor polynomial is therefore

$$\ln 2 + (-1)x + \frac{(-1)x^2}{2!} = \ln 2 - x - \frac{x^2}{2}.$$

This is choice (D).

Notes: (1) The nth degree **Taylor polynomial** about $x = 0$ for the function f is

$$P_n(x) = f(0) + f'(0)x + \frac{f''(0)}{2!}x^2 + \frac{f'''(0)}{3!}x^3 + \cdots + \frac{f^n(0)}{n!}x^n$$

For this problem we are being asked for the second degree Taylor polynomial $P_2(x) = f(0) + f'(0)x + \frac{f''(0)}{2!}x^2$.

(2) The following is not needed for this problem but may be useful in similar problems.

More generally, the nth degree **Taylor polynomial** about $x = a$ for the function f is

$$P_n(x) = f(a) + f'(a)(x - a) + \frac{f''(a)}{2!}(x - a)^2 + \frac{f'''(a)}{3!}(x - a)^3 + \cdots + \frac{f^n(a)}{n!}(x - a)^n$$

Using summation notation, we can write

$$P_n(x) = \sum_{k=0}^{n} \frac{f^{(k)}(a)}{k!}(x - a)^k$$

Note that we define $f^{(0)}(a) = f(a)$, and recall that $0!$ is defined to be 1.

63. If $\sum_{n=0}^{\infty} a_n x^n$ is a Maclaurin series that converges to $g(x)$ for all x. then $g''(1) =$

(A) 1
(B) a_2
(C) $\sum_{n=2}^{\infty} a_n$
(D) $\sum_{n=2}^{\infty} n(n - 1)a_n$

Solution: $g(x) = \sum_{n=0}^{\infty} a_n x^n$. So we have $g'(x) = \sum_{n=1}^{\infty} n a_n x^{n-1}$ and $g''(x) = \sum_{n=2}^{\infty} n(n - 1)a_n x^{n-2}$.

So $g''(1) = \sum_{n=2}^{\infty} n(n - 1)a_n$, choice (D).

Notes: (1) The **Maclaurin series** for the function f is

$$\sum_{n=0}^{\infty} \frac{f^n(0)}{n!}x^n = f(0) + f'(0)x + \frac{f''(0)}{2!}x^2 + \cdots + \frac{f^n(0)}{n!}x^n + \cdots$$

(2) A Maclaurin series is a special case of a **Taylor series**. More specifically a Maclaurin series is a Taylor series about $x = 0$. See problem 93 for the more general definition.

(3) Taylor series, and more specifically, Maclaurin series can be differentiated term by term. Since the derivative of $a_n x^n$ is $n a_n x^{n-1}$, it follows that the derivative of

$$g(x) = \sum_{n=0}^{\infty} a_n x^n = a_0 + a_1 x + a_2 x^2 + \cdots + a_n x^n + \cdots$$

is

$$g'(x) = \sum_{n=1}^{\infty} n a_n x^{n-1} = a_1 + 2a_2 x + 3a_3 x^2 \ldots + n a_n x^{n-1} + \cdots$$

Note that the $n = 0$ term "went away" because the derivative of the constant a_0 is 0.

(4) Differentiating again yields

$$g''(x) = \sum_{n=2}^{\infty} n(n-1) a_n x^{n-1}$$

$$= 2a_2 + 3 \cdot 2a_3 x + 4 \cdot 3a_4 x^2 \ldots + n(n-1) a_n x^{n-2} + \cdots$$

Once again, note that the $n = 1$ term "went away" because the derivative of the constant a_1 is zero.

Substituting 1 in for x yields

$$g''(1) = \sum_{n=2}^{\infty} n(n-1) a_n$$

$$= 2a_2 + 3 \cdot 2a_3 + 4 \cdot 3a_4 \ldots + n(n-1) a_n + \cdots$$

64. The function h has derivatives of all orders at $x = 0$, and the Maclaurin series for h is $\sum_{n=2}^{\infty} \frac{\ln n}{2^n n^4} x^n$. Find $h'''(0)$.

Solution: $\frac{h'''(0)}{3!} = \frac{\ln 3}{2^3 \cdot 3^4}$. So $h'''(0) = \frac{\ln 3}{2^3 \cdot 3^4} \cdot 3! = \frac{\ln 3}{108} \approx .01$

Notes: (1) See problem 63 for the definition of a Maclaurin series.

(2) The coefficient of x^3 in the Maclaurin series for h is $\frac{h'''(0)}{3!}$.

Since we are given the Maclaurin series for h in this problem, we can also get the coefficient of x^3 by substituting 3 for n in the expression $\frac{\ln n}{2^n n^4}$ to get $\frac{\ln 3}{2^3 \cdot 3^4}$.

These two quantities are equal so that we have $\frac{h'''(0)}{3!} = \frac{\ln 3}{2^3 \cdot 3^4}$.

LEVEL 3: DIFFERENTIATION

65. A point (x, y) is moving along the curve $y = f(x)$. At the instant when the slope of the curve is $-\frac{2}{5}$, the y-coordinate of the point is decreasing at the rate of 4 units per minute. The rate of change, in units per minute, of the x-coordinate of the point is

   (A) 10

   (B) $\frac{1}{10}$

   (C) $-\frac{1}{10}$

   (D) -10

Solution: $\frac{dy}{dt} = f'(x) \cdot \frac{dx}{dt}$. So we have $-4 = -\frac{2}{5} \cdot \frac{dx}{dt}$. It follows that $\frac{dx}{dt} = (-4)\left(-\frac{5}{2}\right) = 10$, choice (A).

Notes: (1) Remember that the word *rate* generally indicates a derivative. "Increasing at a rate of" indicates a positive derivative, and "decreasing at a rate of" indicates a negative derivative.

So "the y-coordinate of the point is decreasing at the rate of 4 units per minute" can be interpreted as $\frac{dy}{dt} = -4$.

(2) This is a **related rates** problem. In a related rates problem we differentiate the independent and dependent variables with respect to a new variable, usually named t, for time.

(3) A *related rates* problem can be pictured as a *dynamic* (moving) process that gets fixed at a specific moment in time.

For this problem we can picture a point moving along a curve. We then *freeze time* at the moment when the slope of the curve is $f'(x) = -\frac{2}{5}$.

At this moment in time we want to know what the rate of change of the x-coordinate of the point is. The word "rate" indicates that we want the derivative $\frac{dx}{dt}$.

Don't forget to apply the chain rule when differentiating the right hand side of the equation $y = f(x)$. In this case, the derivative of $f(x)$ is $f'(x) \cdot \frac{dx}{dt}$.

66. * Let K be defined by $K(t) = 70 + 15 \cos\left(\frac{\pi t}{4}\right) + 5 \sin(\frac{\pi t}{3})$. For $0 \leq t \leq 6$, K is decreasing most rapidly when $t =$

Solution: $K'(t) = -\frac{15\pi}{4} \sin\left(\frac{\pi t}{4}\right) + \frac{5\pi}{3} \cos(\frac{\pi t}{3})$. We graph K' in our calculator in the window $[0,6] \times [-20,20]$ and use the "minimum" feature to find that $t \approx 2.431$.

Note: K is decreasing most rapidly when K' is as small as possible.

67. If the line $7x - 4y = 3$ is tangent in the first quadrant to the curve $y = x^3 + x + c$, then c is

(A) $-\frac{1}{2}$

(B) $-\frac{1}{4}$

(C) $\frac{1}{4}$

(D) $\frac{1}{2}$

Solution: The slope of the line $7x - 4y = 3$ is $\frac{7}{4}$, and the derivative of the given function is $y' = 3x^2 + 1$. So we must have $3x^2 + 1 = \frac{7}{4}$.

We subtract 1 from each side of this equation to get $3x^2 = \frac{7}{4} - 1 = \frac{3}{4}$. We divide by 3 to get $x^2 = \frac{1}{4}$. By the square root property, $x = \pm\frac{1}{2}$.

Since we want the first quadrant solution, we take $x = \frac{1}{2}$.

We substitute $x = \frac{1}{2}$ into the equation of the line to get

$$7\left(\tfrac{1}{2}\right) - 4y = 3.$$

87

So $4y = \frac{7}{2} - 3 = \frac{1}{2}$, and therefore $y = \frac{1}{2} \cdot \frac{1}{4} = \frac{1}{8}$. It follows that the point of tangency is $(\frac{1}{2}, \frac{1}{8})$. We plug $x = \frac{1}{2}$ and $y = \frac{1}{8}$ into the equation for the curve and solve for c.

$$\frac{1}{8} = \left(\frac{1}{2}\right)^3 + \frac{1}{2} + c$$

$$\frac{1}{8} = \frac{1}{8} + \frac{1}{2} + c$$

$$c = -\frac{1}{2}$$

This is choice (A).

Notes: (1) One way to find the slope of the line $7x - 4y = 3$ is to put the equation into slope-intercept form by solving for y:

$$7x - 4y = 3$$
$$-4y = -7x + 3$$
$$y = \frac{7}{4}x - \frac{3}{4}$$

We can now see that the slope is $\frac{7}{4}$.

(2) The slope of a line in the general form $ax + by = c$ is $-\frac{a}{b}$.

In this problem $a = 7$ and $b = -4$, so that the slope is $-\frac{7}{(-4)} = \frac{7}{4}$.

(3) The derivative of a curve at a point is equal to the slope of the tangent line to the curve at that point. This is why we set the derivative equal to $\frac{7}{4}$.

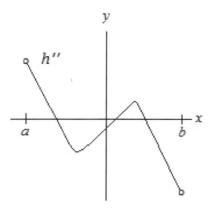

68. Let h be a function whose domain is the open interval (a, b). The figure above shows the graph of h''. Which of the following describes the relative extrema of h' and the points of inflection of the graph of h' ?

(A) 1 relative maximum, 1 relative minimum, 2 points of inflection

(B) 1 relative maximum, 2 relative minima, 2 points of inflection

(C) 1 relative maximum, 2 relative minima, 2 points of inflection

(D) 2 relative maxima, 1 relative minimum, 2 points of inflection

Solution: h' has 3 critical numbers. These are the x-values where $h''(x) = 0$. At each of the leftmost and rightmost critical numbers, h' has a relative maximum. At the other critical number, h' has a relative minimum. So h' has 2 relative maxima and 1 relative minimum.

The graph of h' has a point of inflection whenever the graph of h'' has a relative maximum or minimum. This occurs twice, and so the graph of h' has 2 points of inflection.

Therefore the answer is choice (D).

Notes: (1) A **critical number** of a function f is a real number c in the domain of f such that $f'(c) = 0$ or $f'(c)$ is undefined.

(2) A function f attains a **relative minimum** (or **local minimum**) at a real number $x = c$ if there is an interval (a, b) containing c such that $f(c) < f(x)$ for all x in the interval.

If a function is decreasing to the left of c, and increasing to the right of c, then f attains a relative minimum at c.

In terms of derivatives, if $f'(x) < 0$ for $x < c$, and $f'(x) > 0$ for $x > c$, then f attains a relative minimum at c.

A similar analysis can be done for a relative maximum. This method of finding the relative extrema of a function is called the **first derivative test**.

(3) Take careful note that in this problem we are trying to find the relative extrema of the *derivative* of h. So we need to be checking $h''(x)$ near $x = c$.

(4) For the leftmost critical number of h' (in other words the leftmost x-intercept of h''), h'' changes from positive to negative as we go from left to right across the critical number. So h' changes from increasing to decreasing, and the leftmost critical number of h' is a relative maximum.

A similar analysis can be made for the other two critical numbers.

(5) A point at which a function changes concavity is called a **point of inflection**. At a point of inflection, the second derivative of the function is either 0 or undefined.

So we are looking for x-values such that $h'''(x) = 0$. This happens when the graph of h'' has a horizontal tangent line. In the given graph of h'' there are two such places, the relative maximum and minimum values of h''.

69. Given the function defined by $f(x) = 5x^3 - 3x^5$, find all values of x for which the graph of f is concave down.

(A) $-\frac{\sqrt{2}}{2} < x < \frac{\sqrt{2}}{2}$

(B) $x > \frac{\sqrt{2}}{2}$

(C) $-\frac{1}{2} < x < 0$ or $x > \frac{1}{2}$

(D) $-\frac{\sqrt{2}}{2} < x < 0$ or $x > \frac{\sqrt{2}}{2}$

Solution: $f'(x) = 15x^2 - 15x^4$ and
$$f''(x) = 30x - 60x^3 = 30x(1 - 2x^2).$$

The second derivative is 0 when $x = 0$ and $1 - 2x^2 = 0$. We solve this last equation for x to get $2x^2 = 1$, or $x^2 = \frac{1}{2}$, or $x = \pm\frac{1}{\sqrt{2}} = \pm\frac{\sqrt{2}}{2}$

Let's draw a sign chart for f'':

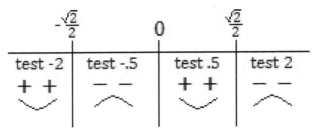

In this case we split up the real line into four pieces. Notice that the cutoff points are $-\frac{\sqrt{2}}{2}$, 0 and $\frac{\sqrt{2}}{2}$, the x-values where $f''(x) = 0$. We then plug a real number from each of these four intervals into f'' to see if the answer is positive or negative. For example, $f''(2) = 30(2)(1 - 2(2)^2) < 0$.

Note that we do not need to finish the computation. We only need to know if the answer is positive or negative. Whenever the answer comes out positive we draw a smiley face with plus signs for eyes. Whenever the answer comes out negative we draw a frowny face with minus signs for eyes. This way we can see the correct concavity right inside the sign chart. We can then clearly see that the function is concave down when $-\frac{\sqrt{2}}{2} < x < 0$ or $x > \frac{\sqrt{2}}{2}$. This is choice (D).

Notes: (1) In the sign chart above, we drew two plus signs (or two minus signs) for visual purposes only (so that we could draw a face). There is no other reason.

(2) Always remember "positive people are happy, and negative people are sad." This will help you to remember to draw a smiley face with the plus signs, and a frowny face with the minus signs.

(3) When the second derivative of a function is positive, the graph of the function is concave up.

(4) When the second derivative is negative, the graph of the function is concave down.

(5) Recall that a point at which a function changes concavity is called a **point of inflection**. In this problem there are three points of inflection. They occur when $x = -\frac{\sqrt{2}}{2}$, $x = 0$, and $x = \frac{\sqrt{2}}{2}$.

(6) At a point of inflection, the second derivative of the function is either 0 or undefined.

(7) If the second derivative of a function is 0 or undefined at $x = c$, then the function may or may not have a point of inflection there. Sometimes the function will change concavity there, and sometimes it will not.

(8) Since each of the three zeros of the second derivative have multiplicity 1 (odd multiplicity), it follows that a point of inflection occurs at each of them.

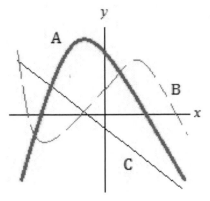

70. Three graphs labeled A, B, and C are shown above. One is the graph of f, one is the graph of f', and one is the graph of f''. Which of the following correctly identifies each of the three graphs in the order f, f', f'' ?

    (A) A, B, C
    (B) A, C, B
    (C) B, A, C
    (D) B, C, A

Solution: Observe that the x-values where graph B has a relative minimum or maximum are x-intercepts of graph A. Similarly, the x-value where graph A has a relative maximum is an x-intercept of graph C.

So B is the graph of f, A is the graph of f', and C is the graph of f'', choice (C).

Notes: (1) It looks as though B is the graph of a cubic function (3rd degree polynomial), A is the graph of a quadratic function (2nd degree polynomial), and C is the graph of a linear function (1st degree polynomial). Since the derivative of a polynomial is a polynomial of 1 less degree, it follows that B must be the graph of f, A is the graph of f', and C is the graph of f''.

(2) Here are some additional observations we can make to confirm that B is the graph of f, A is the graph of f', and C is the graph of f''.

- When graph B is increasing, graph A is above the x-axis, and when graph B is decreasing, graph A is below the x-axis.

- When graph B is concave up, graph C is above the x-axis, and when graph B is concave down, graph C is below the x-axis.

- When graph A is increasing, graph C is above the x-axis, and when graph A is decreasing, graph C is below the x-axis.

71. $\frac{d}{dx}\left[\sin^{-1}\left(\frac{x}{2}\right)\right] =$

(A) $-\dfrac{1}{\sqrt{4-x^2}}$

(B) $\dfrac{1}{\sqrt{4-x^2}}$

(C) $-\dfrac{1}{2\sqrt{1-x^2}}$

(D) $\dfrac{1}{2\sqrt{1-x^2}}$

Solution:

$$\frac{d}{dx}\left[\sin^{-1}\left(\frac{x}{2}\right)\right] = \frac{1}{\sqrt{1-\left(\frac{x}{2}\right)^2}}\cdot\left(\frac{1}{2}\right) = \frac{1}{2\cdot\sqrt{1-\frac{x^2}{4}}} = \frac{1}{\sqrt{4}\cdot\sqrt{1-\frac{x^2}{4}}} = \frac{1}{\sqrt{4\left(1-\frac{x^2}{4}\right)}} = \frac{1}{\sqrt{4-x^2}}.$$

This is choice (B).

Notes: (1) Note that $\sin^{-1}x$ is the same thing as $\arcsin x$. This is the *inverse* of the function $\sin x$, $-\frac{\pi}{2} \le x \le \frac{\pi}{2}$.

(2) This notation can actually be confusing. To see why I say this, note that $\sin^2 x$ is an abbreviation for $(\sin x)^2$. But $\sin^{-1}x$ is *not* an abbreviation for $(\sin x)^{-1} = \frac{1}{\sin x}$.

93

$\sin^{-1} x$ is the inverse function, whereas $(\sin x)^{-1}$ is the reciprocal of $\sin x$.

(3) You should know the derivatives of the six basic inverse trig functions:

$$\frac{d}{dx}[\sin^{-1} x] = \frac{1}{\sqrt{1-x^2}} \qquad \frac{d}{dx}[\csc^{-1} x] = -\frac{1}{|x|\sqrt{x^2-1}}$$

$$\frac{d}{dx}[\cos^{-1} x] = -\frac{1}{\sqrt{1-x^2}} \qquad \frac{d}{dx}[\sec^{-1} x] = \frac{1}{|x|\sqrt{x^2-1}}$$

$$\frac{d}{dx}[\tan^{-1} x] = \frac{1}{1+x^2} \qquad \frac{d}{dx}[\cot^{-1} x] = -\frac{1}{1+x^2}$$

(4) Let $f(x) = \sin^{-1}(\frac{x}{2})$. Then $f(x) = g(h(x))$, where $g(x) = \sin^{-1} x$ and $h(x) = \frac{x}{2}$.

To take the derivative of f requires the chain rule. We have

$$f'(x) = g'(h(x)) \cdot h'(x) = \frac{1}{\sqrt{1-\left(\frac{x}{2}\right)^2}} \cdot \left(\frac{1}{2}\right).$$

(5) To get from $\dfrac{1}{\sqrt{1-\left(\frac{x}{2}\right)^2}} \cdot \left(\frac{1}{2}\right)$ to the expression $\dfrac{1}{2 \cdot \sqrt{1-\frac{x^2}{4}}}$ we simply multiplied the two numerators together $(1 \cdot 1 = 1)$, and we multiplied the two denominators together $\left(\sqrt{1-\left(\frac{x}{2}\right)^2} \cdot 2 = 2 \cdot \sqrt{1-\frac{x^2}{4}}\right)$.

(6) We would now like to move the 2 in the denominator inside of the square root. to do this we write $2 = \sqrt{4}$, and use the fact that for any nonnegative real numbers a and b, we have $\sqrt{a}\sqrt{b} = \sqrt{ab}$.

So we have $\dfrac{1}{2 \cdot \sqrt{1-\frac{x^2}{4}}} = \dfrac{1}{\sqrt{4} \cdot \sqrt{1-\frac{x^2}{4}}} = \dfrac{1}{\sqrt{4\left(1-\frac{x^2}{4}\right)}}.$

(7) Finally, we distribute the 4 to get $4\left(1-\frac{x^2}{4}\right) = 4 - 4\left(\frac{x^2}{4}\right) = 4 - x^2$.

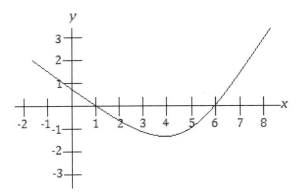

72. The **derivative** of g is graphed above. Give a value of x where g has a local minimum.

   (A) 0
   (B) 1
   (C) 4
   (D) 6

Solution: From the graph of g' we see that $g'(6) = 0$, so that $x = 6$ is a critical number of g.

We have $g'(x) < 0$ for x near 6 and to the left of 6, and $g'(x) > 0$ for x near 6 and to the right of 6.

It follows that $g(x)$ is decreasing for x a little less than 6, and $g(x)$ is increasing for x a little greater than 6. Therefore g has a local minimum at $x = 6$, choice (D).

Notes: (1) Recall that a **critical number** of a function f is a real number c in the domain of f such that $f'(c) = 0$ or $f'(c)$ is undefined.

The function g here has two critical numbers: $x = 1$ and $x = 6$.

(2) If a function is decreasing to the left of c, and increasing to the right of c, then f attains a local minimum at c.

In terms of derivatives, if $f'(x) < 0$ for $x < c$, and $f'(x) > 0$ for $x > c$, then f attains a local minimum at c.

This happens at $x = 6$.

(3) If a function is increasing to the left of c, and decreasing to the right of c, then f attains a local maximum at c.

In terms of derivatives, if $f'(x) > 0$ for $x < c$, and $f'(x) < 0$ for $x > c$, then f attains a local maximum at c.

This happens at $x = 1$.

(4) This method of finding the local minima and maxima of a function is called the **first derivative test**.

(5) Let's make a sign chart

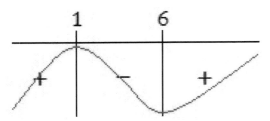

In this case we split up the real line into three pieces. Notice that the cutoff points are 1 and 6, the critical numbers of g. We then note that $g'(x) > 0$ for $x < 1$ and $x > 6$, and $g'(x) < 0$ for $1 < x < 6$ (just look at the given graph of g'). Finally we make a quick sketch that decreases across the interval where there is a minus sign, and increases across the intervals where there is a plus sign. We can then clearly see that there is a local maximum at $x = 1$ (not needed in this problem) and a local minimum at $x = 6$.

(5) The sketch of the graph in the sign chart is not meant to be completely accurate. It is only being used to demonstrate where the function is increasing and decreasing, so we can determine if there is a minimum or maximum (or neither) at each critical number.

(6) Many students get confused about the distinction between g and g'. The graph that is given in the problem is the graph of g', the *derivative* of g, whereas the graph that we sketched in the sign chart gives the general shape of the graph of g.

Note that the graph of g in the sign chart is increasing precisely when the given graph of g' is above the x-axis, and the graph of g in the sign chart is decreasing precisely when the given graph of g' is below the x-axis.

The maximum and minimum points of g in the sign chart at $x = 1$ and $x = 6$, respectively, correspond to the zeros of g', ie. where the given graph of g' crosses the x-axis.

73. If $\sec(x^2 y) = y$, then $\frac{dy}{dx} =$

(A) $\frac{-2y\sec(x^2 y)}{1 - x\sec(x^2 y)}$

(B) $\frac{2xy\tan(x^2 y)}{\cos(x^2 y) - x^2 \tan(x^2 y)}$

(C) $\frac{1}{\sec(x^2 y)\tan(x^2 y)}$

(D) $\frac{1 - y\tan^2(x^2 y)}{x\tan^2(x^2 y)}$

Solution: We have

$$\sec(x^2 y)\tan(x^2 y)\left(x^2 \frac{dy}{dx} + 2xy\right) = \frac{dy}{dx}$$

$$x^2 \sec(x^2 y)\tan(x^2 y)\frac{dy}{dx} + 2xy\sec(x^2 y)\tan(x^2 y) = \frac{dy}{dx}$$

$$2xy\sec(x^2 y)\tan(x^2 y) = \frac{dy}{dx} - x^2 \sec(x^2 y)\tan(x^2 y)\frac{dy}{dx}$$

$$2xy\sec(x^2 y)\tan(x^2 y) = \frac{dy}{dx}(1 - x^2 \sec(x^2 y)\tan(x^2 y))$$

$$\frac{2xy\sec(x^2 y)\tan(x^2 y)}{1 - x^2 \sec(x^2 y)\tan(x^2 y)} = \frac{dy}{dx}$$

$$\frac{2xy\tan(x^2 y)}{\cos(x^2 y) - x^2 \tan(x^2 y)} = \frac{dy}{dx}$$

This is choice (B).

Notes: (1) The given equation defines the dependent variable y **implicitly** as a function of x. We therefore used implicit differentiation to find the derivative $\frac{dy}{dx}$. See problem 35 for more information on implicit differentiation.

(2) Recall that the derivative of $\sec x$ is $\sec x \tan x$.

To differentiate $x^2 y$, we use the product rule to get $x^2 \frac{dy}{dx} + 2xy$.

We then used the chain rule to get the derivative of $\sec(x^2 y)$.

(3) After differentiating we must solve for $\frac{dy}{dx}$.

We first distributed on the left as follows:

$$\sec(x^2 y)\tan(x^2 y)\left(x^2 \frac{dy}{dx} + 2xy\right) = x^2 \sec(x^2 y)\tan(x^2 y)\frac{dy}{dx} + 2xy\sec(x^2 y)\tan(x^2 y)$$

We then brought the term on the left with $\frac{dy}{dx}$ over to the right hand side of the equation, and then factored out $\frac{dy}{dx}$. This gave the following:

$$2xy\sec(x^2y)\tan(x^2y) = \frac{dy}{dx}(1 - x^2\sec(x^2y)\tan(x^2y)).$$

We then got $\frac{dy}{dy}$ by itself by dividing by $1 - x^2\sec(x^2y)\tan(x^2y)$:

$$\frac{2xy\sec(x^2y)\tan(x^2y)}{1-x^2\sec(x^2y)\tan(x^2y)} = \frac{dy}{dx}$$

Unfortunately, this expression doesn't look like any of the answer choices. This is easily fixed however by multiplying both the numerator and denominator by $\cos(x^2y)$.

Note that $\cos(x^2y)\sec(x^2y) = 1$ (because $\sec(x^2y) = \frac{1}{\cos(x^2y)}$).

So we have

$$\frac{\cos(x^2y)[2xy\sec(x^2y)\tan(x^2y)]}{\cos(x^2y)[1-x^2\sec(x^2y)\tan(x^2y)]} = \frac{2xy\tan(x^2y)}{\cos(x^2y)-x^2\tan(x^2y)}.$$

Alternative solution using partial derivatives:

Let $F(x,y) = \sec(x^2y) - y$. Then

$$\frac{dy}{dx} = -\frac{\frac{\partial F}{\partial x}}{\frac{\partial F}{\partial y}} = -\frac{\sec(x^2y)\tan(x^2y)(2xy)}{\sec(x^2y)\tan(x^2y)(x^2)-1} = \frac{\sec(x^2y)\tan(x^2y)(2xy)}{1-\sec(x^2y)\tan(x^2y)(x^2)}$$

$$= \frac{\tan(x^2y)(2xy)}{\cos(x^2y)-\tan(x^2y)(x^2)} = \frac{2xy\tan(x^2y)}{\cos(x^2y)-x^2\tan(x^2y)}.$$

This is choice (B).

Note: Partial differentiation is *not* an AP Calculus topic, and therefore a full explanation of this solution lies outside of the scope of this book.

74. A point moves in a straight line so that its distance at time t from a fixed point of the line is $2t^3 - 9t^2 + 12t$. The *total* distance that the point travels from $t = 0$ to $t = 4$ is

(A) 32
(B) 33
(C) 34
(D) 35

Solution: The velocity of the point is

$$v(t) = 6t^2 - 18t + 12 = 6(t^2 - 3t + 2) = 6(t - 1)(t - 2).$$

So the point might change direction at $t = 1$ and $t = 2$.

Let $s(t) = 2t^3 - 9t^2 + 12t$.

We have $s(0) = 0$, $s(1) = 5$, $s(2) = 4$, and $s(4) = 32$.

So the total distance traveled is

$$(5 - 0) + (5 - 4) + (32 - 4) = 5 + 1 + 28 = 34.$$

This is choice (C).

Notes: (1) A common mistake here would be to compute $s(4) - s(0)$. This gives the *total displacement* of the point. In other words it tells us how far the point is from its starting point ($t = 0$) at the time $t = 4$.

If the point is travelling to the right, and never changes direction, then this computation would give the correct answer. In this problem however the point *does* change direction.

(2) To find out when the point changes direction, we set the velocity $v(t) = s'(t)$ equal to 0.

In this case the position function is $s(t) = 2t^3 - 9t^2 + 12t$. It follows that the velocity function is $v(t) = s'(t) = 6t^2 - 18t + 12$.

(3) Just because $v(t) = 0$, it is not necessarily true that the point changes direction. For this particular problem it is not necessary to determine if the point actually changes direction, so we will *not* need to make a sign chart.

(4) Once we find out that the velocity is 0 at $t = 1$ and $t = 2$, we can just compute the distance traveled from $t = 0$ to $t = 1$, then from $t = 1$ to $t = 2$, and then from $t = 2$ to $t = 4$. Adding up these three distances gives us the total distance traveled by the point.

So we wish to compute

$$|s(1) - s(0)| + |s(2) - s(1)| + |s(4) - s(2)|.$$

The quickest way to do this is to first compute $s(0)$, $s(1)$, $s(2)$, and $s(4)$, then perform the three subtractions, dropping any minus signs, and finally adding up the three resulting distances.

75. * Two particles start at the origin and move along the x-axis. For $0 \le t \le 10$, their position functions are given by $x = \cos t$ and $y = \ln(2t) + 1$. For how many values of t do the particles have the same velocity?

(A) None
(B) One
(C) Two
(D) Three

Solution: $x' = -\sin t$ and $y' = \frac{2}{2t} = \frac{1}{t}$. We want to find out for how many values of t between 0 and 5 that $x' = y'$, ie. $-\sin t = \frac{1}{t}$. Now we use our graphing calculator. First make sure that your calculator is in radian mode (Press MODE and select Radian). Next press Y= and next to Y_1 enter $-\sin$ X, and next to Y_2 enter 1/X. Then press WINDOW and set Xmin to 0 and Xmax to 10. Press GRAPH to display the graph (if you do not see the graph well, you may have to adjust Ymin and Ymax as well, perhaps Ymin = -2, and Ymax = 2).

You will see that the two graphs intersect three times, choice (D).

76. Consider the equation $x^2 + e^{xy} + y^2 = 2$. Find $\frac{d^2y}{dx^2}$ at $(0,1)$.

Solution: We differentiate implicitly to get

$$2x + e^{xy}\left(x\frac{dy}{dx} + y\right) + 2y\frac{dy}{dx} = 0$$

$$2x + xe^{xy}\frac{dy}{dx} + ye^{xy} + 2y\frac{dy}{dx} = 0$$

$$xe^{xy}\frac{dy}{dx} + 2y\frac{dy}{dx} = -2x - ye^{xy}$$

$$\frac{dy}{dx}(xe^{xy} + 2y) = -2x - ye^{xy}$$

$$\frac{dy}{dx} = \frac{-2x - ye^{xy}}{xe^{xy} + 2y}.$$

So we have $\frac{d^2y}{dx^2}$

$$= \frac{(xe^{xy}+2y)(-2-\left[ye^{xy}\left(x\frac{dy}{dx}+y\right)+e^{xy}\cdot\frac{dy}{dx}\right])-(-2x-ye^{xy})(xe^{xy}\left(x\frac{dy}{dx}+y\right)+e^{xy}+2\frac{dy}{dx})}{(xe^{xy}+2y)^2}$$

At $(0,1)$, we have $\frac{dy}{dx} = -\frac{1}{2}$, and so

$$\frac{d^2y}{dx^2} = \frac{(2)\left(-2-\left[1(1)+1(-\frac{1}{2})1\right]\right)-(-1)\left(1+2(-\frac{1}{2})\right)}{2^2} = \frac{2\left(-2-\frac{1}{2}\right)+(0)}{4} = -\frac{5}{4}.$$

77. The area of the region in the first quadrant bounded by the graph of $y = x^2\sqrt{1 - x^3}$, the line $x = 1$, and the x-axis is

(A) $\frac{2}{9}$

(B) $\frac{2\sqrt{2}}{9}$

(C) $\frac{2\sqrt{3}}{9}$

(D) $\frac{4}{9}$

Solution: $\int_0^1 x^2\sqrt{1 - x^3}\, dx = -\frac{1}{3} \cdot \frac{2}{3}(1 - x^3)^{\frac{3}{2}}\big|_0^1 = \frac{2}{9}$, choice (A).

Notes: (1) To compute the area under the graph of a function that lies entirely above the x-axis (the line $y = 0$) from $x = a$ to $x = b$, we simply integrate the function from a to b.

In this problem, the function is $y = x^2\sqrt{1 - x^3}$, $a = 0$, and $b = 1$.

Note that $x^2 \geq 0$ for all x, $\sqrt{1 - x^3} \geq 0$ for all x in the interval $[0,1]$, and therefore $x^2\sqrt{1 - x^3} \geq 0$ for all x in the interval $[0,1]$. It follows that the graph of $y = x^2\sqrt{1 - x^3}$ lies entirely above the x-axis for $0 \leq x \leq 1$.

(2) $x = 0$ and $x = 1$ are the only two zeros of $y = x^2\sqrt{1 - x^3}$.

(3) To evaluate $\int x^2\sqrt{1 - x^3}\,dx$, we can formally make the substitution $u = 1 - x^3$. It then follows that $du = -3x^2 dx$.

Since there is no -3 multiplying $x^2 dx$ we place -3 to the left of x^2, and we place $-\frac{1}{3}$ outside of the integral sign as follows:

$$\int x^2\sqrt{1 - x^3}\,dx = -\frac{1}{3}\int \sqrt{1 - x^3}(-3)x^2 dx$$

We now have

$$\int x^2\sqrt{1 - x^3}\,dx = -\frac{1}{3}\int \sqrt{1 - x^3}(-3)x^2 dx = -\frac{1}{3}\int \sqrt{u}\, du =$$

$$-\frac{1}{3}\int u^{\frac{1}{2}}\, du = -\frac{1}{3}\frac{u^{\frac{3}{2}}}{\frac{3}{2}} + C = -\frac{1}{3} \cdot \frac{2}{3}u^{\frac{3}{2}} + C = -\frac{2}{9}(1 - x^3)^{\frac{3}{2}} + C$$

We get the second equality by replacing $1 - x^3$ by u, and $-3x^2 dx$ by du.

We get the fourth equality by applying the power rule for integrals

$$\int u^n du = \frac{u^{n+1}}{n+1} + C.$$

And we get the rightmost equality by replacing u with $1 - x^3$.

(4) With a little practice, we can evaluate an integral like this very quickly with the following reasoning: The derivative of $1 - x^3$ is $-3x^2$. So we artificially insert a factor of -3 next to x^2, and $-\frac{1}{3}$ outside the integral sign. Now to integrate $-3x^2\sqrt{1 - x^3}$ we simply pretend we are integrating $\sqrt{x}$ but as we do it we leave the $1 - x^3$ where it is. This is essentially what was done in the above solution.

Note that the $-3x^2$ "goes away" because it is the derivative of $1 - x^3$. We need it to be there for everything to work.

(5) If we are doing the substitution formally, we can save some time by changing the limits of integration. We do this as follows:

$$\int_0^1 x^2 \sqrt{1 - x^3}\ dx = -\frac{1}{3} \int_0^1 \sqrt{1 - x^3}\ (-3)x^2 dx = -\frac{1}{3} \int_1^0 \sqrt{u}\ du$$

$$= -\frac{1}{3} \cdot \frac{2}{3} u^{\frac{3}{2}} \Big|_1^0 = -\frac{2}{9}(0) - \left(-\frac{2}{9}\right)(1) = \frac{2}{9}.$$

Notice that the limits 0 and 1 were changed to the limits 1 and 0, respectively. We made this change using the formula that we chose for the substitution: $u = 1 - x^3$. When $x = 0$, we have $u = 1 - 0^3 = 1$. And when $x = 1$, we have $u = 1 - 1^3 = 0$.

Note that this method has the advantage that we do not have to change back to a function of x at the end.

78. A particle moves in a straight line with velocity $v(t) = t - \sqrt{t}$ beginning at time $t = 0$. How far is the particle from its starting point at time $t = 4$?

   (A) 0

   (B) 2

   (C) $\frac{8}{3}$

   (D) $\frac{40}{3}$

Solution: $\int_0^4 (t - \sqrt{t})dt = (\frac{t^2}{2} - \frac{2}{3}t^{\frac{3}{2}})\Big|_0^4 = 8 - \frac{16}{3} = \frac{24}{3} - \frac{16}{3} = \frac{8}{3}$

This is choice (C).

Notes: (1) The particle actually changes direction at time $t = 1$. To see this note that $v(1) = 0$, $v(t) < 0$ for $0 < t < 1$, and $v(t) > 0$ for $t > 1$.

We do not actually need to worry about the particle changing direction in this problem since we only want the particle's position relative to its starting point.

(2) If we know the velocity function v of a particle, then we can find its position function s by integrating the velocity v. That is $s(t) = \int v(t)dt$.

(3) $\int_a^b v(t)dt = s(b) - s(a)$ gives the distance between the position of the particle at time a and the position of the particle at time b.

(3) If we were asked to find the *total distance* traveled by the particle, then we would need to be more careful. In this case we would compute $\int_0^4 |t - \sqrt{t}|dt$. See problem 82 for an example like this.

79. The acceleration $a(t)$ of a body moving in a straight line is given in terms of time t by $a(t) = 3 - 2t$. If the velocity of the body is 10 at $t = 1$ and if $s(t)$ is the distance of the body from the origin at time t, then $s(5) - s(1) =$

   (A) $\frac{10}{3}$

   (B) $\frac{20}{3}$

   (C) $\frac{40}{3}$

   (D) $\frac{80}{3}$

Solution: $v(t) = \int a(t)dt = \int(3 - 2t)dt = 3t - t^2 + C.$

We are given that $10 = v(1) = 3(1) - 1^2 + C = 3 - 1 + C = 2 + C.$
So $C = 10 - 2 = 8.$ It follows that $v(t) = 3t - t^2 + 8.$

$$s(5) - s(1) = \int_1^5 v(t)dt = \int_1^5 (3t - t^2 + 8)dt = \left(\frac{3}{2}t^2 - \frac{t^3}{3} + 8t\right)\Big|_1^5$$

$$= \left(\frac{3}{2}(5)^2 - \frac{5^3}{3} + 8 \cdot 5\right) - \left(\frac{3}{2}(1)^2 - \frac{(1)^3}{3} + 8 \cdot 1\right) = \frac{80}{3}.$$

This is choice (D).

Notes: (1) s, v, and a are generally used for *position, velocity,* and *acceleration,* respectively.

(2) The velocity function is the derivative of the position function, and the acceleration function is the derivative of the velocity function.

That is $v(t) = s'(t)$ and $a(t) = v'(t) = s''(t).$

In terms of integrals, $v(t) = \int a(t)dt$ and $s(t) = \int v(t)dt.$

80. The area of the region completely bounded by the curve $y = -x^2 + 2x + 5$ and the line $y = 2$ is

(A) $\frac{32}{3}$

(B) $\frac{24}{3}$

(C) $\frac{16}{3}$

(D) $\frac{8}{3}$

Solution: Let's draw a picture:

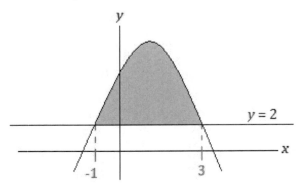

The area of the shaded region is

104

$$\int_{-1}^{3}[(-x^2 + 2x + 5) - 2]\,dx = \int_{-1}^{3}(-x^2 + 2x + 3)\,dx = \left(-\frac{x^3}{3} + x^2 + 3x\right)\Big|_{-1}^{3}$$

$$= \left(-\frac{3^3}{3} + 3^2 + 3\cdot 3\right) - \left(-\frac{(-1)^3}{3} + (-1)^2 + 3(-1)\right) = \frac{32}{3}.$$

This is choice (A).

Notes: (1) The area between the curves $y = f(x)$ and $y = g(x)$ from $x = a$ to $x = b$ is $\int_a^b |f(x) - g(x)|\,dx$. The x-values a and b are usually the x-coordinates of points of intersection of the two graphs.

(2) If we are allowed to use our graphing calculator to solve this problem, we can simply graph the functions $f(x) = -x^2 + 2x + 5$ and $g(x) = 2$ in our calculator, use the intersect feature under the CALC menu to find that $a = -1$ and $b = 3$. We would then see that $f(x)$ lies above $g(x)$, and so we would compute $\int_{-1}^{3}[(-x^2 + 2x + 5) - 2]\,dx$.

We can do this last computation by hand (as was done in the solution above), or by using the integration feature in our calculator.

(3) If we cannot use a calculator, we can find a and b by setting $f(x)$ equal to $g(x)$. We have $-x^2 + 2x + 5 = 2$, so that

$$0 = x^2 - 2x - 3 = (x + 1)(x - 3).$$

This last equation has solutions $x = -1$ and $x = 3$. So $a = -1$ and $b = 3$.

(4) The graph of the quadratic function $q(x) = ax^2 + bx + c$ is a parabola with vertex at $x = -\frac{b}{2a}$. If $a > 0$, the parabola opens upwards. If $a < 0$, the parabola opens downwards.

In this problem we have that the graph of $f(x) = -x^2 + 2x + 5$ is a downward facing parabola with vertex at $x = -\frac{2}{2(-1)} = 1$.

The y-coordinate of this point is then $f(1) = -1^2 + 2(1) + 5 = 6$.

So the vertex of the parabola is the point (1,6).

(5) Notes (3) and (4) allow us to sketch the region shown above without using a calculator.

81. * Calculate the approximate area under the curve $f(x) = x^2$ and bounded by the lines $x = 2$ and $x = 3$ by the trapezoidal rule, using three equal subintervals.

(A) 1.285
(B) 3.176
(C) 6.352
(D) 12.704

Solution: $\int_2^3 f(x)\, dx \approx \frac{1}{2} \cdot \frac{1}{3} \left[f(2) + 2f\left(\frac{7}{3}\right) + 2f\left(\frac{8}{3}\right) + f(3) \right]$

$$= \frac{1}{6} \left[4 + 2\left(\frac{49}{9}\right) + 2\left(\frac{64}{9}\right) + 9 \right] \approx 6.352$$

This is choice (C).

Notes: (1) The **trapezoidal rule** says

$$\int_a^b f(x)\, dx \approx \frac{1}{2} \cdot \frac{b-a}{n} [f(x_0) + 2f(x_1) + \cdots + 2f(x_{n-1}) + f(x_n)],$$

where the interval $[a, b]$ is partitioned into n equal subintervals with endpoints $a = x_0, x_1, \ldots, x_{n-1}, x_n = b$.

In this problem, we have $a = 2$, $b = 3$, $n = 3$, and $f(x) = x^2$.

So $\frac{b-a}{n} = \frac{1}{3}$ is the length of each subinterval.

(2) Recall the formula for the area of a trapezoid: $A = \left(\frac{b_1+b_2}{2}\right)h$. In other words we take the average of the bases times the height.

(3) Here is a picture of the trapezoidal rule being used in this problem:

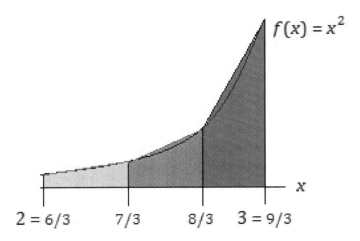

$$f(x) = x^2$$

$$2 = 6/3 \qquad 7/3 \qquad 8/3 \qquad 3 = 9/3$$

Note that all three trapezoids have a height of $\frac{1}{3}$ (the height runs along the x-axis).

The two bases of the leftmost trapezoid are $f(2)$ and $f(\frac{7}{3})$. It follows that the area of the leftmost trapezoid is $\frac{f(2)+f(\frac{7}{3})}{2} \cdot \frac{1}{3}$.

The two bases of the middle trapezoid are $f(\frac{7}{3})$ and $f(\frac{8}{3})$. It follows that the area of the middle trapezoid is $\frac{f(\frac{7}{3})+f(\frac{8}{3})}{2} \cdot \frac{1}{3}$.

The two bases of the rightmost trapezoid are $f(\frac{8}{3})$ and $f(3)$. It follows that the area of the rightmost trapezoid is $\frac{f(\frac{8}{3})+f(3)}{2} \cdot \frac{1}{3}$.

Finally, we get the area of the shaded region by adding these three areas:

$$\int_2^3 f(x)\,dx \approx \frac{f(2)+f(\frac{7}{3})}{2} \cdot \frac{1}{3} + \frac{f(\frac{7}{3})+f(\frac{8}{3})}{2} \cdot \frac{1}{3} + \frac{f(\frac{8}{3})+f(3)}{2} \cdot \frac{1}{3}$$

$$= \frac{1}{2} \cdot \frac{1}{3}\left[f(2) + 2f\left(\frac{7}{3}\right) + 2f\left(\frac{8}{3}\right) + f(3)\right].$$

82. A point moves in a straight line so that its velocity at time t is $2t^3 - 5t^2 + 2t$. What is the *total* distance that the point travels from $t = 0$ to $t = 3$?

Solution: The velocity of the point is

$$v(t) = 2t^3 - 5t^2 + 2t = t(2t^2 - 5t + 2) = t(2t - 1)(t - 2)$$

107

So the point might change direction at $t = \frac{1}{2}$ and $t = 2$.

$$\int v(t)\, dt = \int (2t^3 - 5t^2 + 2t)\, dt = \frac{t^4}{2} - \frac{5t^3}{3} + t^2 + C.$$

Let $x(t) = \frac{t^4}{2} - \frac{5t^3}{3} + t^2$.

We have $x(0) = 0$, $x\left(\frac{1}{2}\right) = \frac{7}{96}$, $x(2) = -\frac{4}{3}$, $x(3) = \frac{9}{2}$.

The total distance traveled by the point is

$$\int_0^3 |v(t)|\, dt = \left|x\left(\tfrac{1}{2}\right) - x(0)\right| + \left|x(2) - x\left(\tfrac{1}{2}\right)\right| + |x(3) - x(2)|$$

$$= \frac{7}{96} + \frac{45}{32} + \frac{35}{6} = \frac{117}{16}, \ \textbf{7.312 or 7.313}.$$

Notes: (1) A common mistake here would be to simply compute $\int_0^3 (2t^3 - 5t^2 + 2t)\, dt$. This gives the *total displacement* of the point. In other words it tells us how far the point is from its starting point ($t = 0$) at the time $t = 3$.

If the point is travelling to the right, and never changes direction, then this computation would give the correct answer. In this problem however the point *does* change direction.

(2) To find out when the point might change direction, we set the velocity $v(t)$ (the given function) equal to 0.

(3) Just because $v(t) = 0$, it is not necessarily true that the point changes direction. For this particular problem it is not necessary to determine if the point actually changes direction, so we will *not* need to make a sign chart.

(4) Once we find out that the velocity is 0 at $t = \frac{1}{2}$ and $t = 2$, we can just compute the distance traveled from $t = 0$ to $t = \frac{1}{2}$, then from $t = \frac{1}{2}$ to $t = 2$, and then from $t = 2$ to $t = 3$. Adding up these three distances gives us the total distance traveled by the point.

So we wish to compute

$$\left|x\left(\tfrac{1}{2}\right) - x(0)\right| + \left|x(2) - x\left(\tfrac{1}{2}\right)\right| + |x(3) - x(2)|.$$

The quickest way to do this is to first compute $x(0)$, $x\left(\frac{1}{2}\right)$, $x(2)$, and $x(3)$, then perform the three subtractions, dropping any minus signs, and finally adding up the three resulting distances.

(5) If we can use a calculator for this problem, we can compute $\int_0^3 |v(t)|\, dt = \int_0^3 |2t^3 - 5t^2 + 2t|\, dt$ using our TI-84 calculator by first selecting fnInt((or pressing 9) under the MATH menu, and then going to the MATH menu again, moving right once to NUM and selecting abs((or pressing 1). The display will show the following:

fnInt(abs(

We then type the following: fnInt(abs(2X^3 − 5X^2 + 2X), X, 0, 3), and press ENTER.

The display will show 7.312502794. So we can answer **7.312** or **7.313**.

83. $\int \frac{1-x}{x^2+3x+2}\, dx =$

(A) $\ln\left|\frac{(x+2)^3}{(x+1)^2}\right| + C$

(B) $\ln\left|\frac{(x+1)^2}{(x+2)^3}\right| + C$

(C) $\ln|(x+1)^2(x+2)^3| + C$

(D) $\ln|(x+1)^3(x+2)^2| + C$

Solution: We do a partial fraction decomposition. First note that $x^2 + 3x + 2 = (x+1)(x+2)$, so that $\frac{1-x}{x^2+3x+2} = \frac{1-x}{(x+1)(x+2)}$.

$\frac{1-x}{(x+1)(x+2)} = \frac{A}{x+1} + \frac{B}{x+2}$ if and only if $1 - x = A(x+2) + B(x+1)$.

Letting $x = -1$ yields $A = 2$, and letting $x = -2$ yields $B = -3$. So we have $\frac{1-x}{(x+1)(x+2)} = \frac{2}{x+1} - \frac{3}{x+2}$. It follows that

$$\int \frac{1-x}{x^2+3x+2}\, dx = \int \frac{2}{x+1} - \frac{3}{x+2}\, dx = 2\ln|x+1| - 3\ln|x+2|$$

$$= \ln|x+1|^2 - \ln|x+2|^3 = \ln\frac{|x+1|^2}{|x+2|^3} = \ln\left|\frac{(x+1)^2}{(x+2)^3}\right| + C.$$

This is choice (B).

Notes: (1) Note that the rational expression $\frac{1-x}{x^2+3x+2}$ is a **proper fraction** because the degree of the polynomial in the numerator is less than the degree of the polynomial in the denominator.

(2) To integrate a rational function that is expressed as a proper fraction, it often helps to do a **partial fraction decomposition**. This means that we rewrite the fraction as a sum of two or more fractions with denominators of smaller degree.

In this case we attempt to rewrite $\frac{1-x}{(x+1)(x+2)}$ as $\frac{A}{x+1} + \frac{B}{x+2}$. We need to figure out the real numbers A and B.

(3) As seen in the solution above, we begin by multiplying each side of the equation $\frac{1-x}{(x+1)(x+2)} = \frac{2}{x+1} - \frac{3}{x+2}$ by the least common denominator $(x+1)(x+2)$ to get $1 - x = A(x+2) + B(x+1)$.

There are now several ways to find A and B.

Method 1: Substitute $x = -1$ to find A and substitute $x = -2$ to find B.

Method 2: Substitute in *any* two real numbers for x and solve the resulting system of equations. Choosing the values used in Method 1 is most efficient of course.

Method 3: Equate coefficients of corresponding terms. To use this method we multiply out the right hand side, and regroup as follows:

$$-x + 1 = (A + B)x + 2A + B.$$

Now, the coefficient of x on the left is -1 and the coefficient of x on the right is $A + B$. So we have $A + B = -1$.

The constant term on the left is 1 and the constant term on the right is $2A + B$. So we have $2A + B = 1$.

We now solve the resulting system of equations. For example, we can subtract the first equation from the second to get

$$\begin{array}{rl} 2A + B = & 1 \\ \underline{A + B = -1} \\ A \quad\;\; = & 2 \end{array}$$

Substituting $A = 2$ into $A + B = -1$ gives $2 + B = -1$, or $B = -3$.

(4) See problem 3 for the laws of logarithms that were used here.

84. * Let G be defined by $G(x) = \int_2^x 35e^{-t^2+t+1}(2t^2 - 3t + 5)dt$, Which of the following statements about G must be true?

    I. G is increasing on $(2,3)$.
    II. G is concave up on $(2,3)$
    III. $G(3) > 0$

    (A) I only
    (B) II only
    (C) III only
    (D) I and III only

Solution: $G'(x) = 35e^{-x^2+x+1}(2x^2 - 3x + 5)$. We graph G' in our calculator in the window $[2,3] \times [0,100]$.

Since the graph of G' lies entirely above the x-axis, $G' > 0$ on $(2,3)$, and therefore G is increasing on $(2,3)$. So I is true.

Since the graph of G' is decreasing, $G'' < 0$ on $(2,3)$, and therefore G is concave down on $(2,3)$. So II is false.

$G(3) = \int_2^3 35e^{-t^2+t+1}(2t^2 - 3t + 5)dt$ is the "net area" between the graph of G' and the x-axis from $x = 2$ to $x = 3$. Since G' lies entirely above the x-axis, $G(3) > 0$. So III is true.

The answer is therefore choice (D).

85. The expression $\frac{1}{100}\left(\sqrt[3]{\frac{1}{100}} + \sqrt[3]{\frac{2}{100}} + \sqrt[3]{\frac{3}{100}} + \cdots + \sqrt[3]{\frac{100}{100}}\right)$ is a Riemann sum approximation for

    (A) $\frac{1}{100}\int_0^{100} \sqrt[3]{x}\, dx$

    (B) $\frac{1}{100}\int_0^1 \sqrt[3]{x}\, dx$

    (C) $\frac{1}{100}\int_0^1 \sqrt[3]{\frac{x}{100}}\, dx$

    (D) $\int_0^1 \sqrt[3]{x}\, dx$

Solution: Let $f(x) = \sqrt[3]{x}$ and partition the interval $[0,1]$ into 100 equal subintervals as follows:

Let $x_0 = \frac{0}{100} = 0$, $x_1 = \frac{1}{100}$, $x_2 = \frac{2}{100}, \ldots, x_{99} = \frac{99}{100}$, $x_{100} = \frac{100}{100} = 1$.

We get the corresponding subintervals $[0, \frac{1}{100}]$, $[\frac{1}{100}, \frac{2}{100}]$, ..., $[\frac{99}{100}, 1]$.

The length of each subinterval (and therefore the base of each rectangle) is $\frac{1-0}{100} = \frac{1}{100}$.

For the height of each rectangle we choose the right endpoint of each subinterval x^*, and compute $f(x^*)$.

So the height of the leftmost rectangle will be $f\left(\frac{1}{100}\right) = \sqrt[3]{\frac{1}{100}}$. It follows that the area of the leftmost rectangle is $\frac{1}{100} \cdot \sqrt[3]{\frac{1}{100}}$.

Similarly, the area of the next rectangle will be $\frac{1}{100} \cdot \sqrt[3]{\frac{2}{100}}$.

Continuing in this fashion, we get that the area of the rightmost rectangle is $\frac{1}{100} \cdot \sqrt[3]{\frac{100}{100}}$.

So we are approximating the area under the graph of $f(x) = \sqrt[3]{x}$ from $x = 0$ to $x = 1$ by

$$\frac{1}{100} \cdot \sqrt[3]{\frac{1}{100}} + \frac{1}{100} \cdot \sqrt[3]{\frac{2}{100}} + \cdots + \frac{1}{100} \cdot \sqrt[3]{\frac{100}{100}}$$

$$= \frac{1}{100}\left(\sqrt[3]{\frac{1}{100}} + \sqrt[3]{\frac{2}{100}} + \cdots + \sqrt[3]{\frac{100}{100}}\right).$$

This is precisely the expression given in the problem. So the answer is choice (D).

Notes: (1) A **Riemann Sum Approximation** of f over the interval $I = [a, b]$ with partition $P = \{[x_0, x_1], [x_1, x_2], \dots, [x_{n-1}, x_n]\}$ where $a = x_0 < x_1 < x_2 < \cdots < x_n = b$ is given by

$$S = \sum_{i=1}^{n} f(x_i^*)(x_i - x_{i-1}), \text{ where } x_{i-1} \leq x^* \leq x_i$$

or equivalently

$$S = f(x_1^*)(x_1 - x_0) + f(x_2^*)(x_2 - x_1) + \cdots + f(x_n^*)(x_n - x_{n-1}).$$

where $x_0 \leq x_1^* \leq x_1$, $x_1 \leq x_2^* \leq x_2$, ..., $x_{n-1} \leq x_n^* \leq x_n$.

(2) Geometrically (and in English), what note (1) says is that we first chop up the interval $[a, b]$ into n pieces, called subintervals.

For each subinterval we then choose an x-value in that subinterval, and draw a rectangle whose base is the length of the subinterval, and whose height is the corresponding y-value on the graph (more precisely, if we choose x^* in the subinterval, then the height is $f(x^*)$).

Finally we add up the areas of all of these rectangles.

(3) Very often (such as in this problem) we want all of the subintervals in our partition to have equal length. In this case, the length of each subinterval is $\frac{b-a}{n}$ (remember that a and b are the left and right endpoints of the original interval, and n is the number of pieces we are chopping it up into). The formula for the Riemann Sum Approximation then simplifies to

$$S = \frac{b-a}{n} \sum_{i=1}^{n} f(x_i^*)$$

or equivalently

$$S = \frac{b-a}{n} [f(x_1^*) + f(x_2^*) + \cdots + f(x_n^*)].$$

(4) Here is a sketch of the Riemann Sum approximation for this problem:

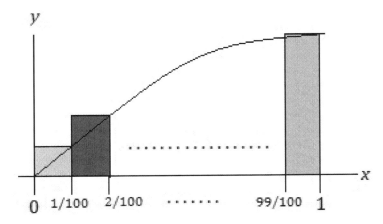

Note that only part of the picture is drawn here. In reality there should be 100 rectangles, each with a base of $\frac{1}{100}$.

113

Also note that for each subinterval we chose the right endpoint of the interval to form the height of the rectangle. For example, the height of the leftmost rectangle is $f\left(\frac{1}{100}\right) = \sqrt[3]{\frac{1}{100}}$. It follows that the area of the leftmost rectangle is $\frac{1}{100} \cdot \sqrt[3]{\frac{1}{100}}$.

Similarly, the area of the second rectangle is $\frac{1}{100} \cdot \sqrt[3]{\frac{2}{100}}$.

Continuing in this fashion, we get that the area of the rightmost rectangle is $\frac{1}{100} \cdot \sqrt[3]{\frac{100}{100}}$.

It follows that the sum of all of these rectangles is

$$\frac{1}{100} \cdot \sqrt[3]{\frac{1}{100}} + \frac{1}{100} \cdot \sqrt[3]{\frac{2}{100}} + \cdots + \frac{1}{100} \cdot \sqrt[3]{\frac{100}{100}}$$

$$= \frac{1}{100}\left(\sqrt[3]{\frac{1}{100}} + \sqrt[3]{\frac{2}{100}} + \cdots + \sqrt[3]{\frac{100}{100}}\right).$$

Observe that this computation led to an approximation of the area under the graph of $f(x) = \sqrt[3]{x}$ from $x = 0$ to $x = 1$. In other words, we approximated $\int_0^1 \sqrt[3]{x}\, dx$.

x	$f'(x)$
-2	1
-1	2
0	3
1	4
2	5

86. The table above gives selected values for the derivative of a function f on the interval $-2 \le x \le 2$. If $f(-2) = 3$ and Euler's method with a step size of 2 is used to approximate $f(2)$, what is the resulting approximation?

(A) 7
(B) 9
(C) 11
(D) 13

114

Solution: Let's make a table:

(x, y)	dx	$\frac{dy}{dx}$	$dx\left(\frac{dy}{dx}\right) = dy$	$(x + dx, y + dy)$
$(-2,3)$	2	1	2	$(0,5)$
$(0,5)$	2	3	6	$(2,11)$

From the last entry of the table we see that $f(2) \approx 11$, choice (C).

Note: See problem 16 for more detailed information on how Euler's method works.

87. Which of the following integrals represents the area enclosed by the smaller loop of the graph of $r = 2 + 4\cos\theta$?

(A) $\int_{\frac{2\pi}{3}}^{\frac{4\pi}{3}} (1 + 2\cos\theta)\, d\theta$

(B) $\int_{\frac{2\pi}{3}}^{\frac{4\pi}{3}} (1 + 2\cos\theta)^2\, d\theta$

(C) $2\int_{\frac{2\pi}{3}}^{\frac{4\pi}{3}} (1 + 2\cos\theta)^2\, d\theta$

(D) $\int_{\frac{4\pi}{3}}^{\frac{7\pi}{3}} (1 + 2\cos\theta)\, d\theta$

Solution: The smaller loop of the graph of $r = 2 + 4\cos\theta$ can be graphed from $\theta = \frac{2\pi}{3}$ to $\theta = \frac{4\pi}{3}$. So the area enclosed by this loop is given by

$$A = \frac{1}{2}\int_{\frac{2\pi}{3}}^{\frac{4\pi}{3}} r^2\, d\theta = \frac{1}{2}\int_{\frac{2\pi}{3}}^{\frac{4\pi}{3}} [2 + 4\cos\theta]^2\, d\theta = 2\int_{\frac{2\pi}{3}}^{\frac{4\pi}{3}} [1 + 2\cos\theta]^2\, d\theta.$$

This is choice (C).

Notes: (1) See problem 48 to learn how to sketch a polar graph in detail.

(2) The graph of the given polar equation is called a **limacon**. Let's sketch it. We will use the usual key points: $\theta = 0, \frac{\pi}{2}, \pi, \frac{3\pi}{2}, 2\pi$. And we will also find any additional values for θ such that $2 + 4\cos\theta = 0$. Subtracting 2 from each side of this equation gives $4\cos\theta = -2$. So $\cos\theta = -\frac{1}{2}$, and so $\theta = \frac{2\pi}{3}$ and $\theta = \frac{4\pi}{3}$. Let's make a table of values and sketch the graph:

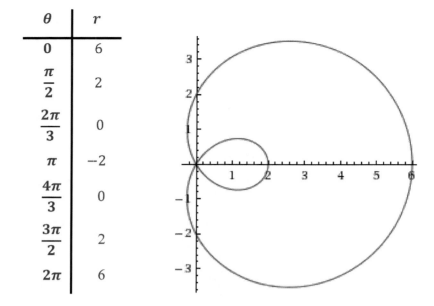

θ	r
0	6
$\dfrac{\pi}{2}$	2
$\dfrac{2\pi}{3}$	0
π	-2
$\dfrac{4\pi}{3}$	0
$\dfrac{3\pi}{2}$	2
2π	6

Note that the smaller loop is traced out from $\theta = \frac{2\pi}{3}$ to $\theta = \frac{4\pi}{3}$. r takes on negative values throughout this whole interval, so there is no danger of positive and negative r-values canceling each other out.

(3) Observe that $\frac{1}{2}\int_{\frac{2\pi}{3}}^{\frac{4\pi}{3}} [2 + 4\cos\theta]^2 \, d\theta = \frac{1}{2}\int_{\frac{2\pi}{3}}^{\frac{4\pi}{3}} [2(1 + 2\cos\theta)]^2 \, d\theta$

$= \frac{1}{2}\int_{\frac{2\pi}{3}}^{\frac{4\pi}{3}} 4(1 + 2\cos\theta)^2 \, d\theta = 2\int_{\frac{2\pi}{3}}^{\frac{4\pi}{3}} [1 + 2\cos\theta]^2 \, d\theta$

88. $\int e^{3x}\cos 2x \, dx =$

Solution: We use integration by parts.

$+$	e^{3x}	$\cos 2x$
$-$	$3e^{3x}$	$\dfrac{1}{2}\sin 2x$
$+$	$9e^{3x}$	$-\dfrac{1}{4}\cos 2x$

So $\int e^{3x}\cos 2x\,dx = \frac{1}{2}e^{3x}\sin 2x + \frac{3}{4}e^{3x}\cos 2x - \frac{9}{4}\int e^{3x}\cos 2x\,dx$.

We add $\frac{9}{4}\int e^{3x}\cos 2x\,dx$ to each side of this equation to get

$$\frac{13}{4}\int e^{3x}\cos 2x\,dx = \frac{1}{2}e^{3x}\sin 2x + \frac{3}{4}e^{3x}\cos 2x,$$

and so $\int e^{3x}\cos 2x\,dx = \frac{4}{13}\left(\frac{1}{2}e^{3x}\sin 2x + \frac{3}{4}e^{3x}\cos 2x\right) + C$.

Finally, $\int e^{3x}\cos 2x\,dx = \frac{2}{13}e^{3x}\sin 2x + \frac{3}{13}e^{3x}\cos 2x + C$.

Notes: (1) See problem 47 to see how to solve a simple integration by parts problem. This problem is a bit more difficult as it requires two iterations of the integration by parts formula. Recall the formula:

$$\int u\,dv = uv - \int v\,du$$

To compute $\int e^{3x}\cos 2x\,dx$, we can let $u = e^{3x}$, and $dv = \cos 2x\,dx$. It then follows that $du = 3e^{3x}dx$ and $v = \frac{1}{2}\sin 2x$. So we have

$$\int e^{3x}\cos 2x\,dx = (e^{3x})\left(\frac{1}{2}\sin 2x\right) - \int\left(\frac{1}{2}\sin 2x\right)(3e^{3x})\,dx + C$$

$$= \frac{1}{2}e^{3x}\sin 2x - \frac{3}{2}\int e^{3x}\sin 2x\,dx + C.$$

We now repeat this procedure to compute $\int e^{3x}\sin 2x\,dx$. We let $u = e^{3x}$, and $dv = \sin 2x\,dx$. It then follows that $du = 3e^{3x}dx$ and $v = -\frac{1}{2}\cos 2x$. So we have

$$\int e^{3x}\sin 2x\,dx = (e^{3x})\left(-\frac{1}{2}\cos 2x\right) - \int\left(-\frac{1}{2}\cos 2x\right)(3e^{3x})\,dx + C$$

$$= -\frac{1}{2}e^{3x}\cos 2x + \frac{3}{2}\int e^{3x}\cos 2x\,dx + C.$$

Putting these two results together, and dropping the constants (for now), we have

$$\int e^{3x}\cos 2x\,dx = \frac{1}{2}e^{3x}\sin 2x - \frac{3}{2}\int e^{3x}\sin 2x\,dx$$

$$= \frac{1}{2}e^{3x}\sin 2x - \frac{3}{2}\left(-\frac{1}{2}e^{3x}\cos 2x + \frac{3}{2}\int e^{3x}\cos 2x\,dx\right)$$

$$= \frac{1}{2}e^{3x}\sin 2x + \frac{3}{4}e^{3x}\cos 2x - \frac{9}{4}\int e^{3x}\cos 2x\,dx$$

Adding $\frac{9}{4}\int e^{3x}\cos 2x\, dx$ to each side of this equation gives

$$\frac{13}{4}\int e^{3x}\cos 2x\, dx = \frac{1}{2}e^{3x}\sin 2x + \frac{3}{4}e^{3x}\cos 2x.$$

Multiplying by $\frac{4}{13}$, and adding an arbitrary constant yields

$$\int e^{3x}\cos 2x\, dx = \frac{2}{13}e^{3x}\sin 2x + \frac{3}{13}e^{3x}\cos 2x + C.$$

(2) In the original solution above, we actually used **tabular integration by parts**. Note that this is a bit more sophisticated than the solution to problem 47.

In the first column we simply alternate signs starting with a plus sign.

In the middle column we put our choice for u, and we differentiate as we go down the column.

In the third column we put our choice for dv, and we integrate as we go down the column.

In this particular example we stop at the third row since the expression $\cos 2x$ appears for the second time in the third column.

Finally we follow the arrow pattern as seen in the original solution above to write down

$$\int e^{3x}\cos 2x\, dx = \frac{1}{2}e^{3x}\sin 2x + \frac{3}{4}e^{3x}\cos 2x - \frac{9}{4}\int e^{3x}\cos 2x\, dx.$$

From here we solve for $\int e^{3x}\cos 2x\, dx$.

LEVEL 3: SERIES

89. If g is a function such that $g'(x) = \cos(x^3)$, then the coefficient of x^{13} in the Maclaurin series for g is

(A) $\frac{1}{13}$

(B) $\frac{1}{24}$

(C) $\frac{1}{52}$

(D) $\frac{1}{312}$

Solution: The Maclaurin series for $\cos x$ is

118

$$\sum_{n=0}^{\infty} \frac{(-1)^n x^{2n}}{(2n)!} = 1 - \frac{x^2}{2!} + \frac{x^4}{4!} - \frac{x^6}{6!} + \cdots + \frac{(-1)^n x^{2n}}{(2n)!} + \cdots$$

So $g'(x) = \cos(x^3)$

$$= \sum_{n=0}^{\infty} \frac{(-1)^n x^{6n}}{(2n)!} = 1 - \frac{x^6}{2!} + \frac{x^{12}}{4!} - \frac{x^{18}}{6!} + \cdots + \frac{(-1)^n x^{6n}}{(2n)!} + \cdots$$

Therefore we have

$$g(x) = C + \sum_{n=0}^{\infty} \frac{(-1)^n x^{6n+1}}{(6n+1)(2n)!} = C + x - \frac{x^7}{7 \cdot 2!} + \frac{x^{13}}{13 \cdot 4!} - \frac{x^{19}}{19 \cdot 6!} + \cdots$$

where C is some constant.

So the coefficient of x^{13} is $\frac{1}{13 \cdot 4!} = \frac{1}{312}$, choice (D).

Notes: (1) See problem 63 for more information on Maclaurin series.

(2) It is worth memorizing the following Maclaurin series:

$$e^x = \sum_{n=0}^{\infty} \frac{x^n}{n!} = 1 + x + \frac{x^2}{2!} + \frac{x^3}{3!} + \frac{x^4}{4!} + \cdots + \frac{x^n}{n!} + \cdots$$

$$\cos x = \sum_{n=0}^{\infty} \frac{(-1)^n x^{2n}}{(2n)!} = 1 - \frac{x^2}{2!} + \frac{x^4}{4!} - \frac{x^6}{6!} + \cdots + \frac{(-1)^n x^{2n}}{(2n)!} + \cdots$$

$$\sin x = \sum_{n=0}^{\infty} \frac{(-1)^n x^{2n+1}}{(2n+1)!} = x - \frac{x^3}{3!} + \frac{x^5}{5!} - \frac{x^7}{7!} + \cdots + \frac{(-1)^n x^{2n+1}}{(2n+1)!} + \cdots$$

(3) If you forget the Maclaurin series for $f(x) = \cos x$, then you can find the series by using the definition. Recall that the **Maclaurin series** for the function f is

$$\sum_{n=0}^{\infty} \frac{f^n(0)}{n!} x^n = f(0) + f'(0)x + \frac{f''(0)}{2!}x^2 + \cdots + \frac{f^n(0)}{n!}x^n + \cdots$$

So $f(x) = \cos x$, $f'(x) = -\sin x$, $f''(x) = -\cos x$, $f'''(x) = \sin x$, $f^{(4)}(x) = \cos x$, …

Notice that the derivatives just cycle through these four functions.

We now substitute 0 for x to get $f(0) = 1$, $f'(0) = 0$, $f''(0) = -1$, $f'''(0) = 0$, $f^{(4)}(0) = 1$, …

119

Once again, we have a cyclical pattern. So using the definition of the Maclaurin series for f we get

$$\cos x = 1 + 0x - \frac{x^2}{2!} + \frac{0x^3}{3!} + \frac{x^4}{4!} + \frac{0x^5}{5!} - \frac{x^6}{6!} + \cdots + \frac{(-1)^n x^{2n}}{(2n)!} + \cdots$$

$$= 1 - \frac{x^2}{2!} + \frac{x^4}{4!} - \frac{x^6}{6!} + \cdots + \frac{(-1)^n x^{2n}}{(2n)!} + \cdots$$

(4) To get the Maclaurin series for $\cos x^3$, we simply replace x by x^3 in the Maclaurin series for $\cos x$.

(5) Taylor series, and more specifically, Maclaurin series, can be integrated term by term. Since an antiderivative of $a_n x^n$ is $\frac{a_n x^{n+1}}{n+1}$, it follows that the integral of

$$g'(x) = \cos(x^3) = 1 - \frac{x^6}{2!} + \frac{x^{12}}{4!} - \frac{x^{18}}{6!} + \cdots + \frac{(-1)^n x^{6n}}{(2n)!} + \cdots$$

is

$$g(x) = C + x - \frac{x^7}{7 \cdot 2!} + \frac{x^{13}}{13 \cdot 4!} - \frac{x^{19}}{19 \cdot 6!} + \cdots$$

where C is some constant. We do not need to know what C is to get the answer to this question.

90. For a series S, let

$$S = \frac{1}{\sqrt{3^3}} - \frac{1}{3} + \frac{1}{\sqrt{5^3}} - \frac{1}{9} + \frac{1}{\sqrt{7^3}} - \frac{1}{27} + \cdots + (-1)^n s_n + \cdots,$$

where $s_n = \begin{cases} \dfrac{1}{(n+2)^{\frac{3}{2}}} & \text{if } n \text{ is odd} \\[2mm] \dfrac{1}{3^{\frac{n}{2}}} & \text{if } n \text{ is even} \end{cases}$

Which of the following statements are true?

I. S converges because the terms of S alternate in sign and $\lim_{n \to \infty} s_n = 0$.

II. S diverges because the sequence (s_n) is not decreasing.

III. S converges even though the sequence (s_n) is not decreasing.

(A) None
(B) I only
(C) II only
(D) III only

Solution: It is not sufficient that $\lim_{n \to \infty} s_n = 0$ for S to converge (in order to guarantee convergence, the sequence (s_n) must also be decreasing). So I is *not* true.

Note that the sequence (s_n) is actually *not* decreasing. For example, we have $s_1 = \frac{1}{(1+2)^{\frac{3}{2}}} = \frac{1}{3^{\frac{3}{2}}} \approx .192$, $s_2 = \frac{1}{3^{\frac{2}{2}}} = \frac{1}{3} \approx .333$, so that $s_1 < s_2$.

Now the series $T = \sum_{n=1}^{\infty} \frac{1}{n^{\frac{3}{2}}}$ is a p-series with $p = \frac{3}{2}$. Since $p > 1$, this series is convergent. The series A consisting of the odd terms of S form a series of positive terms with each term less than the corresponding term of T. It follows that A converges.

The series $B = \sum_{n=1}^{\infty} \left(\frac{1}{3}\right)^n$ is geometric with common ratio $r = \frac{1}{3}$. Since $r < 1$, this series is convergent.

Since A and B are both convergent series consisting of positive terms it follows that $A + B$ is convergent. Therefore S is absolutely convergent, thus convergent.

121

So S converges even though the sequence (s_n) is not decreasing. It follows that II is not true, and III is true. So the answer is choice (D).

Notes: (1) Recall that an **alternating series** has one of the forms $\sum_{n=1}^{\infty}(-1)^n a_n$ or $\sum_{n=1}^{\infty}(-1)^{n+1} a_n$ where $a_n > 0$ for each positive integer n.

The series S in this problem is an alternating series.

The **alternating series test** says that if (a_n) is a decreasing sequence with $\lim_{n\to\infty} a_n = 0$, then the alternating series converges.

The series S in this problem satisfies $\lim_{n\to\infty} s_n = 0$, but the sequence (s_n) is *not* decreasing. It follows that the alternating series test cannot be applied.

Note that the fact that the alternating series test cannot be applied does *not* tell us whether the series converges or diverges. We need to use a different method.

(2) See problem 60 for more information about p-series.

(3) See problems 27 and 30 for more information on geometric series.

(4) See problem 31 for more information on absolute convergence.

91. What is the approximation of the value e^5 obtained by the fifth-degree Taylor Polynomial about $x = 0$ for $f(x) = e^x$?

Solution: The fifth-degree Taylor Polynomial about $x = 0$ for $f(x) = e^x$ is $1 + x + \dfrac{x^2}{2!} + \dfrac{x^3}{3!} + \dfrac{x^4}{4!} + \dfrac{x^5}{5!}$.

So $e^5 \approx 1 + 5 + \dfrac{5^2}{2!} + \dfrac{5^3}{3!} + \dfrac{5^4}{4!} + \dfrac{5^5}{5!}$.

Notes: (1) See problem 62 for more information about Taylor Polynomials.

(2) See problem 89 (note (2)) for the Maclaurin series for e^x (remember that a Maclaurin series is the same thing as a Taylor series about $x = 0$).

The fifth-degree Taylor Polynomial about $x = 0$ for $f(x) = e^x$ is just the sum of the first six terms of the Maclaurin series for e^x.

92. * Using the Maclaurin Series for $\cos x$, approximate $\cos(0.3)$ to five decimal places.

Solution: The Maclaurin Series for $\cos x$ is

$$\sum_{n=0}^{\infty} \frac{(-1)^n x^{2n}}{(2n)!} = 1 - \frac{x^2}{2!} + \frac{x^4}{4!} - \frac{x^6}{6!} + \cdots + \frac{(-1)^n x^{2n}}{(2n)!} + \cdots$$

So $\cos(0.3) = 1 - \frac{(0.3)^2}{2!} + \frac{(0.3)^4}{4!} - \frac{(0.3)^6}{6!} + \cdots + \frac{(-1)^n (0.3)^{2n}}{(2n)!} + \cdots$

Since $\frac{(0.3)^6}{6!} \approx .000001 < .000005$, to five decimal place, we have

$\cos(0.3) \approx 1 - \frac{(0.3)^2}{2!} + \frac{(0.3)^4}{4!} = .9553375 \approx \mathbf{.95534}$.

Notes: (1) See problem 89 (note (2)) for the Maclaurin series for $\cos x$.

(2) The series representation for $\cos(0.3)$ is an alternating series that passes the alternating series test. Indeed, it is easy to see that the sequence $(\frac{(0.3)^{2n}}{(2n)!})$ is decreasing with limit 0.

(3) If the alternating series $\sum_{n=1}^{\infty}(-1)^n a_n$ or $\sum_{n=1}^{\infty}(-1)^{n+1} a_n$ converges by the alternating series test, then the sum of the first n terms is an approximation to the total sum of the series whose accuracy can be determined by the next term.

More precisely, $a_1 - a_2 + \cdots + (-1)^{n+1} a_n$ is an approximation to $\sum_{n=1}^{\infty}(-1)^{n+1} a_n$ whose error is less than or equal to a_{n+1}.

In this problem, $1 - \frac{(0.3)^2}{2!} + \frac{(0.3)^4}{4!}$ is an approximation of $\cos(0.3)$ whose error is less than $\frac{(0.3)^6}{6!}$.

(4) To guarantee that an approximation is accurate to five decimal places, we need the error to satisfy $|error| < .000005$.

Observe that there are five zeros after the decimal point.

In general to get an approximation accurate to n decimal places, there should be n zeros after the decimal point followed by a 5.

93. The Taylor series for a function g about $x = 2$ is given by $\sum_{n=1}^{\infty} \frac{(-1)^n \, 3^n}{n}(x - 2)^n$ and converges to $g(x)$ for $|x - 2| < R$, where R is the radius of convergence of the Taylor series. Find R and the interval of convergence of the Taylor series.

123

Solution: We have

$$\lim_{n\to\infty} \left| \frac{\frac{(-1)^{n+1} 3^{n+1}}{n+1}(x-2)^{n+1}}{\frac{(-1)^n 3^n}{n}(x-2)^n} \right| = \lim_{n\to\infty} \frac{n}{n+1} \cdot 3|x-2| = 3|x-2|.$$

$$3|x-2| < 1 \text{ when } |x-2| < \tfrac{1}{3}.$$

So $R = \tfrac{1}{3}$.

Now, $|x-2| < \tfrac{1}{3}$ if and only if $-\tfrac{1}{3} < x-2 < \tfrac{1}{3}$ if and only if $\tfrac{5}{3} < x < \tfrac{7}{3}$.

We still need to check the endpoints. When $x = \tfrac{7}{3}$, we get the convergent alternating series $\sum_{n=1}^{\infty} \frac{(-1)^n}{n}$, and when $x = \tfrac{5}{3}$ we get the divergent harmonic series $\sum_{n=1}^{\infty} \frac{1}{n}$. So the series converges for $\tfrac{5}{3} < x \le \tfrac{7}{3}$.

Therefore the interval of convergence is $(\tfrac{5}{3}, \tfrac{7}{3}]$.

Notes: (1) The **Taylor series** for the function f about $x = a$ is

$$\sum_{n=0}^{\infty} \frac{f^n(a)}{n!}(x-a)^n$$

$$= f(a) + f'(a)(x-a) + \frac{f''(a)}{2!}(x-a)^2 + \cdots + \frac{f^n(a)}{n!}(x-a)^n + \cdots$$

(2) A Taylor series is a special case of a power series. See problem 32 to learn how to find the radius of convergence and interval of convergence of a power series.

(3) See problem 28 for more information on the harmonic series and the alternating series test.

94. The nth-degree Taylor polynomial for a function h about $x = 0$ is given by by $P_n(x) = \sum_{n=1}^{\infty} \frac{(-1)^k x^k}{2k^2+3k+1}$ and the corresponding Taylor series for h about $x = 0$ converges for $-1 \leq x \leq 1$. Of the following, which is the smallest number M for which the alternating series error bound guarantees that we have $|h(1) - P_3(1)| \leq M$?

(A) $\frac{1}{28}$

(B) $\frac{1}{45}$

(C) $\frac{1}{56}$

(D) $\frac{1}{6} \cdot \frac{1}{45}$

Solution: $|h(1) - P_3(1)| \leq \frac{1}{2(4)^2+3\cdot4+1} = \frac{1}{45}$, choice (B).

Note: If the alternating series $\sum_{n=1}^{\infty}(-1)^n a_n$ or $\sum_{n=1}^{\infty}(-1)^{n+1} a_n$ converges by the alternating series test, then the sum of the first n terms is an approximation to the total sum of the series whose accuracy can be determined by the next term.

More precisely, $-a_1 + a_2 - a_3 + \cdots + (-1)^n a_n$ is an approximation to $\sum_{n=1}^{\infty}(-1)^n a_n$ whose error is less than or equal to a_{n+1}.

In this problem, $P_3(1) = \sum_{k=1}^{3} \frac{(-1)^k}{2k^2+3k+1}$ is an approximation of $h(1) = \sum_{n=1}^{\infty} \frac{(-1)^n}{2n^2+3n+1}$ whose error is less than $a_4 = \frac{1}{2(4)^2+3\cdot4+1} = \frac{1}{45}$.

Observe that we replaced x by 1 in the expressions for $P_3(1)$ and the Taylor series expansion for $h(1)$.

95. The function h has derivatives of all orders at $x = 0$, and the Maclaurin series for h is $\sum_{n=2}^{\infty} \frac{\ln n}{2^n n^4} x^n$. Does h have a relative minimum, a relative maximum, or neither at $x = 0$? Justify your answer.

Solution: $h'(0) = 0$ and $\frac{h''(0)}{2!} = \frac{\ln 2}{2^2 \cdot 2^4}$, so that $h''(0) = \frac{\ln 2}{2^2 \cdot 2^4} \cdot 2 = \frac{\ln 2}{2^5}$. So $h''(0) > 0$. By the second derivative test, h has a relative minimum at $x = 0$.

Notes: (1) See problem 63 for the definition of a Maclaurin series.

(2) The coefficient of x in the Maclaurin series for h is $h'(0)$. Since the series begins with the x^2 term, it follows that this coefficient is 0. So $h'(0) = 0$.

(3) The coefficient of x^2 in the Maclaurin series for h is $\frac{h''(0)}{2!}$.

Since we are given the Maclaurin series for h in this problem, we can also get the coefficient of x^2 by substituting 2 for n in the expression $\frac{\ln n}{2^n n^4}$ to get $\frac{\ln 2}{2^2 \cdot 2^4}$.

These two quantities are equal so that we have $\frac{h''(0)}{2!} = \frac{\ln 2}{2^2 \cdot 2^4}$.

(4) The **Second Derivative Test** says that if f is a differentiable function with $f'(c) = 0$, then

(i) $f''(c) > 0 \Rightarrow f$ has a relative minimum at $x = c$.

(ii) $f''(c) < 0 \Rightarrow f$ has a relative maximum at $x = c$.

Note that if $f''(c) = 0$, then the test cannot be used.

$$g(x) = \begin{cases} \dfrac{\sin x - x}{x^3} & \text{for } x \neq 0 \\ -\dfrac{1}{6} & \text{for } x = 0 \end{cases}$$

96. The function g, defined above, has derivatives of all orders. Write the first five nonzero terms and the general term for the Maclaurin series for g. Then determine whether g has a relative extremum at $x = 0$. Justify your answer.

Solution: $\sin x = x - \dfrac{x^3}{3!} + \dfrac{x^5}{5!} - \dfrac{x^7}{7!} + \dfrac{x^9}{9!} - \dfrac{x^{11}}{11!} + \cdots + \dfrac{(-1)^n x^{2n+1}}{(2n+1)!} + \cdots$

So $\sin x - x = -\dfrac{x^3}{3!} + \dfrac{x^5}{5!} - \dfrac{x^7}{7!} + \dfrac{x^9}{9!} - \dfrac{x^{11}}{11!} + \cdots + \dfrac{(-1)^n x^{2n+1}}{(2n+1)!} + \cdots$

Therefore $g(x) = -\dfrac{1}{3!} + \dfrac{x^2}{5!} - \dfrac{x^4}{4!} + \dfrac{x^6}{9!} - \dfrac{x^8}{11!} + \cdots + \dfrac{(-1)^n x^{2n-2}}{(2n+1)!} + \cdots$

From the Maclaurin series for g we see that $g'(0) = 0$ and $\frac{g''(0)}{2!} = \frac{1}{5!}$, so that $g''(0) = \frac{2!}{5!} = \frac{1}{60} > 0$. So by the Second Derivative Test, g has a **relative minimum** at $x = 0$.

Notes: (1) See problem 63 for more information about Maclaurin series.

(2) See problem 89 (note (2)) for the Maclaurin series for $\sin x$.

(3) See problem 95 for an explanation of the second derivative test.

LEVEL 4: DIFFERENTIATION

97. The function $g(x) = 10x^4 - 7e^{x-1}$, $x > \frac{1}{2}$ is invertible. The derivative of g^{-1} at $x = 3$ is

(A) $-\frac{7}{e}$

(B) $-\frac{e}{7}$

(C) 1

(D) $\frac{1}{33}$

Solution: First note that $g(1) = 10(1)^4 - 7e^{1-1} = 10 - 7 = 3$. It follows that $g^{-1}(3) = 1$.

Now, $g'(x) = 40x^3 - 7e^{x-1}$, so that

$$(g^{-1})'(x) = \frac{1}{g'(g^{-1}(x))} = \frac{1}{40y^3 - 7e^{y-1}}$$

where $y = g^{-1}(x)$.

So $(g^{-1})'(3) = \frac{1}{40(1)^3 - 7e^{1-1}} = \frac{1}{40-7} = \frac{1}{33}$, choice (D).

Notes: (1) Many students find it tricky to find the derivative of an inverse, but the procedure is fairly simple.

Suppose we want to find $(f^{-1})'(x)$. First find $f'(x)$. Then take the reciprocal to get $\frac{1}{f'(x)}$. Finally, replace x by $y = f^{-1}(x)$ to get $\frac{1}{f'(f^{-1}(x))}$.

Now the trickiest part comes when we need to plug in a value. We need to remember that to compute $(f^{-1})'(x)$ we plug in $f^{-1}(x)$, and not x. This is why we started the given problem by figuring out what $g^{-1}(3)$ was.

(2) The question "what is $g^{-1}(3)$?" is equivalent to "g of what is equal to 3?" Equivalently, we need to find x such that $g(x) = 3$.

127

Often in calculus problems on the AP exam, this value can be found fairly easily by simple observation, or guessing and checking simple numbers. In this example, it is not too hard to see that $g(1) = 3$, so that $g^{-1}(3) = 1$.

(3) If a calculator were allowed to be used for this problem, then we could solve the equation $g(x) = 3$ by graphing $y = 10x^4 - 7e^{x-1}$ and $y = 3$ in our graphing calculator, and using the intersect button to find the x-coordinate of the point of intersection.

Be careful to find the x-value that is greater than $\frac{1}{2}$, since this is the restriction placed on the given function (this was done to ensure that the function passes the horizontal line test, and therefore is invertible).

(4) Another notation that is used that some students find helpful is

$$\frac{dx}{dy} = \frac{1}{\frac{dy}{dx}} \cdot$$

In this problem, $\frac{dy}{dx} = 40x^3 - 7e^{x-1}$.

So $\frac{dx}{dy} = \frac{1}{40x^3 - 7e^{x-1}}$.

But remember that we are plugging in 1 for x (and *not* the given value of 3). So we get $\frac{dx}{dy}\Big|_{x=1} = \frac{1}{40(1)^3 - 7e^{1-1}} = \frac{1}{40-7} = \frac{1}{33}$.

98. The radius of a spherical balloon is decreasing at a constant rate of 0.5 centimeters per second. At the instant when the volume V becomes 288π cubic centimeters, what is the rate of decrease, in square centimeters per second, of the surface area of the balloon?

   (A) 24π
   (B) 48π
   (C) 64π
   (D) 72π

Solution: First recall that the volume of a sphere with radius r is $V = \frac{4}{3}\pi r^3$, and the surface area of a sphere with radius r is $S = 4\pi r^2$. We are given that $\frac{dr}{dt} = -0.5$, and we are being asked to find $\frac{dS}{dt}$ when $V = 288\pi$.

Note that when $V = 288\pi$, we have

$$288\pi = \frac{4}{3}\pi r^3$$
$$\frac{3}{4} \cdot 288\pi = \pi r^3$$
$$216 = r^3$$
$$6 = r$$

Now,

$$\frac{dS}{dt} = 8\pi r \cdot \frac{dr}{dt} = 8\pi r(-0.5) = -4\pi r.$$

$$\frac{dS}{dt}\Big|_{r=6} = -4\pi(6) = -24\pi.$$

So the surface area of the balloon is decreasing at a rate of 24π cm^2/sec. Therefore the answer is choice (A).

Notes: (1) Observe that one can get the formula for the surface area of a sphere by differentiating the formula for the volume of a sphere. This is just a little trick that can be used to reduce the number of formulas to memorize.

(2) Remember that the word *rate* generally indicates a derivative. "Increasing at a rate of" indicates a positive derivative, and "decreasing at a rate of" indicates a negative derivative.

(3) A radius is a length and is therefore measured in single units (in this case centimeters). Area (and in particular surface area) is measured in square units. Volume is measured in cubic units.

The type of units being mentioned usually gives a big hint as to what measurement is being given or asked for.

(4) This is a **related rates** problem. In a related rates problem we differentiate the independent and dependent variables with respect to a new variable, usually named t, for time.

(5) A *related rates* problem can be pictured as a *dynamic* (moving) process that gets fixed at a specific moment in time.

For this problem we can picture a sphere shaped balloon deflating. We then *freeze time* at the moment when the volume is 288π cm^3.

At this moment in time we want to know what the *rate of decrease* of the surface area is. The word "rate" indicates that we want the derivative of surface area with respect to time, $\frac{dS}{dt}$.

Don't forget to apply the chain rule when differentiating the right hand side. In this case, the derivative of r is $\frac{dr}{dt}$.

99. For small values of h, the function $\frac{1}{\sqrt[3]{27+h}}$ is best approximated by

(A) $\frac{27-h}{81}$

(B) $\frac{81-h}{81}$

(C) $\frac{27-h}{243}$

(D) $\frac{81-h}{243}$

Solution: We are being asked to find the **linear approximation** of $f(x) = \frac{1}{\sqrt[3]{x}} = x^{-\frac{1}{3}}$ when $x = 27$. Well we have $f'(x) = -\frac{1}{3}x^{-\frac{4}{3}}$. So $f'(27) = -\frac{1}{3}(27)^{-\frac{4}{3}} = -\frac{1}{3}\cdot\frac{1}{81} = -\frac{1}{243}$.

Now,

$$f(x + h) - f(x) \approx f'(x) \cdot h$$
$$f(27 + h) - f(27) \approx f'(27) \cdot h$$
$$\frac{1}{\sqrt[3]{27+h}} - \frac{1}{3} \approx -\frac{1}{243}h$$
$$\frac{1}{\sqrt[3]{27+h}} \approx \frac{1}{3} - \frac{1}{243}h = \frac{81}{243} - \frac{h}{243} = \frac{81-h}{243}.$$

This is choice (D).

Notes: (1) Recall the definition of the derivative:

$$f'(x) = \lim_{h\to 0}\frac{f(x+h)-f(x)}{h}$$

So for small values of h we have $f'(x) \approx \frac{f(x+h)-f(x)}{h}$. Equivalently,

$$hf'(x) \approx f(x + h) - f(x).$$

(2) Geometrically $f'(x)$ is the slope of the tangent line to the graph of f at the point $(x, f(x))$, whereas $\frac{f(x+h)-f(x)}{h}$ is the slope of the secant line passing through the points $(x, f(x))$ and $(x + h, f(x + h))$. For very small values of h these two slopes are *almost* the same. For a picture of this, see the figures in the notes following problem 100.

x	2.5	2.6	2.7	2.8
$f(x)$	7	7.4	7.7	7.9

100. Let f be a function that is concave down for all x in the closed interval [2,3], with selected values shown in the above table. Which of the following inequalities must be true?

(A) $f'(2.7) > 3$
(B) $2 < f'(2.7) < 3$
(C) $1 < f'(2.7) < 2$
(D) $0 < f'(2.7) < 1$

Solution: Since f is concave down in the interval [2,3], the tangent line to f when $x = 2.7$ lies above the graph of f in this interval.

So $f'(2.7) > \frac{f(2.8)-f(2.7)}{2.8-2.7} = \frac{7.9-7.7}{.1} = \frac{.2}{.1} = 2$.

Also $f'(2.7) < \frac{f(2.7)-f(2.6)}{2.7-2.6} = \frac{7.7-7.4}{.1} = \frac{.3}{.1} = 3$.

So $2 < f'(2.7) < 3$, choice (B).

Notes: (1) Here is a sketch of the graph of the function together with the tangent line to the graph at $x = 2.7$.

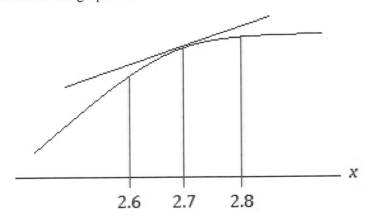

Observe that the graph is below the tangent line in the interval [2,3].

(2) Now let's also look at the secant line through the points (2.7, 7.7) and (2.8, 7.9).

131

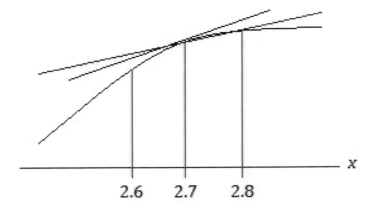

2.6   2.7   2.8

Notice that the tangent line has a greater slope than the secant line.

The slope of the tangent line is $f'(2.7)$, and the slope of the secant line is $\frac{f(2.8)-f(2.7)}{2.8-2.7}$. So we have $f'(2.7) > \frac{f(2.8)-f(2.7)}{2.8-2.7}$.

(3) Now let's also look at the secant line through the points $(2.6, 7.4)$ and $(2.7, 7.7)$.

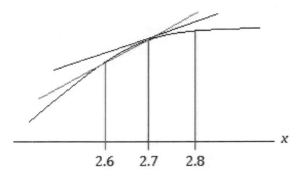

2.6   2.7   2.8

Notice that the tangent line has a smaller slope than the secant line.

The slope of the tangent line is $f'(2.7)$, and the slope of the secant line is $\frac{f(2.7)-f(2.6)}{2.7-2.6}$. So we have $f'(2.7) < \frac{f(2.7)-f(2.6)}{2.7-2.6}$.

101. Consider the differential equation $\frac{dy}{dx} = e^{y-1}(2x^3 - 5)$. Let $y = f(x)$ be the particular solution to the differential equation that passes through $(1,1)$. Write an equation for the line tangent to the graph of f at the point $(1,1)$, and use the tangent line to approximate $f(1.1)$.

Solution: The slope of the tangent line at $(1,1)$ is

$$m = \frac{dy}{dx}\big|_{(1,1)} = e^{1-1}(2(1)^3 - 5) = e^0(2 - 5) = (1)(-3) = -3.$$

So an equation of the tangent line in point–slope form is

$$y - 1 = -3(x - 1).$$

When $x = 1.1$, we have $y - 1 = -3(1.1 - 1) = -3(.1) = -.3$.

So $y = -.3 + 1 = .7$.

It follows that $f(1.1) \approx .7$.

Notes: (1) To find the slope of the tangent line to a function $y = f(x)$ at a point (x_0, y_0), we take the derivative $\frac{dy}{dx} = f'(x)$, and substitute in x_0 for x and y_0 for y.

In this problem, we were already given $\frac{dy}{dx}$, and so we simply needed to substitute in the x-coordinate of the point for x and the y-coordinate of the point for y.

(2) The **point-slope form of an equation of a line** is

$$y - y_0 = m(x - x_0)$$

where m is the slope of the line and (x_0, y_0) is any point on the line.

It is generally easiest to write an equation of a line in point-slope form once the slope of the line and a point on the line are known.

In this problem, the slope is -3 and the point is $(1,1)$.

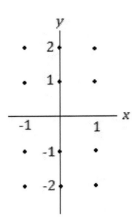

102. Consider the differential equation $\frac{dy}{dx} = -\frac{x^2}{y}$. On the axes provided above, sketch a slope field for the differential equation at the twelve points indicated.

Solution:

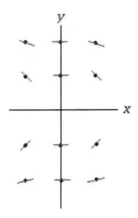

Notes: (1) When $x = 0$, we have $\frac{dy}{dx} = -\frac{0^2}{y} = 0$ (as long as $y \neq 0$). So at each of the four points on the y-axis, the slope is 0. That is, the the tangent line is horizontal. So we draw a horizontal line segment at the points $(0,1)$, $(0,2)$, $(0,-1)$, and $(0,-2)$.

(2) At the points $(1,1)$ and $(-1,1)$, we have $\frac{dy}{dx} = -\frac{1}{1} = -1$.

(3) At the points $(1,-1)$ and $(-1,-1)$, we have $\frac{dy}{dx} = -\frac{1}{-1} = 1$.

(4) At the points $(1,2)$ and $(-1,2)$, we have $\frac{dy}{dx} = -\frac{1}{2}$.

(5) At the points $(1, -2)$ and $(-1, -2)$, we have $\frac{dy}{dx} = -\frac{1}{-2} = \frac{1}{2}$.

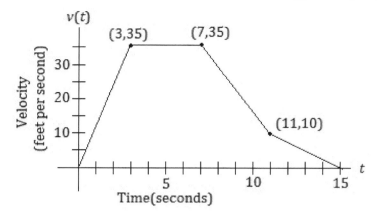

103. A bus is traveling on a straight road. For $0 \le t \le 15$ seconds, the bus's velocity $v(t)$, in feet per second, is modeled by the function shown in the graph above. For each of $v'(3)$, $v'(8)$, and $v'(11)$, find the value or explain why it does not exist. Indicate units of measure.

Solution: $\lim_{x \to 3^-} \left(\frac{v(t) - v(3)}{t - 3} \right) = \frac{35}{3}$ and $\lim_{x \to 3^+} \left(\frac{v(t) - v(3)}{t - 3} \right) = 0$.

Since $\lim_{x \to 3^-} \left(\frac{v(t) - v(3)}{t - 3} \right) \ne \lim_{x \to 3^+} \left(\frac{v(t) - v(3)}{t - 3} \right)$, $v'(3)$ **does not exist**.

$v'(8) = \frac{10 - 35}{11 - 7} = -\frac{25}{4}$ **ft/sec^2**.

$\lim_{x \to 11^-} \left(\frac{v(t) - v(11)}{t - 11} \right) = -\frac{25}{4}$ and $\lim_{x \to 11^+} \left(\frac{v(t) - v(11)}{t - 11} \right) = \frac{-10}{4} = -\frac{5}{2}$.

Since $\lim_{x \to 11^-} \left(\frac{v(t) - v(3)}{t - 3} \right) \ne \lim_{x \to 11^+} \left(\frac{v(t) - v(3)}{t - 3} \right)$, $v'(11)$ **does not exist**.

Notes: (1) At $t = 3$ and $t = 11$ (as well as $t = 7$) there are "sharp edges." A function of t is *not* differentiable at any such t-value. The reason is that these "sharp edges" indicate a disagreement in the slope of the graph from the left and from the right.

For example, to the left of 3, the slope of the line is positive (in fact it is $\frac{35 - 0}{3 - 0} = \frac{35}{3}$), whereas, to the right of 3, the slope of the line is 0.

135

Symbolically, we can write $v'(3)^- = \frac{35}{3}$ and $v'(3)^+ = 0$. Since the slopes from the left and the right disagree, there is no well-defined slope at $t = 3$.

Note that $v'(3)^-$ is just a shorthand notation for $\lim_{x\to 3^-} \left(\frac{v(t)-v(3)}{t-3}\right)$, and similarly $v'(3)^+$ is shorthand for $\lim_{x\to 3^+} \left(\frac{v(t)-v(3)}{t-3}\right)$.

(2) To compute $v'(3)^-$, we simply compute the slope of the leftmost line segment. This line segment passes through the points $(0,0)$ and $(3,35)$. So the slope is $v'(3)^- = \frac{35-0}{3-0} = \frac{35}{3}$.

Similarly, to compute $v'(8)$, we simply compute the slope of the third line segment from the left. This line segment passes through the points $(7,35)$ and $(11,10)$. So the slope is $v'(8) = \frac{10-35}{11-7} = -\frac{25}{4}$.

We can compute all the other slopes in a similar fashion.

104. Two particles are moving along the x-axis. For $0 \le t \le 10$, the position of particle A at time t is given by $a(t) = 3\sin t$, and the position of particle B at time t is given by $b(t) = t^3 - 12t^2 + 21t - 1$. For $0 \le t \le 10$, find all times t during which the two particles travel in opposite directions.

Solution: $a'(t) = 3\cos t$ and

$$b'(t) = 3t^2 - 24t + 21 = 3(t^2 - 8t + 7) = 3(t - 1)(t - 7).$$

Now, $a'(t) = 0$ when $t = \frac{\pi}{2}, \frac{3\pi}{2}$, and $\frac{5\pi}{2}$ on the interval $[0,10]$, and $b'(t) = 0$ when $t = 1$, and 7.

$a'(t) > 0$ for $0 \le t < \frac{\pi}{2}$, and $\frac{3\pi}{2} < t < \frac{5\pi}{2}$

$a'(t) < 0$ for $\frac{\pi}{2} < t < \frac{3\pi}{2}$, and $\frac{5\pi}{2} < t \le 10$

$b'(t) > 0$ for $0 \le t < 1$, and $7 < t \le 10$

$b'(t) < 0$ for $1 < t < 7$

So the particles are travelling in opposite directions for $1 < t < \frac{\pi}{2}$, $\frac{3\pi}{2} < t < 7$, and $\frac{5\pi}{2} < t \le 10$.

136

In interval notation, the two particles are travelling in opposite directions for t in $\left(1, \frac{\pi}{2}\right) \cup \left(\frac{3\pi}{2}, 7\right) \cup \left(\frac{5\pi}{2}, 10\right]$.

Notes: (1) We can determine which direction a particle is moving by looking at its velocity function. If the velocity is positive, the particle is moving to the right. If the velocity is negative, the particle is moving to the left.

(2) The velocity function of a particle is the derivative of its position function. So in this problem we want to determine when a' and b' have opposite signs.

(3) Here is a sketch of the graph of $y = \cos x$:

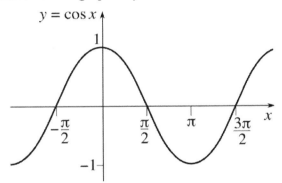

Note that the domain of $y = \cos x$ is $-\infty < x < \infty$. So the graph continues to oscillate between -1 and 1 as x goes to $-\infty$ and ∞.

(4) We start by finding the **critical numbers** of a and b. In other words we want to find all real numbers t such that $a'(t) = 0$ and $b'(t) = 0$.

Finding the critical numbers of b is straightforward.

To find the critical numbers of a, recall that $\cos t = 0$ whenever t is an odd multiple of $\frac{\pi}{2}$. In other words, $t = \pm\frac{\pi}{2}, \pm\frac{3\pi}{2}, \pm\frac{5\pi}{2}, \dots$

It follows that the critical numbers of a on $[0,10]$ are $t = \frac{\pi}{2}, \frac{3\pi}{2}$, and $\frac{5\pi}{2}$ (use your calculator if allowed, or estimate π as a little more than 3 to see this).

(5) Here is a sign chart for a':

	0	π/2		3π/2		5π/2		10
	test π/4		test π	test 2π		test 3π		
	+		−	+		−		

And here is a sign chart for b':

	0	1		7		10
	test .5		test 2		test 9	
	+		−		+	

Let's combine these two sign charts into a single chart:

	0	1	π/2		3π/2	7	5π/2		10
a'	+	+	−		+	+	−		
b'	+	−	−		−	+	+		

From this last chart it is easy to see where a' and b' have opposite signs.

105. * Let r be the polar curve defined by $r(\theta) = 5\theta + \cos\theta$, where $0 \le \theta \le \pi$. A particle is travelling along r so that its position at time t is $\langle x(t), y(t) \rangle$ and such that $\frac{d\theta}{dt} = 3$. Find $\frac{dx}{dt}$ at the instant that $\theta = \frac{3\pi}{4}$, and interpret the meaning of your answer in the context of the problem.

Solution: $x = r(\theta)\cos\theta = (5\theta + \cos\theta)\cos\theta$.

$$\frac{dx}{dt} = \frac{dx}{d\theta} \cdot \frac{d\theta}{dt} = [-(5\theta + \cos\theta)\sin\theta + (5 - \sin\theta)\cos\theta] \cdot \frac{d\theta}{dt}.$$

So $\frac{dx}{dt} \big|_{\theta=\frac{3\pi}{4}} = \left[-\left(\frac{15\pi}{4} - \frac{1}{\sqrt{2}}\right)\left(\frac{1}{\sqrt{2}}\right) + \left(5 - \frac{1}{\sqrt{2}}\right)\left(-\frac{1}{\sqrt{2}}\right)\right] \cdot 3$

$= 3\left(-\frac{15\pi}{4\sqrt{2}} + \frac{1}{2} - \frac{5}{\sqrt{2}} + \frac{1}{2}\right) = 3\left(-\frac{15\pi}{4\sqrt{2}} + \frac{4\sqrt{2}}{4\sqrt{2}} - \frac{20}{4\sqrt{2}}\right) = 3\left(\frac{4\sqrt{2} - 20 - 15\pi}{4\sqrt{2}}\right)$

$$\approx -32.598.$$

138

The x-coordinate of the particle is decreasing at a rate of 32.598.

Note: You should know the formulas for changing from polar to rectangular coordinates:

$$x = r\cos\theta \quad \text{and} \quad y = r\sin\theta.$$

106. * A particle moves along the curve defined by the equation $y = x^2 - x$. The x-coordinate of the particle satisfies $x(t) = \sqrt{7t + 2}$, for $t \geq 0$. Find the speed of the particle at time $t = 2$.

Solution: $\frac{dx}{dt} = \frac{7}{2\sqrt{7t+2}}$ and $\frac{dy}{dt} = \frac{dy}{dx} \cdot \frac{dx}{dt} = \frac{7(2x-1)}{2\sqrt{7t+2}}$.

When $t = 2$, $x(t) = 4$, $\frac{dx}{dt} = \frac{7}{8}$, and $\frac{dy}{dt} = \frac{49}{8}$.

$$\text{Speed} = \sqrt{\left(\frac{dx}{dt}\right)^2 + \left(\frac{dy}{dt}\right)^2} = \sqrt{\left(\frac{7}{8}\right)^2 + \left(\frac{49}{8}\right)^2} \approx \mathbf{6.187}.$$

Notes: (1) Here is an alternative method for finding $\frac{dy}{dt}$ at $t = 2$:

$$y(t) = (x(t))^2 - x(t) = (7t + 2) - \sqrt{7t + 2}$$

So $\frac{dy}{dt} = 7 - \frac{7}{2\sqrt{7t+2}}$, and $\frac{dy}{dt}\big|_{t=2} = 7 - \frac{7}{8} = \frac{49}{8}$.

(2) The speed of a particle with parametric equations $x = x(t)$, $y = y(t)$

is $\sqrt{\left(\frac{dx}{dt}\right)^2 + \left(\frac{dy}{dt}\right)^2}$

107. * A particle moves in the xy-plane so that its position at any time t, $0 \leq t \leq 2\pi$, is given by $x(t) = 2\cos t$, $y(t) = e^{t^2} - t$. Find the acceleration vector at the time t when $x(t)$ attains its minimum value.

Solution: $x'(t) = -2\sin t$ changes sign from negative to positive at $x = \pi$. Since $x = \pi$ is the only critical number of $x(t)$ in the interval $0 \leq t \leq 2\pi$, it follows that $x(t)$ attains its minimum value at $t = \pi$.

The position vector of the particle is $\langle 2\cos t, e^{t^2} - t \rangle$. It follows that the velocity vector of the particle is $\langle -2\sin t, 2te^{t^2} - 1 \rangle$, and so the acceleration vector of the particle is $\langle -2\cos t, 4t^2 e^{t^2} + 2e^{t^2} \rangle$.

When $t = \pi$, the acceleration vector is $\langle \mathbf{2}, (\mathbf{4\pi^2 + 2})e^{\pi^2} \rangle$.

Notes: (1) See problem 68 for more information on the method used here to minimize $x(t)$.

(2) To differentiate a vector we simply differentiate each component separately. So the derivative of the vector $\langle x(t), y(t) \rangle$ is the vector $\langle x'(t), y'(t) \rangle$.

(3) Given a position vector $\langle x(t), y(t) \rangle$, the velocity vector is the derivative $\langle x'(t), y'(t) \rangle$, and the acceleration vector is the derivative of the velocity vector $\langle x''(t), y''(t) \rangle$.

108. The polar curve $r = f(\theta)$ satisfies $r > 0$ and $\frac{dr}{d\theta} < 0$ for $a < \theta < b$. What do these facts tell us about r? What do these facts tell us about the curve?

Solution: For $a < \theta < b$, the length of the radius r is decreasing. Therefore the curve gets closer to the origin as the angle θ increases from a to b.

LEVEL 4: INTEGRATION

109. The region in the xy-plane bounded by the graph of $y = \frac{\ln(x)}{\sqrt{x}}$, $x = 1$, $x = 4$, and the x-axis is rotated about the x-axis. What is the volume of the solid generated?

(A) $\frac{(\ln 4)^3}{3} - 1$

(B) $\frac{\pi (\ln 4)^3}{3} - 1$

(C) $\frac{\pi (\ln 4)^3 - 1}{3}$

(D) $\frac{\pi (\ln 4)^3}{3}$

Solution:

$\pi \int_1^4 \left(\frac{\ln(x)}{\sqrt{x}} \right)^2 dx = \pi \int_1^4 \frac{(\ln x)^2}{x} dx = \pi \frac{(\ln x)^3}{3} \Big|_1^4 = \frac{\pi}{3} ((\ln 4)^3 - (\ln 1)^3)$

$= \frac{\pi}{3} ((\ln 4)^3 - (0)^3) = \frac{\pi}{3} (\ln 4)^3 = \frac{\pi (\ln 4)^3}{3}$, choice (D).

140

Notes: (1) It is helpful to begin by drawing a picture of the region. We do not need an accurate sketch of the function. We need only show where it lies above and below the x-axis. In this case, we have $\frac{\ln(1)}{\sqrt{1}} = 0$, and for all $x > 1$, we have $\frac{\ln(x)}{\sqrt{x}} > 0$.

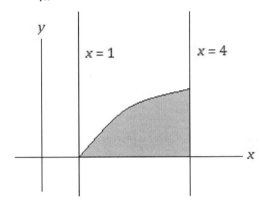

(2) We will use the **disk method** to find the requested volume. A *disk* is a circle together with its interior. A typical disk can be described as follows:

First we take a value x between 1 and 4. Find this number on the x-axis.

We then draw the radius of the disk by drawing a vertical segment from the x-axis straight up until we hit the curve.

Next we draw a circle from the top of this line segment that sweeps below the x-axis, and who's radius is as specified in the last step.

Here is a picture:

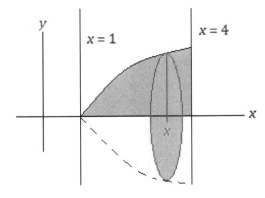

The radius of this disk is $\frac{\ln(x)}{\sqrt{x}}$. It follows that the area of this disk is $\pi r^2 = \pi(\frac{\ln(x)}{\sqrt{x}})^2$.

The disk method requires us to integrate this area over the given interval, in this case from 1 to 4.

$$V = \pi \int_1^4 r^2\, dx = \pi \int_1^4 (\frac{\ln(x)}{\sqrt{x}})^2\, dx = \pi \int_1^4 \frac{(\ln x)^2}{x}\, dx$$

(3) To evaluate $\int \frac{(\ln x)^2}{x}\, dx$, we can formally make the substitution $u = \ln x$. It then follows that

$$du = \frac{1}{x}\, dx$$

We now have

$$\int \frac{(\ln x)^2}{x}\, dx = \int (\ln x)^2 \cdot \frac{1}{x}\, dx = \int u^2\, du = \frac{u^3}{3} + C = \frac{(\ln x)^3}{3} + C$$

It follows that $\pi \int \frac{(\ln x)^2}{x}\, dx = \pi \frac{(\ln x)^3}{3} + C$.

(4) If we are doing the substitution formally, we can save some time by changing the limits of integration. We do this as follows:

$$\pi \int_1^4 \frac{(\ln x)^2}{x}\, dx = \pi \int_0^{\ln 4} u^2\, du = \pi \frac{u^3}{3} \Big|_0^{\ln 4} = \frac{\pi}{3}((\ln 4)^3 - 0^3) = \frac{\pi(\ln 4)^3}{3}.$$

Notice that the limits 1 and 4 were changed to the limits 0 and $\ln 4$, respectively. We made this change using the formula that we chose for the substitution: $u = \ln x$. When $x = 1$, we have $u = 0$ and when $x = 4$, we have $u = \ln 4$.

110. * If $f'(x) = \cos(\frac{\ln(x+1)}{4})$ and $f(0) = 2$, then $f(3) =$

    (A) 4.919
    (B) 2.919
    (C) -0.75
    (D) -1.5

Solution: $f(3) = 2 + \int_0^3 f'(x)\, dx = 2 + \int_0^3 \cos(\frac{\ln(x+1)}{4})\, dx \approx 4.919$.

This is choice (A).

Notes: (1) Given a continuous function g with G an antiderivative of g, and initial condition $G(a) = k$, it follows that

$$G(b) = k + \int_a^b g(x)\,dx.$$

To see why this is true, simply observe that $\int_a^b g(x)\,dx = G(b) - G(a)$, so that $k + \int_a^b g(x)\,dx = G(a) + \big(G(b) - G(a)\big) = G(b)$.

The formula given above is especially useful when you cannot easily find a closed form for G. In other words, this form is very useful when solving this type of problem with a calculator.

(2) In this problem, we have $g = f'$, $G = f$, $a = 0$, $b = 3$, and $k = 2$, so that

$$f(3) = 2 + \int_0^3 f'(x)\,dx.$$

111. * Let D be the region enclosed by $y = \sin x$ and $y = \cos x$ for $0 \le x \le \frac{\pi}{4}$. The volume of the solid generated when D is revolved around the line $x = 4$ is

    (A) 9.715
    (B) 4.857
    (C) 1.793
    (D) 0.897

Solution: $2\pi \int_0^{\frac{\pi}{4}} (4 - x)(\cos x - \sin x)\,dx \approx 9.715$, choice (A).

Notes: (1) It is helpful to begin by drawing a picture of the region D and the line $x = 4$.

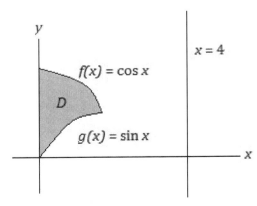

(2) We will use the **shell method** to find this volume. A *shell* is cylinder. A typical shell can be described as follows:

First we take a value x between 0 and $\frac{\pi}{4}$. Find this number on the x-axis.

We then draw the height of the shell directly above this number between the two graphs.

Next we draw circles from the top and bottom of this line segment (the height) that sweep across the line $x = 4$, and who's radius is the distance from the height to the line $x = 4$.

Here is a picture:

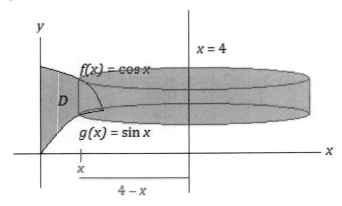

The height of this cylinder is $f(x) - g(x) = \cos x - \sin x$, and the radius of this cylinder is $4 - x$. It follows that the volume of this cylinder is $2\pi rh = 2\pi(4 - x)(\cos x - \sin x)$.

The shell method requires us to integrate this volume over the given interval, in this case from 0 to $\frac{\pi}{4}$.

$$V = 2\pi \int_0^{\frac{\pi}{4}} rh\, dx = 2\pi \int_0^{\frac{\pi}{4}} (4 - x)(\cos x - \sin x)\, dx.$$

112. A solid has a rectangular base that lies in the first quadrant and is bounded by the x- and y-axes and the lines $x = 3$ and $y = 1$. The height of the solid above the point (x, y) is $(2 + 5x)^2$. Which of the following is a Riemann sum approximation for the volume of the solid?

(A) $\sum_{i=1}^{n} \frac{3i}{n}\left(2 + \frac{15i}{n}\right)^2$

(B) $\sum_{i=1}^{n} \frac{3}{n}\left(2 + \frac{15i}{n}\right)^2$

(C) $\sum_{i=1}^{n} \frac{3i}{n}\left(2 + \frac{3i}{n}\right)^2$

(D) $\sum_{i=1}^{n} \frac{3}{n}\left(2 + \frac{3i}{n}\right)^2$

Solution: Let $f(x) = (2 + 5x)^2$ and partition the interval $[0,3]$ into n equal subintervals as follows:

Let $x_0 = \frac{3 \cdot 0}{n} = 0$, $x_1 = \frac{3 \cdot 1}{n}$, $x_2 = \frac{3 \cdot 2}{n}$, ..., $x_{n-1} = \frac{3(n-1)}{n}$, $x_{100} = \frac{3n}{n} = 3$.

We get the corresponding subintervals $[0, \frac{3}{n}]$, $[\frac{3}{n}, \frac{3 \cdot 2}{n}]$, ..., $[\frac{3(n-1)}{n}, 3]$.

The length of each subinterval (and therefore the base of each rectangle) is $\frac{3-0}{n} = \frac{3}{n}$.

For the height of each rectangle we choose the right endpoint of each subinterval x^*, and compute $f(x^*)$.

So the height of the leftmost rectangle will be $f\left(\frac{3}{n}\right) = \left(2 + \frac{15}{n}\right)^2$. It follows that the area of the leftmost rectangle is $\frac{3}{n}\left(2 + \frac{15}{n}\right)^2$.

Similarly, the area of the next rectangle will be $\frac{3}{n}\left(2 + \frac{15 \cdot 2}{n}\right)^2$.

Continuing in this fashion, we get that the area of the rightmost rectangle is $\frac{3}{n}\left(2 + \frac{15 \cdot n}{n}\right)^2$

So we are approximating the volume under the graph of $f(x) = (2 + 5x)^2$ from $x = 0$ to $x = 3$ by

$$\frac{3}{n}\left(2 + \frac{15}{n}\right)^2 + \frac{3}{n}\left(2 + \frac{15 \cdot 2}{n}\right)^2 + \cdots + \frac{3}{n}\left(2 + \frac{15 \cdot n}{n}\right)^2$$

$$= \sum_{i=1}^{n} \frac{3}{n}\left(2 + \frac{15i}{n}\right)^2.$$

145

This is choice (B).

Notes: (1) For more information on Riemann sums, see problem 85.

(2) The standard geometrical application of Riemann sums is to approximate the area under a curve. This problem is a bit trickier because we are approximating a volume of a solid instead. But in this case, because the height of the rectangle is 1, approximating this volume is exactly the same as approximating the area under the curve $f(x) = (2 + 5x)^2$ from $x = 0$ to $x = 3$.

113. * Let R be the region in the first and second quadrants bounded above by the graph of $y = \dfrac{48}{2+x^4}$ and below by the horizontal line $y = 4$. The region R is the base of a solid whose cross sections perpendicular to the x-axis are semicircles. Find the volume of this solid.

Solution: We first find the x-values where the graph of $y = \dfrac{48}{2+x^4}$ intersects the line $y = 4$. To do this we solve the equation $\dfrac{48}{2+x^4} = 4$. Multiplying by the denominator on the left hand side gives the equation $48 = 8 + 4x^4$. We subtract 8 to get $40 = 4x^4$, divide by 4 to get $10 = x^4$, and finally take the fourth root of each side to get $x = \pm\sqrt[4]{10}$.

So the volume we are looking for is

$$\frac{\pi}{2} \int_{-\sqrt[4]{10}}^{\sqrt[4]{10}} \left[\frac{1}{2}\left(\frac{48}{2+x^4} - 4\right)\right]^2 dx \approx 284.202.$$

Notes: (1) It is helpful to begin by drawing a picture of the region R

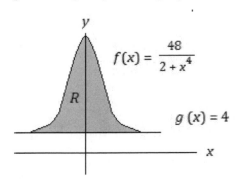

(2) Let's draw a cross section that is perpendicular to the x-axis.

146

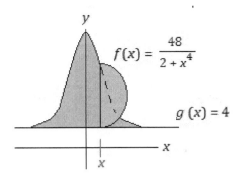

$$f(x) = \frac{48}{2 + x^4}$$

$$g(x) = 4$$

First we take a value x between $-\sqrt[4]{10}$ and $\sqrt[4]{10}$ and find this number on the x-axis.

We then draw the diameter of the semicircle. This diameter has a length of $f(x) - g(x) = \frac{48}{2+x^4} - 4$. It follows that the length of a radius of this semicircle is $r = \frac{1}{2}(\frac{48}{2+x^4} - 4)$. So the area of the semicircle is

$$A = \frac{\pi}{2}r^2 = \frac{\pi}{2}\left[\frac{1}{2}\left(\frac{48}{2+x^4} - 4\right)\right]^2.$$

To get the desired volume, we now simply integrate this expression over the interval $[-\sqrt[4]{10}, \sqrt[4]{10}]$:

$$V = \frac{\pi}{2}\int_{-\sqrt[4]{10}}^{\sqrt[4]{10}} \left[\frac{1}{2}\left(\frac{48}{2+x^4} - 4\right)\right]^2 dx.$$

(3) We can compute $\int_{-\sqrt[4]{10}}^{\sqrt[4]{10}} \left[\frac{1}{2}\left(\frac{48}{2+x^4} - 4\right)\right]^2 dx$ directly in our TI-84 calculator as follows:

Press MATH, followed by 9 (or scroll up 2 times and select 9:fnInt( ). Type ((1 / 2(48 / (2 + X^4) − 4))^2, X, −4$\sqrt[x]{}$10, 4$\sqrt[x]{}$10) followed by ENTER. The display will show 180.9284648. Multiply this result by $\pi / 2$, and the display will show 284.201768.

(4) We can compute $\sqrt[4]{10}$ in our TI-84 calculator by typing 4, then selecting $\sqrt[x]{}$ from the MATH menu, then typing 10 followed by ENTER. We needed to do this for the calculator computation in note (3).

114. For what value of a is $\int_0^\infty axe^{-5x} dx = 2$?

Solution: We begin with integration by parts.

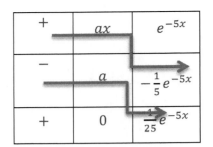

$+$	ax	e^{-5x}
$-$	a	$-\dfrac{1}{5}e^{-5x}$
$+$	0	$\dfrac{1}{25}e^{-5x}$

So we have $\left[-\dfrac{ax}{5}e^{-5x} - \dfrac{1}{25}ae^{-5x}\right]\Big|_0^\infty = 2$. So we have $\dfrac{1}{25}a = 2$, and so $a = 2 \cdot 25 = 50$.

(1) See problem 47 for more information on integration by parts and problem 15 for more information on this type of improper integral.

(2) $\left[-\dfrac{ax}{5}e^{-5x} - \dfrac{1}{25}ae^{-5x}\right]\Big|_0^\infty = -\dfrac{ax}{5}e^{-5x}\Big|_0^\infty - \dfrac{1}{25}ae^{-5x}\Big|_0^\infty$

(3) $\lim_{b\to\infty}(\dfrac{1}{25}ae^{-5b}) = \dfrac{1}{25}a\lim_{b\to\infty}(e^{-5b}) = \dfrac{1}{25}a\cdot 0 = 0$.

Here we have used the fact that as $b \to \infty$, $e^{-b} \to 0$. This can be verified easily by looking at the graph of $y = e^x$ (see problem 3).

(4) $-\dfrac{1}{25}ae^{-5x}\Big|_0^\infty = \lim_{b\to\infty}\left(-\dfrac{1}{25}ae^{-5b}\right) + \dfrac{1}{25}ae^0 = 0 + \dfrac{1}{25}a = \dfrac{1}{25}a$.

Recall that $\lim_{b\to\infty}(\dfrac{1}{25}ae^{-5b}) = 0$ by note (3).

(5) $\lim_{b\to\infty}(-\dfrac{ax}{5}e^{-5x}) = -\dfrac{a}{5}\lim_{b\to\infty}\dfrac{x}{e^{5x}} = -\dfrac{a}{5}\lim_{b\to\infty}\dfrac{1}{5e^{5x}} = 0$.

For the first equality we moved e^{-5x} to the denominator of the expression by negating the exponent.

For the second equality we used L'Hôpital's rule.

For the third equality we used the fact that as x gets large, so does e^{5x}. Therefore as x gets large, $\dfrac{1}{e^{5x}} \to 0$.

(6) $-\dfrac{ax}{5}e^{-5x}\Big|_0^\infty = \lim_{b\to\infty}\left(-\dfrac{ax}{5}e^{-5x}\right) + a\cdot\dfrac{0}{5}e^{-5\cdot 0} = 0 + 0 = 0$.

115. * A particle moves in the xy-plane so that its velocity at any time t, $0 \le t \le 2\pi$, is given by $\dfrac{dx}{dt} = 2\cos t$, $\dfrac{dy}{dt} = e^{t^2} - t$. At time $t = 0$, the particle is at the point $(3,5)$. Find the y-coordinate of the position of the particle at time $t = 2$.

148

Solution: $y(2) = 5 + \int_0^2 (e^{t^2} - t)\, dt \approx \mathbf{19.453}$

Notes: (1) We do not need to worry about the particle changing direction in this problem since we only want the y-coordinate of the particle's position relative to its starting point.

(2) If we know the velocity vector $\langle \frac{dx}{dt}, \frac{dy}{dt} \rangle$ of a particle, then we can find its position vector $\langle x(t), y(t) \rangle$ by integrating each component of the velocity vector.

(3) $\int_a^b \frac{dy}{dt}\, dt = y(b) - y(a)$ gives the vertical distance between the position of the particle at time a and the position of the particle at time b.

So $\int_0^2 \frac{dy}{dt}\, dt$ is the vertical distance between the position of the particle at time 0 and the position of the particle at time 2.

Since the y-coordinate of the particle started at position $y(0) = 5$, we must add 5 to $\int_0^2 \frac{dy}{dt}\, dt$ to get the y-coordinate of the final position.

(4) We can compute $\int_0^2 (e^{t^2} - t)\, dt$ directly in our TI-84 calculator as follows:

Press MATH, followed by 9 (or scroll up 2 times and select 9:fnInt( ). Type e^(X^2 − X), X, 0, 2) followed by ENTER. The display will show 14.45262777.

(5) Remember to add 5 to get

$$5 + \int_0^2 (e^{t^2} - t)\, dt = 19.45262777.$$

We can then truncate this to **19.452** or round to **19.453** if we wish.

116. Let R be the region in the first and fourth quadrants bounded by the graph of $y = x^2 e^{x^3}$, the line $y = -3x$, and the vertical line $x = 2$. Write, but do not evaluate, an expression involving one or more integrals that gives the perimeter of R.

Solution: $\frac{d}{dx}\left[x^2 e^{x^3}\right] = 2xe^{x^3} + 3x^4 e^{x^3} = xe^{x^3}(2 + 3x^3)$. It follows that the perimeter of R is

$$\sqrt{2^2 + 6^2} + 6 + 4e^8 + \int_0^2 \sqrt{1 + \left[xe^{x^3}(2 + 3x^3)\right]^2}\, dx$$

$$= 2\sqrt{10} + 6 + 4e^8 + \int_0^2 \sqrt{1 + x^2 e^{2x^3}(2 + 3x^3)^2}\, dx$$

Notes: (1) Let's sketch the region

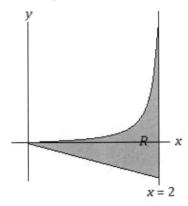

(2) The perimeter of the region R given in the sketch is the sum of the lengths of the two line segments and the curve shown.

(3) The length of the vertical line segment is $2^2 e^{2^3} - (-3 \cdot 2) = 4e^8 + 6$

(4) The diagonal line segment passes through the points $(0,0)$ and $(2, -6)$. So we can use the distance formula to find its length:

$$\sqrt{2^2 + (-6)^2} = \sqrt{4 + 36} = \sqrt{40} = \sqrt{4 \cdot 10} = \sqrt{4}\sqrt{10} = 2\sqrt{10}.$$

(5) The length of the curve is given by the arc length formula:

$$\text{Arc length} = \int_a^b \sqrt{1 + \left(\frac{dy}{dx}\right)^2}\, dx = \int_0^2 \sqrt{1 + \left(\frac{dy}{dx}\right)^2}\, dx.$$

See problem 18 for more information on arc length.

117. The arc length for the graph of the differentiable function f between $x = 0$ and $x = 10$ is 4. Define the function h by $h(x) = \frac{f(2x)}{2}$. Find the arc length of the graph of $y = h(x)$ from $x = 0$ to $x = 5$.

150

Solution:

Arc length of $h = \int_0^5 \sqrt{1 + (h'(x))^2}\, dx = \int_0^5 \sqrt{1 + (f'(2x))^2}\, dx$

If we let $u = 2x$, then $du = 2dx$, and we have

$$\int_0^5 \sqrt{1 + (f'(2x))^2}\, dx = \frac{1}{2}\int_0^{10} \sqrt{1 + (f'(u))^2}\, du = \frac{1}{2}(4) = 2.$$

Note: See problem 18 for more information on computing arc length.

118. The average value of a function f on the unbounded interval $a \leq x \leq \infty$ is defined to be $\lim_{b \to \infty}\left[\frac{\int_a^b f(x)dx}{b-a}\right]$. Let h be the function given by $h(x) = \frac{2}{3\sqrt{x}}$. Show that the improper integral $\int_1^\infty h(x)\, dx$ diverges, but the average value of h on the interval $1 \leq x \leq \infty$ converges.

Solution: $\int_1^\infty h(x)\, dx = \int_1^\infty \frac{2}{3\sqrt{x}}\, dx = \frac{2}{3}\int_1^\infty x^{-\frac{1}{2}}\, dx = \frac{2}{3} \cdot 2x^{\frac{1}{2}}\, \Big|_1^\infty = \infty.$

$$\lim_{b \to \infty}\left[\frac{\int_1^b h(x)dx}{b-1}\right] = \lim_{b \to \infty}\left[\frac{\int_1^b \frac{2}{3\sqrt{x}}dx}{b-1}\right] = \lim_{b \to \infty}\left[\frac{\frac{4}{3}x^{\frac{1}{2}}\big|_1^b}{b-1}\right]$$

$$= \frac{4}{3}\lim_{b \to \infty}\left(\frac{b^{\frac{1}{2}}-1}{b-1}\right) = \frac{4}{3} \cdot 0 = 0.$$

Notes: (1) See problem 15 for more information on this type of improper integral.

(2) To compute $\lim_{b \to \infty}\left(\frac{b^{\frac{1}{2}}-1}{b-1}\right)$, we can multiply both the numerator and denominator of the fraction under the limit by $\frac{1}{b}$ to get

$$\frac{b^{\frac{1}{2}}-1}{b-1} = \frac{\left(\frac{1}{b}\right)}{\left(\frac{1}{b}\right)} \cdot \frac{(b^{\frac{1}{2}}-1)}{(b-1)} = \frac{\frac{1}{\sqrt{b}}-\frac{1}{b}}{1-\frac{1}{b}}.$$

It follows that $\lim_{b \to \infty}\frac{b^{\frac{1}{2}}-1}{b-1} = \frac{\lim_{b \to \infty}\left(\frac{1}{\sqrt{b}}\right)-\lim_{b \to \infty}\left(\frac{1}{b}\right)}{\lim_{b \to \infty}1-\lim_{b \to \infty}\left(\frac{1}{b}\right)} = \frac{0-0}{1-0} = \frac{0}{1} = 0.$

151

(3) L'Hôpital's rule can also be used to compute $\lim\limits_{b\to\infty}\left(\dfrac{b^{\frac{1}{2}}-1}{b-1}\right)$ since the limit has the form $\dfrac{\infty}{\infty}$:

$$\lim_{b\to\infty}\frac{b^{\frac{1}{2}}-1}{b-1}=\lim_{b\to\infty}\frac{\frac{1}{2}b^{-\frac{1}{2}}}{1}=\lim_{b\to\infty}\frac{1}{2\sqrt{b}}=0.$$

119. * A particle moves in the xy-plane so that its velocity at any time t, $0\le t\le 2\pi$, is given by $\dfrac{dx}{dt}=2\cos t$, $\dfrac{dy}{dt}=e^{t}-t$. Find the total distance traveled by the particle over the time interval $0\le t\le 2\pi$.

Solution: Distance $=\int_{0}^{2\pi}\sqrt{(2\cos t)^2+(e^{t}-t)^2}\,dt\approx\mathbf{515.892}$

Notes: (1) The total distance traveled by a particle with parametric equations $x=x(t)$, $y=y(t)$, $a\le t\le b$ is equal to the arc length of the parametric curve from a to b.

(2) Recall that the **arc length** of the differentiable curve with parametric equations $x=x(t)$ and $y=y(t)$ from $t=a$ to $t=b$ is

$$\text{Arc length}=\int_{a}^{b}\sqrt{\left(\frac{dx}{dt}\right)^2+\left(\frac{dy}{dt}\right)^2}\,dt$$

(3) See problem 115 to learn how to use your calculator to approximate the integral.

120. Consider the polar equations $r_1=\sqrt{3}$ and $r_2=2\sin\theta$. Let D be the region in the first quadrant bounded the graphs of the two equations and the y-axis. Set up an expression involving one or more integrals with respect to the polar angle θ that represents the area of D.

Solution: Area $=\dfrac{1}{2}\int_{0}^{\frac{\pi}{3}}(2\sin\theta)^2\,d\theta+\dfrac{1}{2}\int_{\frac{\pi}{3}}^{\frac{\pi}{2}}(\sqrt{3})^2\,d\theta$

Notes: (1) The graph of r_1 is a circle centered at the origin with radius $\sqrt{3}$, and the graph of r_2 is a circle centered at $(0,1)$ with radius 1 (see problem 48 to see how to sketch a polar graph in detail).

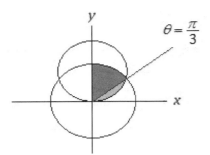

Observe that $r_1 = r_2$ when $\sqrt{3} = 2 \sin \theta$, or equivalently $\sin \theta = \frac{\sqrt{3}}{2}$. This gives $\theta = \frac{\pi}{3}$ in the first quadrant.

(3) Recall that the area of the polar curve $r(\theta)$ from $\theta = a$ to $\theta = b$ is $A = \frac{1}{2} \int_a^b r^2 \, d\theta$.

(4) The light gray region is the area of r_2 from $\theta = 0$ to $\theta = \frac{\pi}{3}$.

(5) The dark gray region is the area of r_1 from $\theta = \frac{\pi}{3}$ to $\theta = \frac{\pi}{2}$.

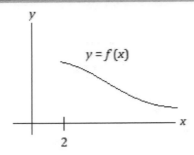

121. For $x \geq 2$, the function $y = f(x)$ is continuous, decreasing and positive. A portion of the graph of f is shown above. Suppose that $\int_{n=2}^{\infty} f(x)\,dx$ converges to 5 and define the nth term of the series $\sum_{n=2}^{\infty} c_n$ by $c_n = f(n)$. Which of the following could be true?

   I. $\sum_{n=2}^{\infty} c_n = 4$
   II. $\sum_{n=2}^{\infty} c_n = 5$
   III. $\sum_{n=2}^{\infty} c_n = 6$

    (A) I only
    (B) II only
    (C) III only
    (D) II and III only

Solution: We must have $\sum_{n=2}^{\infty} c_n > \int_{n=2}^{\infty} f(x)\,dx$. So only III is a possibility. Therefore the answer is choice (C).

Notes: (1) Geometrically, $\int_{n=2}^{\infty} f(x)\,dx$ gives the area under the graph of f. Here is a picture:

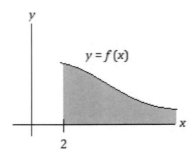

154

(2) Geometrically $\sum_{n=2}^{\infty} c_n$ is a sum of areas of rectangles as shown below:

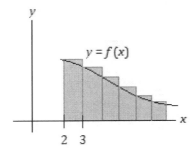

Notice how the area in this figure is greater than the area in the previous figure.

122. A function h has derivatives of all orders at $x = 0$. Let $P_n(x)$ denote the nth-degree Taylor polynomial for h about $x = 0$. It is known that $h(0) = -2$, $h''(0) = -\frac{4}{5}$, $h'''(0) = \frac{5}{2}$, and $P_1\left(\frac{1}{4}\right) = -1$. Find $h'(0)$ and $P_3(x)$.

Solution: We have $P_1(x) = h(0) + h'(0)x = -2 + h'(0)x$. It follows that $-1 = P_1\left(\frac{1}{4}\right) = -2 + h'(0)\left(\frac{1}{4}\right)$. So $h'(0)\left(\frac{1}{4}\right) = -1 + 2 = 1$, and therefore $h'(0) = 1(4) = 4$.

$$P_3(x) = h(0) + h'(0)x + \frac{h''(0)x^2}{2!} + \frac{h'''(0)x^3}{3!} = -2 + 4x - \frac{4}{5} \cdot \frac{x^2}{2!} + \frac{5}{2} \cdot \frac{x^3}{3!}$$

$$= -2 + 4x - \frac{2}{5}x^2 + \frac{5}{12}x^3.$$

Note: See problem 62 for more information about Taylor Polynomials.

123. The Taylor series for a function g about $x = 2$ is given by $\sum_{n=1}^{\infty} \frac{(-1)^n 3^n}{n}(x - 2)^n$ and converges to $g(x)$ for $|x - 2| < \frac{1}{3}$. Find the first four nonzero terms and the general term of the Taylor series for g', the derivative of g, about $x = 2$. Find the function g' to which the series converges for $|x - 2| < \frac{1}{3}$, and use this function to determine g for $|x - 2| < \frac{1}{3}$.

Solution: The first four terms of the Taylor series for g are

$$-3(x - 2) + \frac{9}{2}(x - 2)^2 - 9(x - 2)^3 + \frac{81}{4}(x - 2)^4.$$

155

It follows that the first four terms of the Taylor series for g' are

$$-3 + 9(x - 2) - 27(x - 2)^2 + 81(x - 2)^3.$$

The general term of the Taylor series for g' is

$$(-1)^n 3^n (x - 2)^{n-1} \text{ for } n \geq 1.$$

This series is geometric with common ratio $r = -3(x - 2)$.

So $g'(x) = \frac{-3}{1+3(x-2)} = \frac{-3}{3x-5} = \frac{3}{5-3x}$ for $|x - 2| < \frac{1}{3}$.

$g(x) = \int \frac{3}{5-3x} dx = -\ln|5 - 3x| + C.$

Since $g(2) = 0$, we have $0 = -\ln 1 + C = 0 + C = C$. So $C = 0$, and therefore $g(x) = -\ln|5 - 3x|$ for $|x - 2| < \frac{1}{3}$.

Note: See problem 93 for more information on Taylor series.

124. Write the first four nonzero terms of the Maclaurin series for $g(x) = \cos(x^2) + x^3 \sin x$. The find the value of $g^{(8)}(0)$.

Solution: $\cos x = 1 - \frac{x^2}{2!} + \frac{x^4}{4!} - \frac{x^6}{6!} + \cdots$

So $\cos(x^2) = 1 - \frac{x^4}{2!} + \frac{x^8}{4!} - \frac{x^{12}}{6!} + \cdots$

$\sin x = x - \frac{x^3}{3!} + \frac{x^5}{5!} - \frac{x^7}{7!} + \cdots$

So $x^3 \sin x = x^4 - \frac{x^6}{3!} + \frac{x^8}{5!} - \frac{x^{10}}{7!} + \cdots$

It follows that the first four terms of the desired Maclaurin series is

$$g(x) \approx 1 + \frac{x^4}{2} - \frac{x^6}{6} + \frac{6x^8}{5!}$$

$\frac{g^{(8)}(0)}{8!}$ is the coefficient of x^8 in the Maclaurin series for g. Therefore, we have $\frac{g^{(8)}(0)}{8!} = \frac{6}{5!}$. So $g^{(8)}(0) = \frac{6 \cdot 8!}{5!} = 6 \cdot 8 \cdot 7 \cdot 6 = \mathbf{2016}$.

Note: See problem 63 for more information on Maclaurin series.

125. Let $h(x) = \ln(1 + x^4)$. Write the first four nonzero terms of the Maclaurin series for $h'(x^2)$.

Solution: Let's begin by writing the first four nonzero terms of the Maclaurin series for $h(x) = \ln(1 + x)$.

$h'(x) = \frac{1}{1+x}$, $h''(x) = -\frac{1}{(1+x)^2}$, $h'''(x) = \frac{2}{(1+x)^3}$, and $h^{(4)}(x) = -\frac{3!}{(1+x)^4}$

So $h(0) = 0$, $h'(0) = 1$, $h''(0) = -1$, $h'''(0) = 2$, and $h^{(4)}(0) = -3!$

It follows that $\ln(1 + x) \approx x - \frac{x^2}{2} + \frac{x^3}{3} - \frac{x^4}{4}$. So

$$h(x) = \ln(1 + x^4) \approx x^4 - \frac{x^8}{2} + \frac{x^{12}}{3} - \frac{x^{16}}{4}$$

$$h'(x) \approx 4x^3 - 4x^7 + 4x^{11} - 4x^{15}$$

$$h'(x^2) \approx 4x^6 - 4x^{14} + 4x^{22} - 4x^{30}.$$

Note: See problem 63 for more information on Maclaurin series.

126. Let $h(x) = \ln(1 + x^4)$. Use the first two nonzero terms of the Maclaurin series for $g(x) = \int_0^x h'(u^2)\, du$ to approximate $g(1)$. Show that this approximation differs from $g(1)$ by less than $\frac{2}{11}$.

Solution: We have seen in the last problem that the Maclaurin series for $h'(u^2)$ is $4u^6 - 4u^{14} + 4u^{22} - 4u^{30} + \cdots + (-1)^{n+1}4u^{8n-2} + \cdots$

It follows that the Maclaurin series for $g(x)$ is

$$\frac{4x^7}{7} - \frac{4x^{15}}{15} + \frac{4x^{23}}{23} - \frac{4x^{31}}{31} + \cdots + \frac{(-1)^{n+1}4x^{8n-1}}{8n - 1} + \cdots$$

So $g(1) \approx \frac{4}{7} - \frac{4}{15} = \frac{32}{105}$.

Note that the Maclaurin series for g at $x = 1$ is the alternating series

$$4\sum_{n=1}^{\infty} \frac{(-1)^{n+1}}{8n - 1}$$

which converges by the alternating series test.

It follows that $g(1)$ exists, and $\left| g(1) - \frac{32}{105} \right| < \frac{4 \cdot 1^{23}}{23} = \frac{4}{23} < \frac{4}{22} = \frac{2}{11}$.

Notes: (1) See problem 63 for more information on Maclaurin series.

(2) See problem 92 for more information on approximating a Maclaurin series using the alternating series test remainder theorem.

127. The function h has derivatives of all orders at $x = 0$, and the Maclaurin series for h is $\sum_{n=2}^{\infty} \frac{\ln n}{2^n n^4} x^n$. Determine the interval of convergence of the Maclaurin series for h. Justify your answer.

Solution: $\lim_{n\to\infty} \left| \frac{\frac{\ln(n+1)}{2^{n+1}(n+1)^4} x^{n+1}}{\frac{\ln n}{2^n n^4} x^n} \right| = \lim_{n\to\infty} \left| \frac{\ln(n+1)}{\ln n} \cdot \left(\frac{n}{n+1}\right)^4 \cdot \frac{x}{2} \right| = \frac{|x|}{2}$. So by the ratio test, the series converges for all x such that $\frac{|x|}{2} < 1$, or equivalently $|x| < 2$. Removing absolute values, we have $-2 < x < 2$.

We still need to check the endpoints. When $x = 2$, we get the series $\sum_{n=2}^{\infty} \frac{\ln n}{n^4}$.

We have $0 < \frac{\ln n}{n^4} < \frac{n}{n^4} = \frac{1}{n^3}$. Since $\sum_{n=2}^{\infty} \frac{1}{n^3}$ is a convergent p-series, $\sum_{n=2}^{\infty} \frac{\ln n}{n^4}$ converges by the comparison test.

When $x = -2$ we get the series $\sum_{n=2}^{\infty} (-1)^n \frac{\ln n}{n^4}$. This series is absolutely convergent because we just showed that $\sum_{n=2}^{\infty} \frac{\ln n}{n^4}$ converges.

Therefore the interval of convergence is $[-2, 2]$.

Notes: (1) See problem 63 for the definition of a Maclaurin series and problem 31 for information on the ratio test.

(2) The **comparison test** says the following:

Let $\sum_{n=1}^{\infty} a_n$ and $\sum_{n=1}^{\infty} b_n$ be series with nonnegative terms such that $a_n \leq b_n$ for all n. Then

(i) if $\sum_{n=1}^{\infty} b_n$ converges, so does $\sum_{n=1}^{\infty} a_n$.

(ii) if $\sum_{n=1}^{\infty} a_n$ diverges, so does $\sum_{n=1}^{\infty} b_n$.

In this problem $a_n = \frac{\ln n}{n^4}$ and $b_n = \frac{1}{n^3}$. Since $\sum_{n=2}^{\infty} \frac{1}{n^3}$ converges (it is a convergent p-series), so does $\sum_{n=2}^{\infty} \frac{\ln n}{n^4}$.

(Don't get hung up on whether the index starts at $n = 1$, $n = 2$, or even $n = 10,000$. Convergence of a series does not depend on where the indexing starts.)

$$g(x) = \begin{cases} \dfrac{\sin x - x}{x^3} & \text{for } x \neq 0 \\ -\dfrac{1}{6} & \text{for } x = 0 \end{cases}$$

128. The function g, defined above, has derivatives of all orders. Define the function h by $h(x) = 3 + \int_0^x g(u)\, du$. Write the fifth degree Taylor polynomial for h about $x = 0$, and then estimate the value of $h(1)$ to 4 decimal place accuracy.

Solution: $\sin x = x - \dfrac{x^3}{3!} + \dfrac{x^5}{5!} - \dfrac{x^7}{7!} + \dfrac{x^9}{9!} - \dfrac{x^{11}}{11!} + \cdots + \dfrac{(-1)^n x^{2n+1}}{(2n+1)!} + \cdots$

So $\sin x - x = -\dfrac{x^3}{3!} + \dfrac{x^5}{5!} - \dfrac{x^7}{7!} + \dfrac{x^9}{9!} - \dfrac{x^{11}}{11!} + \cdots + \dfrac{(-1)^n x^{2n+1}}{(2n+1)!} + \cdots$

Therefore $g(x) = -\dfrac{1}{3!} + \dfrac{x^2}{5!} - \dfrac{x^4}{7!} + \dfrac{x^6}{9!} - \dfrac{x^8}{11!} + \cdots + \dfrac{(-1)^n x^{2n-2}}{(2n+1)!} + \cdots$

The fifth degree Taylor polynomial for h about $x = 0$ is

$$P_5(x) = 3 - \frac{x}{3!} + \frac{x^3}{3 \cdot 5!} - \frac{x^5}{5 \cdot 7!}$$

Since $\dfrac{1^5}{5 \cdot 7!} \approx .00003 < .00005$, and the Maclaurin series for h evaluated at $x = 1$ is an alternating series whose terms decrease in absolute value to 0, we have $|h(1) - P_3(1)| < .00005$. So to 4 decimal place accuracy we have $g(1) = P_3(1) = 3 - \dfrac{1}{3!} + \dfrac{1}{3 \cdot 5!} = \mathbf{2.8361}$.

Notes: (1) See problem 63 for more information on Maclaurin series.

(2) See problem 92 for more information on approximating a Maclaurin series using the alternating series test remainder theorem.

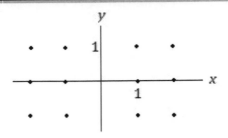

129 – 132 Consider the differential equation $\frac{dy}{dx} = \frac{y+1}{x}$ and the figure above.

129. On the axes provided, sketch a slope field for the differential equation at the twelve points indicated, and for $y > -1$, sketch the solution curve passing through the point $(-1,0)$. Then describe all points in the xy-plane, $x \neq 0$, for which $\frac{dy}{dx} = -1$.

Solution:

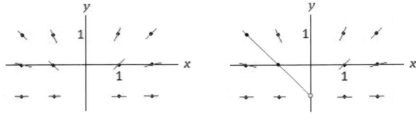

$$\frac{dy}{dx} = -1 \Leftrightarrow \frac{y+1}{x} = -1 \Leftrightarrow y + 1 = -x \Leftrightarrow y = -x - 1.$$

Notes: (1) The figure above on the left gives the slope field for the differential equation at the twelve indicated points. For more information on how to draw this slope field see problem 102.

(2) The figure on the right shows the solution curve that passes through the point $(-1,0)$. Observe that at any point of the form $(x, -x - 1)$, the slope is $\frac{dy}{dx} = \frac{(-x-1)+1}{x} = \frac{-x}{x} = -1$. So the solution curve is a line with slope -1.

130. Write an equation for the line tangent to the solution curve at the point $(-2,0)$. Use the equation to approximate $f(-1.5)$ where $y = f(x)$ is the particular solution of the differential equation with initial condition $f(-2) = 0$.

Solution: The slope of the tangent line at $(-2,0)$ is

$$m = \frac{dy}{dx}\Big|_{(-2,0)} = \frac{0+1}{-2} = -\frac{1}{2}.$$

So an equation of the tangent line in point–slope form is

$$y - 0 = -\frac{1}{2}(x - (-2)), \text{ or equivalently}$$

$$y = -\frac{1}{2}x - 1$$

When $x = -1.5$, we have $y = -\frac{1}{2}(-1.5) - 1 = -\frac{1}{4}$.

It follows that $f(-1.5) \approx -\frac{1}{4}$ or $-.25$.

Notes: (1) To find the slope of the tangent line to a function $y = f(x)$ at a point (x_0, y_0), we take the derivative $\frac{dy}{dx} = f'(x)$, and substitute in x_0 for x and y_0 for y.

In this problem, we were already given $\frac{dy}{dx}$, and so we simply need to substitute in the x-coordinate of the point for x and the y-coordinate of the point for y.

(2) The **point-slope form of an equation of a line** is

$$y - y_0 = m(x - x_0)$$

where m is the slope of the line and (x_0, y_0) is any point on the line.

It is generally easiest to write an equation of a line in point-slope form once the slope of the line and a point on the line are known.

In this problem, the slope is $-\frac{1}{2}$ and the point is $(-2,0)$.

131. Find $y = f(x)$, the particular solution to the differential equation with the initial condition $f(-2) = 0$.

Solution: We separate variables to get $\frac{dy}{y+1} = \frac{dx}{x}$. Now we integrate both sides of this equation to get $\ln|y + 1| = \ln|x| + C$. So we have that

161

$\ln|y + 1| - \ln|x| = C$, and so $\ln\left|\frac{y+1}{x}\right| = C$. Changing to exponential form yields $\frac{y+1}{x} = \pm e^C$. We can simply rename the constant $\pm e^C$ as D.

So we have $\frac{y+1}{x} = D$.

Now we substitute in $x = -2$ and $y = 0$ to get $\frac{1}{-2} = D$. So we have $\frac{y+1}{x} = -\frac{1}{2}$, and so $y + 1 = -\frac{1}{2}x$, and finally, $y = -\frac{1}{2}x - 1$.

So $f(x) = -\frac{1}{2}x - 1$.

Notes: (1) See problem 43 for more information on separable differential equations.

(2) Observe that in this problem, the solution curve is a line, and therefore it is equal to its tangent line (so the approximation found in problem 130 is actually the exact value).

132. Describe the region in the xy-plane in which all solution curves to the differential equation are concave down.

Solution: $\frac{d^2y}{dx^2} = \frac{x\frac{dy}{dx} - (y+1)(1)}{x^2} = \frac{x\left(\frac{y+1}{x}\right) - (y+1)}{x^2} = \frac{(y+1) - (y+1)}{x^2} = \frac{0}{x^2} = 0.$

Since $\frac{d^2y}{dx^2}$ is always 0, it follows that there are no solution curves which are concave down. So the region is empty.

Notes: (1) The graph of a function $y = f(x)$ is concave down at x-values such that $\frac{d^2y}{dx^2} = f''(x) < 0$. Therefore, we are looking for solutions y to the differential equation for which $\frac{d^2y}{dx^2} < 0$.

(2) We get the third expression above by replacing $\frac{dy}{dx}$ with $\frac{y+1}{x}$.

(3) Since $\frac{d^2y}{dx^2} = 0$, all solutions to this differential equation are in fact linear. Only linear functions have second derivatives that are 0 everywhere.

To see this, we integrate each side of $\frac{d^2y}{dx^2} = 0$ to get $\frac{dy}{dx} = C$ where C is some constant. We integrate again to get $y = Cx + D$, where D is another constant.

133 – 136 * Suppose that the average annual salary of an NBA player is modeled by the function $S(t) = 161.4(1.169^t)$, where $S(t)$ is measured in thousands of dollars and t is measured in years since 1980 (for example, since $S(0) = 161.4$, the average salary of an NBA player in 1980 was $161,400).

133. * Find the average rate of change of $S(t)$ over the interval $0 \le t \le 20$. Interpret this answer and indicate units of measure.

Solution: The average rate of change of $S(t)$ over $0 \le t \le 20$ is

$$\frac{S(20)-S(0)}{20-0} = \mathbf{175.230} \text{ (or } \mathbf{175.231}\text{)}$$

So the average rate of change in the annual salary of an NBA player from 1980 through 2000 was $175,230 (or $175,231) per year

Notes: (1) The **average rate of change** of the function f on the interval $a \le x \le b$ is $\frac{f(b)-f(a)}{b-a}$.

(2) $S(20) = 161.4(1.169^{20})$ and $S(0) = 161.4(1.169^0) = 161.4$.

(3) We perform the computation $\frac{S(20)-S(0)}{20-0}$ right in our calculator.

(4) When $t = 0$ the year is 1980, and when $t = 20$ the year is 2000.

(5) Since $S(t)$ is measured in *thousands of dollars*, we interpret the answer 175.230 as $175,230.

134. * Find the value of $S'(10)$. Using correct units, interpret the meaning of the value in the context of the problem.

Solution: We use our calculator to compute

$$S'(10) = \mathbf{120.112}$$

So the average annual salary of an NBA player is increasing at a rate of $120,112 per year at the beginning of 1990.

Notes: (1) We can compute $S'(10)$ directly in our TI-84 calculator as follows:

Press MATH, followed by 8 (or scroll up 3 times and select 8:nDeriv( ). Type 161.4(1.169^X), X, 10) followed by ENTER. The display will show 120.1121575. We truncate this number to 120.112.

(2) As an alternative, we can first compute the derivative

$$S'(x) = 161.4(1.169^t)(\ln(1.169))$$

and then use our calculator to get

$$S'(10) = 161.4(1.169^{10})(\ln(1.169))$$

(3) Since $S'(10)$ is positive, it follows that the average annual salary of an NBA player is *increasing* when $t = 10$.

(4) $t = 10$ at the beginning of the year 1990.

(5) Since $S(t)$ is measured in *thousands of dollars*, we interpret the answer 120.112 as $120,112.

> 135. * Use a right Riemann sum with five equal subintervals to approximate $\frac{1}{20}\int_0^{20} S(t)dt$. Does this approximation overestimate or underestimate the average salary from the beginning of 1980 through the end of 2000? Explain your reasoning.

Solution:

$$\frac{1}{20}\int_0^{20} S(t)dt \approx \frac{1}{20} \cdot 4[S(4) + S(8) + S(12) + S(16) + S(20)]$$

$$\approx \mathbf{1508.911} \text{ or } \mathbf{1508.912}.$$

This approximation is an overestimate, because a right Riemann sum is used and the function S is strictly increasing.

Note: See problem 85 for information about Riemann Sum Approximations.

> 136. * Find the year in which it occurs that the average annual salary is equal to the average salary from the beginning of 1980 through the end of 2000.

Solution: The average salary from the beginning of 1980 through the end of 2000 is

$$\frac{1}{20-0}\int_0^{20} S(t)dt \approx 1122.203$$

So we solve the equation $S(t) = \frac{1}{20}\int_0^{20} S(t)dt$ and get $t \approx 12.418$ or $t \approx 12.419$.

It follows that the average annual salary is equal to the average salary from the beginning of 1980 through the end of 2000 in **1992**.

Notes: (1) We can compute $\int_0^{20} S(t)dt$ directly in our TI-84 calculator as follows:

Press MATH, followed by 9 (or scroll up 2 times and select 9:fnInt( ). Type 161.4(1.169^X), X, 0, 20) followed by ENTER. The display will show 22444.0633.

(2) Remember to multiply 22444.0633 by $\frac{1}{20}$ to get

$$\frac{1}{20} \int_0^{20} S(t)dt = 1122.203165.$$

(3) We can solve the equation $S(t) = \frac{1}{20} \int_0^{20} S(t)dt$ using the graphing features of our TI-84 calculator as follows:

Press Y=, and next to Y_1 type 161.4(1.169^X), and next to Y_2 type 1122.203. Then press WINDOW, set Xmin to 0, Xmax to 20, Ymin to 0, and Ymax to a number greater than 1122.203 (such as 1500). Next press GRAPH. After the two graphs appear press CALC (2nd TRACE), followed by 5 (or scroll down and select 5:intersect). Press ENTER three times, and we see that X is approximately 12.418.

(4) $t = 12$ at the beginning of the year 1992. It follows that the average annual salary is equal to the average salary from the beginning of 1980 through the end of 2000 in 1992.

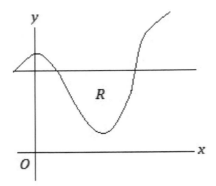

137 – 140 * Let R be the region in the first quadrant enclosed by the graph of $f(x) = x^6 - 3.5x^4 + 7$ and the horizontal line $y = 5$, as shown in the figure above.

137. * Write an equation for the tangent line to the graph of f at $x = -0.5$.

Solution: $f(-0.5) = (-0.5)^6 - 3.5(-0.5)^4 + 7 \approx 6.797$.

$f'(x) = 6x^5 - 14x^3$.

So $f'(-0.5) = 6(-0.5)^5 - 14(-0.5)^3 \approx 1.563$.

So the line passes through $(-0.5, 6.797)$ and has slope $m = 1.563$. An equation of the line in point-slope form is then

$$y - 6.797 = 1.563(x + 0.5).$$

138. * Find the volume of the solid generated when R is rotated about the horizontal line $y = -3$.

Solution: $V = \pi \int_{.934}^{1.822} [(5 - (-3))^2 - (x^6 - 3.5x^4 + 7 - (-3))^2]\, dx$

$= \pi \int_{.934}^{1.822} [64 - (x^6 - 3.5x^4 + 10)^2]\, dx \approx \mathbf{93.216}$.

Notes: (1) We begin by finding the x-values where f intersects the line $y = 5$. We can do this in our calculator as follows:

Press Y=, and next to Y_1 type X^6 – 3.5X^4 + 7 and next to Y_2 type 5. Then press WINDOW, set Xmin to 0, Xmax to 5, Ymin to 0, and Ymax to 10 (other windows will work, of course – you may need to experiment a bit to find the right window). Next press GRAPH. After the two graphs appear press CALC (2nd TRACE), followed by 5 (or scroll down and

166

select 5:intersect).Press ENTER twice, then place the cursor close to the leftmost point of intersection and press ENTER again. The display will show that $x \approx .934$. Repeat the procedure again, but this time place the cursor close to the rightmost point of intersection before pressing ENTER the third time. This time the display will show that $x \approx 1.822$.

(2) We will use the **washer method** to find the requested volume. A *washer* is a disk with a hole in it. A typical washer can be described as follows:

First we take a value x between .934 and 1.822 Find this number on the x-axis.

We then draw the outer radius of the washer by drawing a vertical segment from the line $y = -3$ straight up until we hit the line $y = 5$.

Next we draw a circle from the top of this line segment that sweeps below the line $x = -3$, and who's radius is as specified in the last step.

We draw the inner radius of the washer by drawing a vertical line segment from the line $y = -3$ straight up until we hit the graph of f.

We then draw a circle from the top of this line segment that sweeps below the line $x = -3$, and who's radius is as specified in the last step.

Here is a picture:

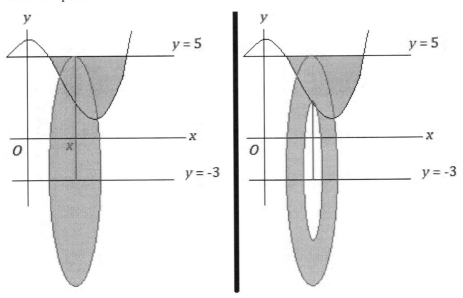

The picture on the left shows the disk formed from the outer radius. This radius is $R = 5 - (-3) = 5 + 3 = 8$. It follows that the area of this disk is $\pi R^2 = \pi(8)^2 = 64\pi$.

The picture on the right shows the formation of the hole from the inner radius. This radius is $r = f(x) - (-3) = f(x) + 3$. It follows that the area of this disk is $\pi r^2 = \pi(f(x) + 3)^2$.

So the area of the washer is "outer disk" – "inner hole." This is

$$\pi R^2 - \pi r^2 = 64\pi - \pi(f(x) + 8)^2 = \pi[64 - (f(x) + 3)^2]$$

The washer method requires us to integrate this area over the given interval, in this case from .934 to 1.822.

$$V = \pi \int_{.934}^{1.822} [64 - (f(x) + 3)^2]\, dx$$

$$= \pi \int_{.934}^{1.822} [64 - (x^6 - 3.5x^4 + 10)^2]\, dx$$

(3) We can compute $\int_{.934}^{1.822} [64 - (x^6 - 3.5x^4 + 10)^2]\, dx$ directly in our TI-84 calculator as follows:

Press MATH, followed by 9 (or scroll up 2 times and select 9:fnInt( ). Type 64 – (X^6 – 3.5X^4 + 10)^2, X, .934, 1.822) followed by ENTER. The display will show 29.67169214.

Remember to multiply this result by π to get approximately **93.216.**

139. * The region R is the base of a solid. For this solid, each cross section perpendicular to the x-axis is an equilateral triangle. Find the volume of the solid.

Solution: $V = \frac{\sqrt{3}}{4} \int_{.934}^{1.822} (-x^6 - 3.5x^4 - 2)^2\, dx \approx \mathbf{454.951}$.

Notes: (1) To see where the limits of integration come from, see note (1) from problem 146.

(2) Let's draw a cross section that is perpendicular to the x-axis.

168

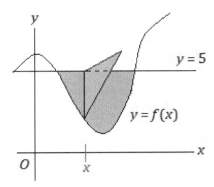

First we take a value x between .934 and 1.822 and find this number on the x-axis.

We then draw a side of the triangle between $y = f(x)$ and $y = 5$. This side has length $5 - f(x) = 5 - (x^6 - 3.5x^4 + 7) = -x^6 - 3.5x^4 - 2$.

The area of an equilateral triangle with side length s is $A = \frac{\sqrt{3}}{4}s^2$ (see note (4) below).

It follows that the area of this triangle is $\frac{\sqrt{3}}{4}(-x^6 - 3.5x^4 - 2)^2$.

To get the desired volume, we now simply integrate this expression over the interval [.934,1.822]:

$$= \frac{\sqrt{3}}{4} \int_{.934}^{1.822} (-x^6 - 3.5x^4 - 2)^2 \, dx.$$

(3) We can compute $\int_{.934}^{1.822} (-x^6 - 3.5x^4 - 2)^2 \, dx$ directly in our TI-84 calculator as follows:

Press MATH, followed by 9 (or scroll up 2 times and select 9:fnInt( ). Type (-X^6 – 3.5X^4 – 2)^2, X, .934, 1.822) followed by ENTER. The display will show 1050.66355.

Remember to multiply this result by $\frac{\sqrt{3}}{4}$ to get approximately **454.951.**

(4) Most students do not know the formula for the area of an equilateral triangle, so here is a quick derivation.

Let's start by drawing a picture of an equilateral triangle with side length s, and draw an **altitude** from a vertex to the opposite base. Note that an altitude of an equilateral triangle is the same as the **median** and **angle bisector** (this is in fact true for any isosceles triangle).

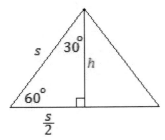

So we get two 30, 60, 90 right triangles with a leg of length $\frac{s}{2}$ and hypotenuse of length s.

We can find h by recalling that the side opposite the 60 degree angle has length $\sqrt{3}$ times the length of the side opposite the 30 degree angle. So $h = \frac{\sqrt{3}s}{2}$.

Alternatively, we can use the Pythagorean Theorem to find h:

$$h^2 = s^2 - \left(\frac{s}{2}\right)^2 = s^2 - \frac{s^2}{4} = \frac{3s^2}{4}. \text{ So } h = \frac{\sqrt{3}s}{2}.$$

It follows that the area of the triangle is

$$A = \frac{1}{2}\left(\frac{s}{2} + \frac{s}{2}\right)\left(\frac{\sqrt{3}s}{2}\right) = \frac{1}{2}s\left(\frac{\sqrt{3}s}{2}\right) = \frac{\sqrt{3}}{4}s^2.$$

140. The vertical line $x = a$ divides R into two regions with equal areas. Write, but do not solve, an equation involving integral expressions whose solution gives the value a.

Solution:

$$\int_{.934}^{a}[5 - f(x)]\,dx = \int_{a}^{1.822}[5 - f(x)]\,dx$$

$$\int_{.934}^{a}[5 - (x^6 - 3.5x^4 + 7)]\,dx = \int_{a}^{1.822}[5 - (x^6 - 3.5x^4 + 7)]\,dx$$

$$\int_{.934}^{a}(-x^6 + 3.5x^4 - 2)\,dx = \int_{a}^{1.822}(-x^6 + 3.5x^4 - 2)\,dx$$

141 – 144 Let h and k be twice-differentiable functions such that $h(1) = -4$, $h(8) = 6$, $k(-3) = 1$, and $k(2) = 8$. Let f be the function given by $f(x) = h(k(x))$.

141. Let b satisfy $-4 < b < 6$. Explain why there must be a value a for $-3 < a < 2$ such that $f(a) = b$.

Solution: Since h and k are twice-differentiable, they are continuous. It follows that f is continuous.

$f(-3) = h(k(-3)) = h(1) = -4$ and $f(2) = h(k(2)) = h(8) = 6$.

Since f is a continuous function satisfying $f(-3) < b < f(2)$, the Intermediate Value Theorem guarantees that there is a value a, with $-3 < a < 2$, such that $f(a) = b$.

Notes: (1) The **Intermediate Value Theorem** says that if f is a continuous function on the interval $[j, k]$ and r is between $f(j)$ and $f(k)$, then there is a real number s with $j < s < k$ such that $f(s) = r$.

Note that "r is between $f(j)$ and $f(k)$" means either $f(j) < r < f(k)$ or $f(k) < r < f(j)$. It depends if $f(j) < f(k)$ or $f(k) < f(j)$.

(2) In this problem the interval is $[-3,2]$, $f(-3) = -4$, and $f(2) = 6$, $r = b$, and $s = a$. Here is a picture:

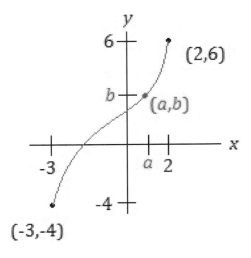

171

Let's just clarify the order of events that take place in this picture. First, b is given between $f(-3) = -4$ and $f(2) = 6$. Since f is continuous, the Intermediate Value theorem guarantees that the graph of f must pass through the point (a, b) for some a between -3 and 2. In other words, there is a real number a, with $-3 < a < 2$, such that $f(a) = b$.

142. Is there a value c for $-3 < c < 2$ such that $f'(c) = 2$. Justify your answer.

Solution: Since h and k are differentiable, so is f. In particular, f is continuous on $[-3,2]$ and differentiable on $(-3,2)$. So the Mean Value Theorem guarantees that there is a value c, with $-3 < c < 2$ such that

$$f'(c) = \frac{f(2)-f(-3)}{2-(-3)} = \frac{h(k(2))-h(k(-3))}{2+3} = \frac{h(8)-h(1)}{5} = \frac{6-(-4)}{5} = \frac{10}{5} = 2.$$

Note: See problem 36 for more information on the Mean Value Theorem.

143. Suppose that $h'(1) = k'(2)$ and $h'(8) = k'(-3)$. Explain why there must be a value d, with $-3 < d < 2$ such that $f''(d) = 0$.

Solution: $f'(x) = h'(k(x)) \cdot k'(x)$

$f'(-3) = h'(k(-3)) \cdot k'(-3) = h'(1) \cdot k'(-3)$

$f'(2) = h'(k(2)) \cdot k'(2) = h'(8) \cdot k'(2)$.

Since $h'(1) = k'(2)$ and $h'(8) = k'(-3)$, we have $f'(-3) = f'(2)$.

Also, since h and k are twice-differentiable, so is f. So f' is differentiable. In particular, f' is continuous on $[-3,2]$ and differentiable on $(-3,2)$. So the Mean Value Theorem guarantees that there is a value d, with $-3 < d < 2$ such that $f''(d) = \frac{f'(2)-f'(-3)}{2-(-3)} = \frac{0}{2+3} = 0$.

Note: See problem 36 for more information on the Mean Value Theorem.

144. Suppose that $h''(x) = k''(x) = 0$ for all x. Find all points of inflection on the graph of f.

Solution 1: Since $h''(x) = k''(x) = 0$ for all x, it follows that h and k are linear functions. The composition of two linear functions is also linear. therefore f is a linear function, and so the graph of f has no points of inflection.

Notes: (1) Since $h''(x) = 0$, it follows by integration that $h'(x) = C$ for some constant C. Integrating again gives $h(x) = Cx + D$ for another constant D. That is h is a linear function.

Similarly, k is a linear function, let's say $k(x) = Ax + B$.

(2) Let's compose h and k as defined in the first note.

$$f(x) = h(k(x)) = h(Ax + B) = C(Ax + B) + D = CAx + (CB + D).$$

So f is a linear function with slope $m = CA$ and y-intercept $(0, CB + D)$.

Solution 2: $f'(x) = h'(k(x)) \cdot k'(x)$

$$f''(x) = h'(k(x)) \cdot k''(x) + k'(x) \cdot h''(k(x)) \cdot k'(x).$$

Since $h''(x) = k''(x) = 0$ for all x, we have

$$f''(x) = h'(k(x)) \cdot 0 + k'(x) \cdot 0 \cdot k'(x) = 0.$$

Since $f''(x) = 0$ for all x, there are no x-values at which f'' changes sign. So the graph of f has no points of inflection.

* 145 – 150 For $t \geq 0$, a particle is moving along a curve so that its position at time t is $(x(t), y(t))$. At time $t = 1$, the particle is at position (3,5). It is known that $\frac{dx}{dt} = \cos^2 t$ and $\frac{dy}{dt} = \frac{e^t}{\sqrt{t+3}}$.

145. * Is the vertical movement of the particle upward or downward at time $t = 1$? Justify your answer. Find the slope of the path of the particle at time $t = 1$.

Solution: $\frac{dy}{dt}\big|_{t=1} = \frac{e^1}{\sqrt{1+3}} = \frac{e}{2} > 0$. So the particle is moving **up** at time $t = 1$.

$\frac{dx}{dt}\big|_{t=1} = \cos^2 1$ and so $\frac{dy}{dx}\big|_{t=1} = \frac{\frac{dy}{dt}\big|_{t=1}}{\frac{dx}{dt}\big|_{t=1}} = \frac{e}{2\cos^2 1} \approx \mathbf{4.655}$ or $\mathbf{4.656}$.

146. * Find the x-coordinate of the particle's position at time $t = \frac{\pi}{2}$.

Solution: $x\left(\frac{\pi}{2}\right) = 3 + \int_1^{\frac{\pi}{2}} \cos^2 t \, dt \approx \mathbf{3.058}$.

147. * Find the speed of the particle at time $t = \frac{\pi}{2}$.

Solution: Speed $= \sqrt{\left(x'\left(\frac{\pi}{2}\right)\right)^2 + \left(y'\left(\frac{\pi}{2}\right)\right)^2} = \sqrt{0^2 + \left(\dfrac{e^{\frac{\pi}{2}}}{\sqrt{\frac{\pi}{2}+3}}\right)^2}$

$$= \dfrac{e^{\frac{\pi}{2}}}{\sqrt{\frac{\pi}{2}+3}} \approx 2.250 = \mathbf{2.25}.$$

148. * Find the acceleration vector of the particle at time $t = \frac{\pi}{2}$.

Solution: $x''(t) = -2\cos t \sin t$ and so $x''\left(\frac{\pi}{2}\right) = -2(0)(1) = 0$

$y''(t) = \dfrac{\sqrt{t+3}e^t - \frac{e^t}{2\sqrt{t+3}}}{t+3}$ and so $y''\left(\frac{\pi}{2}\right) = \dfrac{\sqrt{\frac{\pi}{2}+3}\cdot e^{\frac{\pi}{2}} - \frac{e^{\frac{\pi}{2}}}{2\sqrt{\frac{\pi}{2}+3}}}{\frac{\pi}{2}+3} \approx 2.004$

Acceleration $= \langle x''\left(\frac{\pi}{2}\right), y''\left(\frac{\pi}{2}\right)\rangle = \langle 0, \mathbf{2.004}\rangle.$

149. * Find the distance traveled by the particle from time $t = 1$ to $t = \frac{\pi}{2}$.

Solution: Distance $= \int_1^{\frac{\pi}{2}} \sqrt{(x'(t))^2 + \left(y'(t)\right)^2}\, dt$

$$= \int_1^{\frac{\pi}{2}} \sqrt{(\cos^2 t)^2 + \left(\frac{e^t}{\sqrt{t+3}}\right)^2}\, dt \approx \mathbf{1.012}.$$

150. * Find the time t, $0 \le t \le 2$, when the line tangent to the path of the particle is vertical. Is the direction of the motion of the particle upward or downward at that time. Justify your answer.

Solution: $\frac{dx}{dt} = 0$ when $\cos^2 t = 0$. On the interval $0 \le t \le 2$, this happens when $t = \frac{\pi}{2}$.

Since $y'\left(\frac{\pi}{2}\right) = \dfrac{e^{\frac{\pi}{2}}}{\sqrt{\frac{\pi}{2}+3}} > 0$, the particle is moving **upward** at time $t = \frac{\pi}{2}$.

151 – 156 The polar curves r_1 and r_2 are given by $r_1(\theta) = 4$ and $r_2(\theta) = 4 - 3\sin(2\theta)$.

151. Sketch the graphs of r_1 and r_2 for $0 \le \theta \le \pi$, and shade the region D that is inside both the graphs of r_1 and r_2.

Solution:

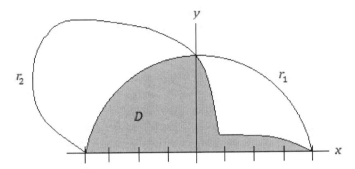

Note: See problem 48 to see how to sketch a polar graph in detail

152. Find the area of the region D that is inside both the graphs of r_1 and r_2 for $0 \le \theta \le \pi$.

Solution: Area $= \frac{16\pi}{4} + \frac{1}{2}\int_0^{\frac{\pi}{2}}(4 - 3\sin(2\theta))^2\, d\theta$

$$= 4\pi + \frac{1}{2}\int_0^{\frac{\pi}{2}}(16 - 24\sin(2\theta) + \frac{9}{2}(1 - \cos(4\theta)))\, d\theta$$

$$= 4\pi + \frac{1}{2}\left(16\theta + 12\cos(2\theta) + \frac{9}{2}(\theta - \frac{1}{4}\sin(4\theta))\right)\Big|_0^{\frac{\pi}{2}}$$

$$= 4\pi + (\frac{41\pi}{8} - 12) = \frac{73\pi}{8} - 12.$$

Note: If a calculator were allowed we could just write down the decimal approximation **16.667**. See problem 115 to learn how to use your calculator to approximate the integral.

153. For the curve r_2, find the value of $\frac{dy}{d\theta}$ at $\theta = \frac{\pi}{3}$.

Solution: $y = r_2\sin\theta = (4 - 3\sin(2\theta))\sin\theta$.

So $\frac{dy}{d\theta} = (4 - 3\sin(2\theta))\cos\theta - 6\cos(2\theta)\sin\theta$.

175

Therefore $\frac{dy}{d\theta}\big|_{\theta=\frac{\pi}{3}} = \left(4 - 3\sin\left(\frac{2\pi}{3}\right)\right)\cos\frac{\pi}{3} - 6\cos\left(\frac{2\pi}{3}\right)\sin\frac{\pi}{3}$

$= \left(4 - \frac{3\sqrt{3}}{2}\right)\left(\frac{1}{2}\right) - 6\left(-\frac{1}{2}\right)\left(\frac{\sqrt{3}}{2}\right) = 2 - \frac{3\sqrt{3}}{4} + \frac{6\sqrt{3}}{4} = 2 + \frac{3\sqrt{3}}{4}$.

Note: If a calculator were allowed we could just write down the decimal approximation **3.299**. See problem 2 to learn how to use your calculator to approximate the derivative.

154. The distance between r_1 and r_2 changes for $0 < \theta < \frac{\pi}{2}$. Find the rate at which the distance between the two curves is changing with respect to θ when $\theta = \frac{\pi}{6}$.

Solution: The distance between r_1 and r_2 is

$$D = 4 - (4 - 3\sin(2\theta)) = 3\sin(2\theta).$$

So $\frac{dD}{d\theta} = 6\cos(2\theta)$, and therefore $\frac{dD}{d\theta}\big|_{\theta=\frac{\pi}{6}} = 6\cos\frac{\pi}{3} = 6\left(\frac{1}{2}\right) = \mathbf{3}$.

155. A particle moves along the curve r_2 so that $\frac{d\theta}{dt} = 4$ for all times $t \geq 0$. Find the value of $\frac{dr_2}{dt}$ at $\theta = \frac{\pi}{6}$.

Solution: $\frac{dr_2}{dt} = \frac{dr_2}{d\theta} \cdot \frac{d\theta}{dt} = \frac{dr_2}{d\theta} \cdot 4$.

Also, $\frac{dr_2}{d\theta} = -6\cos(2\theta)$, so that $\frac{dr_2}{d\theta}\big|_{\theta=\frac{\pi}{6}} = -6\cos\left(\frac{\pi}{3}\right) = -3$.

So $\frac{dr_2}{dt}\big|_{\theta=\frac{\pi}{6}} = (-3)(4) = \mathbf{-12}$.

156. * A particle moves along the curve r_2 so that at time t, $\theta = t^3$. Find the times t in the interval $2 \leq t \leq 2.5$ for which the y-coordinate of the particle's position is -3. Then find the particle's position and velocity vectors in terms of t.

Solution: $y = r_2 \sin\theta$. So $y(\theta) = (4 - 3\sin(2\theta))\sin\theta$.

$y(t) = (4 - 3\sin(2t^3))\sin(t^3)$ and $y(t) = -3$ when $t \approx \mathbf{2.213}$ and $t \approx \mathbf{2.295}$.

Now, $x = r_2 \cos\theta$. So $x(\theta) = (4 - 3\sin(2\theta))\cos\theta$.

$x(t) = (4 - 3\sin(2t^3))\cos(t^3)$.

Position vector $= \langle x(t), y(t) \rangle$

$$= \langle (4 - 3\sin(2t^3))\cos(t^3), (4 - 3\sin(2t^3))\sin(t^3) \rangle.$$

Velocity vector $= \langle x'(t), y'(t) \rangle =$

$$\langle -3t^2\sin(t^3)(4 - 3\sin(2t^3)) - 18t^2\cos(2t^3)\cos(t^3),$$
$$3t^2\cos(t^3)(4 - 3\sin(2t^3)) - 18t^2\cos(2t^3)\sin(t^3) \rangle$$

Note: You will need to use the graphing features of your calculator to determine when $y(t) = -3$. We graph $(4 - 3\sin(2t^3))\sin(t^3)$ and -3 in our calculator in the window $[2, 2.5] \times [-5, 5]$ and use the "intersect" feature twice to find that $t \approx 2.213$ and $t \approx 2.295$.

157 – 160 The function g has a Taylor series about $x = 3$ that converges to $g(x)$ for all x in the interval of convergence. The nth derivative of g at $x = 3$ is given by $g^{(n)}(3) = \frac{(n+2)!}{5^n}$ for $n \geq 1$, and $g(3) = 2$.

157. Write the first four terms and the general term of the Taylor series for g about $x = 3$.

Solution: $g(3) = 2$, $g'(3) = \frac{3!}{5}$, $g''(3) = \frac{4!}{5^2}$, $g'''(3) = \frac{5!}{5^3}$. So

$$g(x) = g(3) + g'(3)(x - 3) + \frac{g''(3)}{2!}(x - 3)^2 + \frac{g'''(3)}{3!}(x - 3)^3 + \cdots$$

$$+ \frac{g^{(n)}(3)}{n!}(x - 3)^n + \cdots$$

$$= 2 + \frac{3!}{5}(x - 3) + \frac{4!}{5^2(2!)}(x - 3)^2 + \frac{5!}{5^3(3!)}(x - 3)^3 + \cdots$$

$$+ \frac{(n + 2)!}{5^n(n!)}(x - 3)^n + \cdots$$

$$= 2 + \frac{3 \cdot 2}{5}(x - 3) + \frac{4 \cdot 3}{5^2}(x - 3)^2 + \frac{5 \cdot 4}{5^3}(x - 3)^3 + \cdots$$

$$+ \frac{(n + 2)(n + 1)}{5^n}(x - 3)^n + \cdots$$

$$\text{or } \sum_{n=0}^{\infty} \frac{(n+2)(n+1)}{5^n}(x - 3)^n.$$

Note: See problem 93 for more information on Taylor series.

158. Find the radius of convergence for the Taylor series for g about $x = 3$. Justify your answer.

Solution: We have

$$\lim_{n \to \infty} \left| \frac{\frac{(n+3)(n+2)}{5^{n+1}}(x-3)^{n+1}}{\frac{(n+2)(n+1)}{5^n}(x-3)^n} \right| = \lim_{n \to \infty} \frac{n^2+5n+6}{n^2+3n+2} \cdot \frac{1}{5}|x-3| = \frac{1}{5}|x-3|.$$

$$\frac{1}{5}|x-3| < 1 \text{ when } |x-3| < 5.$$

So the radius of convergence is **5**.

159. Find the interval of convergence for the Taylor series for g about $x = 3$. Justify your answer.

Solution: We have $|x - 3| < 5$. This is equivalent to $-5 < x - 3 < 5$ or $-2 < x < 8$.

When $x = 8$, the series is $\sum_{n=0}^{\infty} \frac{(n+2)(n+1)}{5^n} 5^n = \sum_{n=0}^{\infty}(n+2)(n+1)$ which diverges by the divergence test.

When $x = -2$, the series is $\sum_{n=0}^{\infty}(-1)^n(n+2)(n+1)$ which also diverges by the divergence test.

It follows that the interval of convergence is $(-2, 8)$.

160. Let G be a function satisfying $G(3) = 1$ and $G'(x) = g(x)$ for all x. Write the first four terms and the general term of the Taylor series for G about $x = 3$. Does this Taylor series converge at $x = -3$?

Solution: $G(3) = 1$, $G'(3) = g(3)$, $G''(3) = g'(3)$, $G'''(3) = g''(3)$.

$$G(x) = G(3) + g(3)(x-3) + \frac{g'(3)}{2!}(x-3)^2 + \frac{g''(3)}{3!}(x-3)^3 + \cdots$$
$$+ \frac{g^{(n-1)}(3)}{n!}(x-3)^n + \cdots$$

$$= 1 + 2(x-3) + \frac{3!}{5(2!)}(x-3)^2 + \frac{4!}{5^2(3!)}(x-3)^3 + \cdots$$
$$+ \frac{(n+1)!}{5^{n-1}(n!)}(x-3)^n + \cdots$$

$$= 1 + 2(x-3) + \frac{3}{5}(x-3)^2 + \frac{4}{5^2}(x-3)^3 + \cdots + \frac{(n+1)}{5^{n-1}}(x-3)^n + \cdots$$

The radius of convergence of this series is $R = 5$. Since we have $|-3 - 3| = |-6| = 6 > 5$, it follows that this Taylor series does not converge at $x = -3$.

178

SUPPLEMENTAL PROBLEMS
QUESTIONS

LEVEL 1: DIFFERENTIATION

1. The instantaneous rate of change at $x = 1$ of the function $f(x) = \sqrt{x}\ln(2x^2 - 1)$ is

   (A) 4

   (B) 2

   (C) $\frac{5}{4}$

   (D) $\frac{1}{2}$

2. $\frac{d}{dx}\left[\frac{\pi^2}{7} + \frac{5}{\sqrt[3]{x^4}} + x^x\right] =$

3. $\frac{d}{dx}\left[\frac{x\arctan\sqrt{x}}{3}\right] =$

4. If $h(x) = \sqrt{\sqrt{x} + x}$, then $h'(1) =$

5. If $y = x^{\cot x}$, then $y' =$

6. Differentiate $f(x) = \frac{(x-2)\log_3 x}{\sqrt[3]{x}}$ and express your answer as a simple fraction.

7. If $x = \sin^{-1}(t^2)$ and $y = e^{3\ln t}$, then find $\frac{dy}{dx}$ in terms of t.

8. If G is the vector-valued function defined by $G(t) = \langle\frac{1+t^3}{1+t}, \cos^2 t - \sin^2 t\rangle$, then $G''(0) =$

LEVEL 1: INTEGRATION

9. $\int_0^1 \frac{x^2 + e^{3x}}{x^3 + e^{3x}}\, dx =$

10. $\int(\frac{3}{x^5} + \frac{5}{x} - 5\sqrt[3]{x} + \frac{3}{\sqrt[5]{x^4}})\, dx =$

11. $\int \frac{x}{(3x^2+1)\ln(3x^2+1)}\, dx =$

179

12. $\int 3^{x \cos x}(x \sin x - \cos x)dx =$

13. $\int_{-3}^{1} \frac{|x|}{x}dx =$

14. * If $1 < b < 10$ and the function h given by $h(x) = \frac{\ln x}{x}$ has an average value of $\frac{1}{4}$ on the interval $[1, b]$, then $b =$

15. $\int_{0}^{\infty} \frac{\arctan x}{x^2+1}dx$ is

16. Let $y = f(x)$ be the solution to the differential equation $\frac{dy}{dx} = \ln(xy)$ with the initial condition $f(1) = 1$. What is the approximation of $f(2)$ if Euler's method is used, starting at $x = 1$ with a step size of 0.5?

17. * What is the area of the closed region bounded by the curve $y = \arctan x$, and the lines $x = -2$ and $y = -\frac{\pi}{4}$?

18. Find the length of the graph of $y = 2\left(x - \frac{1}{9}\right)^{3/2}$ between $x = 1$ and $x = 4$?

LEVEL 1: LIMITS AND CONTINUITY

19. $\lim_{x \to \infty} \frac{\sqrt{3x^2-1}}{2x-5} =$

   (A) $\frac{1}{2}$

   (B) $\frac{\sqrt{3}}{2}$

   (C) ∞

   (D) The limit does not exist

20. The graph of the rational function r where $r(x) = \frac{x^2-2x-1}{x^2-4}$ has asymptotes $x = a$, $x = b$, and $y = c$. What is the value of $a + b + c$?

   (A) $-\frac{1}{4}$

   (B) $\frac{1}{4}$

   (C) 1

   (D) 3

21. If the function g is continuous for all real numbers and if $g(x) = \frac{x^3+2x^2-15x}{x-3}$ for all $x \neq 3$, then $g(3) =$

    (A) 12
    (B) 24
    (C) $+\infty$
    (D) $g(3)$ does not exist.

22. $\lim_{x \to 0} \frac{\tan^4 2x}{x^4}$

23. $\lim_{x \to 0} \frac{5 \sin x - 5 \sec^2 x \sin x}{x^3}$

24. What is $\lim_{h \to 0} \frac{\ln(e+h) - \ln e}{h}$?

25. $\lim_{x \to \infty} (3 - e^{\frac{1}{2} - \frac{1}{x^2}}) =$

26. $\lim_{x \to 11^-} \frac{x+2}{(x-11)^3} =$

LEVEL 1: SERIES

27. The sum of the infinite geometric series $\frac{1}{3} + \frac{4}{15} + \frac{16}{75} + \cdots$ is

28. Which of the following series converge?

    I. $\sum_{n=1}^{\infty} \frac{(-3)^n}{n}$

    II. $\sum_{n=1}^{\infty} \frac{e^n}{2e^n+5}$

    III. $\sum_{n=1}^{\infty} \frac{1}{n^{\frac{3}{2}}}$

    (A) I only
    (B) II only
    (C) III only
    (D) I and III only

29. If $\lim_{b \to \infty} \int_1^b \frac{1}{x^p} dx = \infty$, then which of the following must be true?

(A) $\sum_{n=1}^{\infty} \frac{1}{n^{p+1}}$ diverges

(B) $\sum_{n=1}^{\infty} \frac{1}{n^p}$ converges

(C) $\sum_{n=1}^{\infty} \frac{1}{n^p}$ diverges

(D) $\sum_{n=1}^{\infty} \frac{1}{n^{p-1}}$ converges

30. Which of the following series converge to $-\frac{5}{4}$?

I. $\sum_{n=1}^{\infty} \frac{5}{(-3)^n}$

II. $\sum_{n=1}^{\infty} \frac{1-5\sqrt{n}}{4\sqrt{n}+2}$

III. $\sum_{n=1}^{\infty} \frac{1}{\sqrt{n}}$

(A) I only
(B) II only
(C) III only
(D) I and III only

31. Which of the following series diverge?

I. $\sum_{n=1}^{\infty} \frac{n^3-n+1}{\ln n}$

II. $\sum_{n=1}^{\infty} (\frac{101}{100})^n$

III. $\sum_{n=1}^{\infty} \frac{n!}{3^n}$

(A) I only
(B) III only
(C) I and III only
(D) I, II, and III

32. What are all values of x for which the series $\sum_{n=1}^{\infty} \frac{(-3)^n x^n}{n^2+1}$ converges?

182

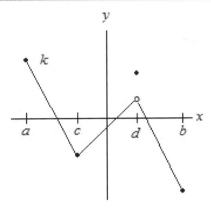

33. The function k, whose graph consists of three line segments, is shown above. Which of the following are false for k on the open interval (a, b) ?

    I. k has a nonremoval discontinuity at $x = d$.
    II. k is differentiable on the open interval (c, d).
    III. The derivative of k is negative on the interval $(c, 0)$.

    (A) I only
    (B) II only
    (C) III only
    (D) I and III only

34. If $f(x) = \dfrac{3x}{\sqrt{2x^2 + 5}}$, then $f'(x) =$

35. If $h(x) = \dfrac{x^2 + \sqrt[3]{x}}{\sqrt[3]{x^2}}$, then $h'(8) =$

36. The *derivative* of $f(x) = xe^x$ attains its minimum value at $x =$

37. Write an equation of the normal line to the curve $y = \sqrt{\ln x}$ at the point $(e, 1)$.

38. A curve is described by the parametric equations $x = \cos t$ and $y = e^{\sqrt{\sin t}}$. An equation of the line tangent to the curve at the point where $t = \dfrac{\pi}{2}$ is

183

39. * The line perpendicular to the tangent line to the curve represented by the equation $y = \ln \sqrt{x}$ at the point $(e^2, 1)$ also intersects the curve at $x =$

40. If $\frac{d}{dx}[k(x)] = h(x)$ and if $g(x) = 2x^3 - 5$, then $\frac{d}{dx}[g(k(x))] =$

    (A) $6(h(x))(k(x))^2$

    (B) $6(h(x))(k(x))^2 - 5h(x)$

    (C) $h'(x)$

    (D) $6x^2 h(x)$

LEVEL 2: INTEGRATION

41. $\int_0^{\ln \sqrt{3}} \frac{e^x dx}{1+e^{2x}} =$

42. $\int_0^{\frac{\pi}{4}} \sec x \, (\tan x - \sec x) dx$

43. $\int_0^2 \frac{x^3 + 2x^2 - x - 2}{x^2 - 1} dx =$

44. A radioactive substance is decaying at a rate of $30e^{-\frac{3t}{5}}$ per year. At $t = 0$ years, there is 100 pounds of this substance. Find the amount present after 5 years.

45. $\int_0^3 \frac{dx}{\sqrt{3-x}} =$

46. Find the length of $y = \ln(\sec x)$ between $x = 0$ and $x = \frac{\pi}{4}$?

47. $\int x^2 e^x dx =$

48. The area enclosed by the graph of the polar equation $r = 2 \cos(3\theta)$ is

184

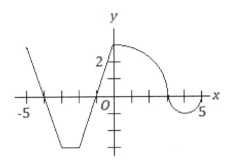

49. Let g be the continuous function defined on $[-5,5]$ whose graph, consisting of three line segments, a quarter circle centered at the origin, and a semicircle centered at $(4,0)$, is shown above. If $G(x) = \int_0^x g(t)\,dt$, where is $G(x)$ negative?

50. Find the length of the arc of the curve defined by $x(t) = 5\sin t$ and $y(t) = 5\cos t$, from $t = 0$ to $t = 2\pi$.

LEVEL 2: LIMITS AND CONTINUITY

51. Suppose that the differentiable function k satisfies $\lim_{h\to 0} \frac{k'(3+h)-k'(3)}{h} = 1$. Which of the following must be true ?

    I. k is continuous at $x = 3$
    II. k' is continuous at $x = 3$
    III. $k''(3)$ exists

    (A) I only
    (B) 1I only
    (C) I and II only
    (D) I, II, and III

52. $\lim_{x\to-\infty} \frac{\sqrt{7x^6+3x^8}}{6-5x^2+2x^4} =$

53. If f is continuous for all c in the interval (a,b), which of the following *can* be false?

    (A) $f(c)$ is defined for all c in (a,b)

    (B) $\lim_{x\to c} f(x) = f(\lim_{x\to c} x)$ for all c in (a,b)

    (C) f is Riemann integrable on (a,b).

    (D) There is a c in (a,b) such that $f'(c) = \frac{f(b)-f(a)}{b-a}$.

185

54. Let g be defined by

$$g(x) = \begin{cases} e^x \cos x & \text{for } -2 \le x \le \pi \\ \dfrac{e^\pi}{\sin(x+\frac{\pi}{2})} & \text{for } \pi < x \le 10 \end{cases}.$$

Is g continuous at $x = \pi$? Use the definition of continuity to explain your answer.

55. A 5000 gallon tank is filled to capacity with water. At time $t = 0$, water begins to leak out of the tank at a rate modeled by $R(t)$, measured in gallons per hour, where

$$R(t) = \begin{cases} \dfrac{300t}{t+1} & , \quad 0 \le t \le 4 \\ 12e^{2-0.5t} + 228, & t > 4 \end{cases}$$

Is $\dfrac{dR}{dt}$ continuous at $t = 4$? Show the work that leads to your answer.

56. Let $g(x) = \dfrac{x^3 - 2x^2 - 3x}{2x^3 - 2x^2 - 4x}$. Find each x-value at which g is discontinuous, and classify each such discontinuity as removable or nonremovable. Define a function G such that G is continuous at each removable discontinuity of g and such that $G(x) = g(x)$ for all x in the domain of g.

LEVEL 2: SERIES

57. $\sum_{n=2}^{\infty} \dfrac{\ln n}{n} =$

    (A) The series diverges.

    (B) $\dfrac{\ln 2}{2}$

    (C) $\ln 2$

    (D) $\dfrac{1}{\ln 2}$

58. If $g(x) = \sum_{n=1}^{\infty} (\cos^2 x)^n$, then $g\left(\dfrac{\pi}{6}\right) =$

59. $\sum_{n=1}^{\infty} \left(\frac{5^n}{(4+n^2)^{80}} \right) \left(\frac{(3+n^2)^{80}}{5^{n+1}} \right) =$

(A) $\frac{1}{5}$

(B) $\frac{1}{4}$

(C) $\frac{3}{4}$

(D) The series diverges.

60. Which of the following statements about the series $\sum_{n=1}^{\infty} \frac{(-1)^n(3n^2-1)}{\sqrt{n^7+2n^3-1}}$ is true?

(A) The series converges absolutely.
(B) The series converges conditionally.
(C) The series converges but neither conditionally nor absolutely.
(D) The series diverges.

61. Find the interval of convergence for the series $\sum_{n=1}^{\infty} \frac{(x-5)^n}{\sqrt{n}(2^n)}$.

62. The third-degree Taylor polynomial about $x = 0$ of $\ln(3 - 3x)$ is

63. If $\sum_{n=0}^{\infty} a_n x^n$ is a Maclaurin series that converges to $g(x)$ for all x. then $g''(-1) =$

(A) -1
(B) $-a_2$
(C) $\sum_{n=2}^{\infty}(-1)^n a_n$
(D) $\sum_{n=2}^{\infty}(-1)^n n(n-1)a_n$

64. The function k has derivatives of all orders at $x = 1$, and the Taylor series for k about $x = 1$ is $\sum_{n=2}^{\infty} \frac{\ln\sqrt{n}}{e^n n^2}(x-1)^n$. Find $h''(1)$.

187

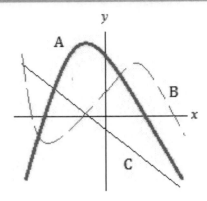

65. Three graphs labeled A, B, and C are shown above. One is the graph of f, one is the graph of f', and one is the graph of f''. When $f''(x) = 0$, what can we say about $f(x)$ and $f'(x)$?

   (A) $f(x) > 0$ and $f'(x) > 0$
   (B) $f(x) > 0$ and $f'(x) < 0$
   (C) $f(x) < 0$ and $f'(x) > 0$
   (D) $f(x) < 0$ and $f'(x) < 0$

66. A point (x, y) is moving along the curve $y = f(x)$. At the instant when the slope of the curve is $\frac{3}{7}$, the y-coordinate of the point is increasing at the rate of 5 units per minute. The rate of change, in units per minute, of the x-coordinate of the point is

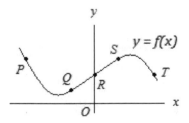

67. At which of the five points on the graph in the figure above are $\frac{dy}{dx}$ and $\frac{d^2y}{dx^2}$ both negative?

   (A) T
   (B) S
   (C) R
   (D) Q

188

68. Given the function defined by $f(x) = x^2e^x$, find all values of x for which the graph of f is concave up.

69. If the line $2x - 3y = 3$ is tangent in the first quadrant to the curve $y = \ln(3x + 1)$, at $x = c$, then c is

70. Find all relative extrema and points of inflection for the function f defined by $f(x) = \ln(x^2 + 1)$.

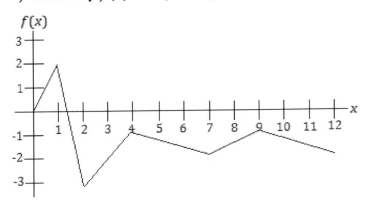

71. The graph of $f(x)$ is given above for $0 \le x \le 12$. On the same set of axes, sketch the graph of f'.

72. If $h(x) = \dfrac{x^{\frac{1}{3}}}{(x+3)^{\frac{1}{2}}}$ for all x, then the domain of h' is

73. If $\sin(xy^3) = e^{xy}$, then $\dfrac{dy}{dx} =$

74. A point moves in a straight line so that its distance at time t from a fixed point of the line is $\dfrac{t^2-1}{e^t}$. The *total* distance that the point travels from $t = 0$ to $t = 3$ is

75. * Two particles start at the origin and move along the x-axis. For $0 \le t \le 2$, their position functions are given by $x = \tan^2 t$ and $y = te^{t^2+1}$. For how many values of t do the particles have the same velocity?

   (A) None
   (B) One
   (C) Two
   (D) Three

189

76. Consider the equation $x \ln(xy) = 1$. Find $\frac{d^2y}{dx^2}$ at $(1,1)$.

LEVEL 3: INTEGRATION

77. The area of the region in the first quadrant bounded by the graph of $y = \frac{\ln(2x+1)}{4x+2}$, the y-axis, and the line $x = 1$ is

78. Let f and g be continuous functions such that $f'(x) = g(x)$ for all x. It follows that $\int_a^b 2x \cdot g(x^2 + 1)dx =$

79. If $\frac{dy}{dx} = \frac{y \cdot e^x}{e^x+1}$ and if $y = 4$ when $x = 0$, then $y =$

80. The average value of $\tan x$ over the interval $\frac{\pi}{6} \le x \le \frac{\pi}{3}$ is

81. Evaluate $\int_{-\frac{1}{2}}^{1} g(x)dx$, where

$$g(x) = \begin{cases} \cos \pi x \sin^2 \pi x & \text{for } x < 0 \\ e^{\sin \pi x} \cos \pi x & \text{for } x \ge 0 \end{cases}$$

82. If $\int_{2j}^{2k} f(x)dx = st$, then $\int_j^k (5f(2x) - 3)dx =$

83. If $f(0) = 1$, $f(1) = e$, then $\int_0^1 \frac{\ln[f(x)] \cdot f'(x)}{f(x)} dx =$

84. Calculate the approximate area under the curve $f(x) = \log_2 x$ and bounded by the lines $x = 1$ and $x = 4$ by the trapezoidal rule, using three equal subintervals.

85. A point moves in a straight line so that its velocity at time t is $\frac{x-1}{x^2-2x-15}$. What is the *total* distance that the point travels from $t = 0$ to $t = 2$?

86. $\int \frac{x+13}{x^2-4x-5} dx =$

      (A) $\ln|(x - 5)^2(x + 1)^3| + C$

      (B) $\ln|(x - 5)^3(x + 1)^2| + C$

      (C) $\ln \left| \frac{(x-5)^3}{(x+1)^2} \right| + C$

      (D) $\ln \left| \frac{(x+1)^2}{(x-5)^3} \right| + C$

87. * Let G be defined by $G(x) = \int_3^x (7 - t^2) \ln(t^2 - 5)\, dt$, Which of the following statements about G must be true?

   I. G is increasing on $(3,4)$.
   II. G is concave up on $(3,4)$
   III. $G(5) > 0$

   (A) None
   (B) I only
   (C) II only
   (D) I, II and III

x	$f'(x)$
-4	0
-3.5	2
-3	1
-2.5	4
-2	3
-1.5	6
-1	5

88. The table above gives selected values for the derivative of a function f on the interval $-4 \le x \le -1$. If $f(-4) = 1$ and Euler's method with a step size of 1 is used to approximate $f(-1)$, what is the resulting approximation?

89. Find the area in the first quadrant between the outer envelope and the smaller loop of the graph of $r = 2 + 4\cos\theta$.

90. $\int e^{2x} \sin 3x\, dx =$

LEVEL 3: SERIES

91. If g is a function such that $g'(x) = e^{x^3}$, then the coefficient of x^{10} in the Maclaurin series for g is

191

92. For a series S, let

$$S = \frac{1}{\sqrt{5^5}} - \frac{1}{5} + \frac{1}{\sqrt{7^5}} - \frac{1}{25} + \frac{1}{\sqrt{9^5}} - \frac{1}{125} + \cdots + (-1)^n s_n + \cdots,$$

where $s_n = \begin{cases} \dfrac{1}{(n+4)^{\frac{5}{2}}} & \text{if } n \text{ is odd} \\ \dfrac{1}{5^{\frac{n}{2}}} & \text{if } n \text{ is even} \end{cases}$

Which of the following statements are true?

    I. S converges because the terms of S alternate in sign and $\lim_{n\to\infty} s_n = 0$.

    II. S diverges because the sequence (s_n) is not decreasing.

    III. S converges even though the sequence (s_n) is not decreasing.

    (A) None
    (B) I only
    (C) II only
    (D) III only

93. What is the approximation of the value $\cos 5$ obtained by the sixth-degree Taylor Polynomial about $x = 0$ for $f(x) = \cos x$?.

94. * Using the Maclaurin Series for $\sin x$, approximate $\sin(0.3)$ to four decimal places.

95. The Taylor series for a function g about $x = 3$ is given by $\sum_{n=1}^{\infty} \frac{(-1)^n 4^n}{n^2}(x-3)^n$ and converges to $g(x)$ for $|x - 3| < R$, where R is the radius of convergence of the Taylor series. Find R and the interval of convergence of the Taylor series.

$$h(x) = \begin{cases} \dfrac{\cos x - 1}{x} & \text{for } x \neq 0 \\ 0 & \text{for } x = 0 \end{cases}$$

96. The function h, defined above, has derivatives of all orders. Write the first five nonzero terms and the general term for the Maclaurin series for h. Then determine whether h has a relative extremum at $x = 0$. Justify your answer.

LEVEL 4: DIFFERENTIATION

97. Suppose that f is an odd function (so that $f(-x) = -f(x)$ for all x), and that $f'(c)$ exists. Then $f'(-c)$ must be equal to

    (A) $f'(c)$

    (B) $-f'(c)$

    (C) $\dfrac{1}{f'(c)}$

    (D) $-\dfrac{1}{f'(c)}$

98. The function $f(x) = 2x^3 + x - 3$ has an inverse function g. Find $g'(15)$.

99. A container is in the form of a right circular cone with radius 4 inches, height 16 inches, vertex pointing downward. Water is being poured into the container at the constant rate of 16 inches^3 per second. How fast is the water level rising when the water is 8 inches deep?

100. If $y = \sin kx$, where k is a nonzero constant, then $\dfrac{d^{73}y}{dx^{73}} =$

101. Consider a differentiable function g with domain $(-\infty, \infty)$, satisfying $g'(x) = \sqrt[3]{x}(x^2 - 7)$. Find the x-coordinates of all relative minima and maxima, find all intervals on which the graph of g is concave up, and find all intervals on which the graph of g is concave down. Justify your answers.

102. Let h be a function with derivative $h'(x) = \sqrt{x^2 + 7}$ such that $h(3) = -1$. Estimate $h(3.1)$ and determine if this estimate is too large or too small. Justify your answer.

103. Does there exist a differentiable function g such that $g(-3) = 3$, $g(5) = 11$, and $g'(x) < 1$ for all x ? Justify your answer.

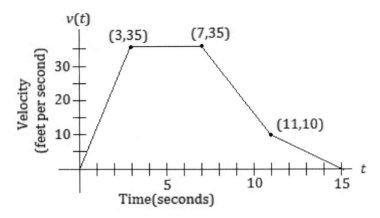

104. A bus is traveling on a straight road. For $0 \le t \le 15$ seconds, the bus's velocity $v(t)$, in feet per second, is modeled by the function defined by the graph above. Find the average rate of change of v over the interval $1 \le t \le 6$. Does the Mean Value Theorem guarantee a value of c for $1 < t < 6$, such that $v'(c)$ is equal to this average rate of change? Why or why not?

105. * Let r be the polar curve defined by $r(\theta) = 7e^{\frac{6}{7}\theta} + \sin 2\theta$, where $0 \le \theta \le 2\pi$. A particle is traveling along r so that its position at time t is $\langle x(t), y(t) \rangle$ and such that $\frac{d\theta}{dt} = 2$. Find $\frac{dy}{dt}$ at the instant that $\theta = \frac{7\pi}{6}$, and interpret the meaning of your answer in the context of the problem.

106. * A particle moves along the curve defined by the equation $y = \ln(x^2 + 1)$. The x-coordinate of the particle satisfies $x(t) = \sqrt{t-1}$, for $t \ge 1$. Find the speed of the particle at time $t = 5$.

107. * A particle moves in the xy-plane so that its position at any time t, $0 \le t \le 2\pi$, is given by $x(t) = 5\sin\frac{t}{2}$, $y(t) = \ln 5t$. Find the acceleration vector at the time t when $x(t)$ attains its maximum value.

108. The polar curve $r = f(\theta)$ satisfies $r > 0$ and $\frac{dr}{d\theta} > 0$ for $a < \theta < b$. What do these facts tell us about r? What do these facts tell us about the curve?

194

109. Consider the differential equation $\frac{dy}{dx} = 2xy^3$ Let $y = f(x)$ be the particular solution to the differential equation that passes through $(2,1)$. Find $y = f(x)$, and the domain of f.

x	0	1	2	3
$f(x)$	2	3	0	4
$f'(x)$	3	3	4	-1
$g(x)$	-1	-2	-3	4
$g'(x)$	2	1	-3	1

110. The differentiable functions f and g are defined for all real numbers x. Values of f, f', g, and g' for various values of x are given in the table above. Evaluate $\int_1^{\sqrt[3]{2}} x^2 g'(f(x^3)) f'(x^3)\, dx$.

111.* The function h is defined for $x > 0$ by $h'(x) = \cos(\frac{1}{x} + x)$ and $h(3) = 1$. Write an equation for the line tangent to the graph of h at $x = 3.2$.

112.* Let $G(x) = \int_0^{x^2} \sin^3 t\, dt$. Find the average value of $G'(x)$ on the interval $[0,2]$.

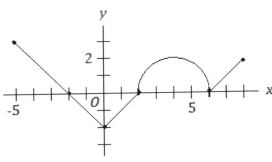

113. Let f be the continuous function defined on $[-5,8]$ whose graph, consisting of three line segments and a semicircle centered at $(4,0)$, is shown above. Compute $\int_{-5}^{8} f(t)\, dt$.

114. * The rate, in tons per hour, at which bricks are arriving at a construction site is modeled by $K(t) = 5 + 32\sin\left(\frac{t^3}{128}\right)$, where t is measured in hours and $0 \le t \le 5$. At time $t = 0$, there are already 10 tons of unused bricks at the site, and bricks are being used (for the construction) at a constant rate of 7 tons per hour. Write an expression for the amount of unused bricks at the construction site at any time t. Then find the maximum amount (in tons) of unused bricks at the site for $0 \le t \le 3$. Justify your answer.

115. * Let R be the region in the first and second quadrants bounded above by the graph of $y = \frac{48}{2+x^4}$ and below by the horizontal line $y = 4$. The region R is the base of a solid whose cross sections perpendicular to the x-axis are rectangles with height twice the length of the base. Find the volume of this solid.

116. * A particle moves in the xy-plane so that its velocity at any time t, $0 \le t \le 2\pi$, is given by $\frac{dx}{dt} = 5\sin\frac{t}{2}$, $\frac{dy}{dt} = \ln 5t$. At time $t = 1$, the particle is at the point $(7,2)$. Find the y-coordinate of the position of the particle at time $t = 3$.

117. Let R be the region in the first and fourth quadrants bounded by the graph of $y = \ln(x^2 + 1)$ the line $y = -4x$, and the vertical line $x = 3$. Write, but do not evaluate, an expression involving one or more integrals that gives the perimeter of R.

118. The arc length for the graph of the differentiable function g between $x = 0$ and $x = 2$ is 11. Define the function k by $k(x) = 5g\left(\frac{x}{5}\right)$. Find the arc length of the graph of $y = k(x)$ from $x = 0$ to $x = 10$.

119. A solid has a rectangular base that lies in the first quadrant and is bounded by the x- and y-axes and the lines $x = 5$ and $y = 1$. The height of the solid above the point (x, y) is $x\ln(x + 1)$. Which of the following is a Riemann sum approximation for the volume of the solid?

(A) $\sum_{i=1}^{n} \frac{25i^2}{n^2} \ln\left(\frac{5i+n}{n}\right)$

(B) $\sum_{i=1}^{n} \frac{25i}{n^2} \ln\left(\frac{5i+n}{n}\right)$

(C) $\sum_{i=1}^{n} \frac{5i}{n^2} \ln\left(\frac{5i+n}{n}\right)$

(D) $\sum_{i=1}^{n} \frac{5}{n} \ln\left(\frac{5i+n}{n}\right)$

120. $\int_1^\infty \frac{x}{x^4+1}\,dx =$

121. * A particle moves in the xy-plane so that its velocity at any time t, $0 < t < 2\pi$, is given by $\frac{dx}{dt} = 5\sin\frac{t}{2}$, $\frac{dy}{dt} = \ln 5t$. Find the total distance traveled by the particle over the time interval $0 < t < 2\pi$.

122. Consider the polar equations $r = \sqrt{2}$ and $r = 2\cos\theta$. Let D be the region in the first quadrant bounded by the graphs of the two equations and the x-axis. Set up an expression involving one or more integrals with respect to the polar angle θ that represents the area of D.

LEVEL 4: SERIES

123. A function h has derivatives of all orders at $x = 2$. Let $P_n(x)$ denote the nth-degree Taylor polynomial for h about $x = 2$. It is known that $h(2) = -1$, $h''(2) = -\frac{1}{2}$, $h'''(2) = 3$, and $P_1(1) = -3$. Find $h'(2)$ and $P_3(x)$.

124. The Taylor series for a function h about $x = 1$ is given by $\sum_{n=1}^\infty \frac{(-1)^n 5^n}{\sqrt{n^3}}(x-1)^n$ and converges to $h(x)$ for $|x-1| < \frac{1}{5}$. Find the first four nonzero terms and the general term of the Taylor series for h', the derivative of h, about $x = 1$. Find the interval of convergence of the Taylor series for h'.

125. Write the first five nonzero terms of the Maclaurin series for $g(x) = x^2 e^{x^3} + 2x\cos x^2$. The find the value of $g^{(11)}(0)$.

126. Let $g(x) = \cos(x^3) + \sin 2x$. Write the first four nonzero terms of the Maclaurin series for $g'(x^3)$.

127. * Let $g(x) = \cos(x^3) + \sin 2x$. Use the first four nonzero terms of the Maclaurin series for $k(x) = \int_0^x g'(u^3)\,du$ to approximate $k(1)$.

197

$$h(x) = \begin{cases} \dfrac{\cos x - 1}{x} & \text{for } x \neq 0 \\ 0 & \text{for } x = 0 \end{cases}$$

128. The function h, defined above, has derivatives of all orders. Define the function k by $k(x) = 2 + \int_0^x h(u)\, du$. Write the sixth degree Taylor polynomial for k about $x = 0$, and then estimate the value of $k(1)$ to 5 decimal place accuracy.

LEVEL 5: FREE RESPONSE QUESTIONS

129 – 132 * Machine A removes salt from a container at a rate modeled by the function M, given by $M(t) = 3 + 2\cos\left(\dfrac{3\pi t}{20}\right)$. Simultaneously, machine B adds salt to the container at a rate modeled by the function N, given by $N(t) = \dfrac{e^t}{2+t}$. Both $M(t)$ and $N(t)$ have units of cubic feet per hour and t is measured in hours for $0 \leq t \leq 5$. At time $t = 0$, the container contains 20 cubic feet of salt.

129. * How much salt will machine A remove from the container during this 5 hour period, and how much salt will machine B add to the container during this 5 hour period? Indicate units of measure.

130. Write an expression for $K(t)$, the total number of cubic feet of salt in the container at time t.

131. * Find the rate at which the total amount of salt in the container is changing at time $t = 2$.

132. For $0 \leq t \leq 5$, at what time t is the amount of salt in the container a minimum? At what time t is the amount of the salt in the container a maximum? What are the maximum and minimum values? Justify your answers.

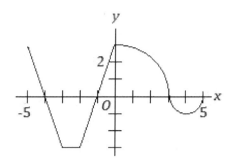

133 – 140 Let g be the continuous function defined on $[-5,5]$ whose graph, consisting of three line segments, a quarter circle centered at the origin, and a semicircle centered at $(4,0)$, is shown above. Let $G(x) = -3x + \int_0^x g(t)\, dt$.

133. Find the values of $G(-2)$ and $G(5)$.

134. Find $G'(x)$. Then evaluate $G'(-1)$ and $G''(-1)$.

135. Determine the x-coordinate of the point at which G has an absolute maximum on the interval $[-5,5]$. Justify your answer.

136. For $-5 < x < 5$, find all values of x for which the graph of G has a point of inflection. Explain your reasoning.

137. On what open intervals contained in $-5 < x < 5$ is the graph of G concave up? Justify your answer.

138. Find the average rate of change of g on the interval $[-5, -2]$. There is no point c with $-5 < c < -2$, for which $g'(c)$ is equal to that average rate of change. Explain why this statement does not contradict the Mean Value Theorem.

139. Suppose that g is defined for all real numbers x and is periodic with a period of length 10. The graph above shows one period of g. Find $G(10)$.

140. The function H is defined by $H(x) = g(\ln(x))$. Find an equation of the tangent line to the graph of H at the point where $x = \dfrac{1}{e}$.

141 – 142 * Let R be the region bounded by the graphs of $f(x) = \ln x$ and $g(x) = x - 3$.

141. * Find the volume of the solid generated when R is rotated about the y-axis.

142. * The region R is the base of a solid. For this solid, each cross section perpendicular to the x-axis is a square. Find the volume of the solid.

143 – 144 Let f be a twice-differentiable function that is defined for all real numbers and satisfies the following conditions:

$$f(1) = 3, f'(1) = 5, f''(1) = -2, f(3) = 2, f'(3) = 1, f''(3) = 0$$

143. Is there a value c for $1 < c < 3$ such that $f''(c) = -2$? Justify your answer.

144. The function g is given by $g(x) = f(x) + xe^{kx}$ for all real x, with k a constant. Find $g''(1)$ in terms of k.

* 145 – 150 For $t \geq 1$, a particle is moving along a curve so that its position at time t is $(x(t), y(t))$. At time $t = 2$, the particle is at position $(1,3)$. It is known that $\frac{dx}{dt} = \frac{\ln t}{\sqrt{t}}$ and $\frac{dy}{dt} = \sin^2 t$.

145. * Is the horizontal movement of the particle left or right at time $t = 2$? Justify your answer. Find the slope of the path of the particle at time $t = 2$.

146. * Find the y-coordinate of the particle's position at time $t = \frac{\pi}{2}$.

147. * Find the speed of the particle at time $t = \frac{\pi}{2}$.

148. * Find the acceleration vector of the particle at time $t = \frac{\pi}{2}$.

149. * Find the distance traveled by the particle from time $t = \frac{\pi}{2}$ to $t = 2$.

150. Find the time t, $1 \leq t \leq 4$, when the line tangent to the path of the particle is horizontal. Is the direction of the motion of the particle to the left or right at that time. Justify your answer.

200

151 – 156 The polar curves r_1 and r_2 are given by $r_1(\theta) = 6$ and $r_2(\theta) = 8 - 4\cos\theta$.

151. Sketch the graphs of r_1 and r_2, and shade the region D that is inside both the graphs of r_1 and r_2.

152. Find the area of the region D that is inside both the graphs of r_1 and r_2.

153. For the curve r_2, find the value of $\frac{dx}{d\theta}$ at $\theta = \frac{\pi}{3}$.

154. The distance between r_1 and r_2 changes for $0 \le \theta \le 2\pi$. Find the rate at which the distance between the two curves is changing with respect to θ when $\theta = \frac{\pi}{6}$.

155. A particle moves along the curve r_2 so that $\frac{d\theta}{dt} = 5$ for all times $t \ge 0$. Find the value of $\frac{dr_2}{dt}$ at $\theta = \frac{\pi}{6}$.

156. * A particle moves along the curve r_2 so that at time t, $\theta = 2t^3$. Find the time t in the interval $0 \le t \le 1$ for which the y-coordinate of the particle's position is 3. Then find the particle's position and velocity vectors in terms of t.

157 – 160 The function h has a Taylor series about $x = 5$ that converges to $h(x)$ for all x in the interval of convergence. The nth derivative of h at $x = 5$ is given by $h^{(n)}(5) = \frac{(-1)^n 2^n (n+1)!}{n3^n}$ for $n \ge 1$, and $h(5) = 1$.

157. Write the first four terms and the general term of the Taylor series for h about $x = 5$.

158. Find the radius of convergence for the Taylor series for h about $x = 5$. Justify your answer.

159. Find the interval of convergence for the Taylor series for h about $x = 5$. Justify your answer.

160. Let H be a function satisfying $H(5) = -6$ and $H'(x) = h(x)$ for all x. Write the first four terms and the general term of the Taylor series for H about $x = 5$. Does this Taylor series converge at $x = 3$?

201

LEVEL 1: DIFFERENTIATION

1. A

2. $\frac{-20}{3\sqrt[3]{x^7}} + x^x(1 + \ln x)$

3. $\frac{1}{3}\left(\frac{\sqrt{x}}{2(x+1)} + \arctan\sqrt{x}\right)$

4. $\frac{3\sqrt{2}}{8}$

5. $x^{\cot x}\left(\frac{\sin x \cos x - x \ln x}{x \sin^2 x}\right)$

6. $\frac{3[(x-2) + x(\ln 3)\log_3 x] - (x-2)(\ln 3)\log_3 x}{3(\ln 3)\sqrt[3]{x^4}}$

7. $\frac{3t\sqrt{1-t^4}}{2}$

8. $\langle 2, -4 \rangle$

LEVEL 1: INTEGRATION

9. $\frac{\ln(1+e^3)}{3}$

10. $-\frac{3}{4x^4} + 5\ln|x| - \frac{15\sqrt[3]{x^4}}{4} + 15\sqrt[5]{x} + C$

11. $\frac{\ln(\ln(3x^2+1))}{6} + C$

12. $= -\frac{3^x \cos x}{\ln 3} + C$

13. -2

14. 2.097 or 2.098

15. $\frac{\pi^2}{8}$

16. $1 + \ln\sqrt{\frac{3}{2}}$

17. .185

18. 14

202

LEVEL 1: LIMITS AND CONTINUITY

19. B
20. C
21. B
22. 16
23. −5
24. $\frac{1}{e}$
25. $3 - \sqrt{e}$
26. $-\infty$

LEVEL 1: SERIES

27. $\frac{5}{3}$
28. C
29. C
30. A
31. D
32. $-\frac{1}{3} \leq x \leq \frac{1}{3}$

LEVEL 2: DIFFERENTIATION

33. D
34. $\dfrac{15}{\sqrt{(2x^2 + 5)^3}}$
35. $\dfrac{127}{48}$
36. −2
37. $y - 1 = -2e(x - e)$ or $y = -2ex + 2e^2 + 1$
38. $y = e$
39. 7.389
40. A

LEVEL 2: INTEGRATION

41. $\frac{\pi}{12}$
42. $\sqrt{2} - 2$
43. 6
44. $50e^{-3} + 50$ pounds

45. $2\sqrt{3}$

46. $\ln(\sqrt{2} + 1)$

47. $(x^2 - 2x + 2)e^x + C$

48. π

49. $(-2,0)$

50. 10π

LEVEL 2: LIMITS AND CONTINUITY

51. D

52. $\frac{\sqrt{3}}{2}$

53. D

54. Yes, $g(\pi) = \lim_{x \to \pi^-} g(x) = \lim_{x \to \pi^+} g(x) = -e^{\pi}$

55. Yes, , $R(4) = \lim_{x \to 4^-} R(x) = \lim_{x \to 4^+} R(x) = 240$

56. $x = -1$ (removable), $x = 0$ (removable), $x = 2$ (nonremovable)

$$G(x) = \begin{cases} \frac{x^3 - 2x^2 - 3x}{2x^3 - 2x^2 - 4x}, & x \neq -1, 0 \\ \frac{2}{3}, & x = -1 \\ \frac{3}{4}, & x = 0 \end{cases}$$

LEVEL 2: SERIES

57. A

58. 3

59. D

60. A

61. $[3,7)$

62. $\ln 3 - x - \frac{x^2}{2} - \frac{x^3}{3}$

63. D

64. $\frac{\ln 2}{4e^2} \approx .023$

LEVEL 3: DIFFERENTIATION

65. A

66. $\frac{35}{3}$, 11.666, or 11.667

67. A

68. $\left(-\infty, -2 - \sqrt{2}\right) \cup \left(-2 + \sqrt{2}, \infty\right)$

69. $\dfrac{7}{6}$

70. rel. max: $(0,0)$, points of inflection: $(\pm 1, \ln 2)$

71.

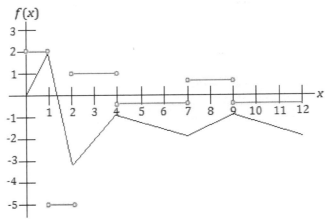

72. $\{x \mid x > -3 \text{ and } x \neq 0\}$

73. $\dfrac{y^3 \cos(xy^3) - ye^{xy}}{xe^{xy} - 3xy^2 \cos(xy^3)}$

74. $\dfrac{e^3 + 8}{e^3}$

75. B

76. 2

LEVEL 3: INTEGRATION

77. $\dfrac{1}{8}(\ln 3)^2$

78. $f(b^2 + 1) - f(a^2 + 1)$

79. $2(e^x + 1)$

80. $\dfrac{3}{\pi}\ln 3$

81. $\dfrac{1}{3\pi}$

82. $\dfrac{5st}{2} + 3j - 3k$

83. $\dfrac{1}{2}$

84. $2 + \log_2 3$

85. $\ln \frac{16}{15}$

86. C

87. A

88. 5

89. $8 + \pi + 3\sqrt{3}$

90. $\frac{2}{13} e^{2x} \sin 3x - \frac{3}{13} e^{2x} \cos 3x + C$

LEVEL 3: SERIES

91. $\frac{1}{60}$

92. D

93. $1 - \frac{5^2}{2!} + \frac{5^4}{4!} - \frac{5^6}{6!}$

94. .2955

95. $R = \frac{1}{4}, I = [\frac{11}{4}, \frac{13}{4}]$

96. $h(x) = -\frac{x}{2!} + \frac{x^3}{4!} - \frac{x^5}{6!} + \frac{x^7}{8!} - \frac{x^9}{10!} + \cdots + \frac{(-1)^n x^{2n-1}}{(2n)!} + \cdots$

   From the Maclaurin series for h we have $h'(0) = -\frac{1}{2!} = -\frac{1}{2}$.
   So $x = 0$ is *not* a critical number for h, and therefore h *does not* have a relative extremum at $x = 0$.

LEVEL 4: DIFFERENTIATION

97. A

98. $\frac{1}{25}$

99. $\frac{4}{\pi}$ in/sec

100. $k^{73} \cos kx$

101. rel max at $x = 0$, rel min at $x = -\sqrt{7}$ and $x = \sqrt{7}$, concave up on $(-\infty, -1)$, $(1, \infty)$, concave down on $(-1, 0)$, $(0, 1)$

102. $h(3.1) \approx -0.6$. The estimate is too small because $h''(x) > 0$ for $x > 0$.

103. No. By the Mean Value Theorem there must exist a c, $-3 < c < 5$ such that $g'(c) = \frac{11-3}{5-(-3)} = 1$.

104. 5, no because v is not differentiable at $t = 3$.

105. $\frac{dy}{dt} \approx -421.910$. The y-coordinate of the particle is decreasing at a rate of 421.91.

106. .320

107. $\langle -\frac{5}{4}, -\frac{1}{\pi^2} \rangle$

108. For $a < \theta < b$, the length of the radius r is increasing. Therefore the curve gets farther from the origin as the angle θ increases from a to b.

LEVEL 4: INTEGRATION

109. $y = \frac{1}{\sqrt{9-2x^2}}$, $-\frac{3}{\sqrt{2}} < x < \frac{3}{\sqrt{2}}$

110. $-\frac{5}{3}$

111. $y - .808 = -.932(x - 3.2)$ or $y = -.932x + 3.79$

112. 0.614

113. $\frac{5}{2} + 2\pi$

114. $A(t) = 10 + \int_0^t (K(u) - 7)\, du$
$A'(t) = K(t) - 7 = 0$ when $t \approx 2$, $A(0) = 10$, $A(2) \approx 7$,
$A(3) \approx 9$. So the maximum amount is 10 tons of bricks.

115. 1447.428

116. 6.514 or 6.515

117. $3\sqrt{17} + 12 + \ln 10 + \int_0^3 \sqrt{1 + \frac{4x^2}{(x^2+1)^2}}\, dx$

118. 55

119. B

120. $\frac{\pi}{8}$

121. 26.348

122. Area $= \frac{1}{2}\int_0^{\frac{\pi}{4}} (\sqrt{2})^2\, d\theta + \frac{1}{2}\int_{\frac{\pi}{4}}^{\frac{\pi}{2}} (2\cos\theta)^2\, d\theta$

LEVEL 4: SERIES

123. $h'(2) = 2$
$P_3(x) = -1 + 2(x - 2) - \frac{1}{4}(x - 2)^2 + \frac{1}{2}(x - 2)^3$

124. The first four terms of the Taylor series for h' are
$$-5 + \frac{25}{\sqrt{2}}(x-1) - \frac{125}{\sqrt{3}}(x-1)^2 + \frac{625}{2}(x-1)^3$$
The general term of the Taylor series for h' is
$$\frac{(-1)^n 5^n}{\sqrt{n}}(x-1)^{n-1} \text{ for } n \geq 1$$
$$I = (\tfrac{4}{5}, \tfrac{6}{5}]$$

125. $g(x) \approx 2x + x^2 + \frac{x^8}{2} + \frac{x^9}{12} + \frac{x^{11}}{6}$, $g^{(11)}(0) = 6{,}652{,}800$

126. $2 - 4x^6 + \frac{4}{3}x^{12} - 3x^{15}$

127. $\frac{5869}{4368}$ or 1.343 or 1.344

128. $P_6(x) = 2 - \frac{x^2}{2 \cdot 2!} + \frac{x^4}{4 \cdot 4!} - \frac{x^6}{6 \cdot 6!}$, $k(1) \approx 1.76019$

LEVEL 5: FREE RESPONSE QUESTIONS

129. $\int_0^5 M(t)dt = 18.001$ ft^3, $\int_0^5 N(t)dt = 25.247$ ft^3

130. $K(t) = 20 + \int_0^t (N(u) - M(u))\, du$

131. decreasing at a rate of 2.328 ft^3/hr

132. $K'(t) = 0$ when $N(t) = M(t)$, ie. when $t \approx 2.82$, $K(0) = 20$, $K(2.82) = 11.514$, $K(5) = 27.246$. So the amount of salt is a minimum when $t \approx 2.82$ hours, and the amount of salt is a maximum when $t = 5$ hours. The minimum value is 11.514 ft^3 and the maximum value is 27.246 ft^3.

133. $G(-2) = 6$, $G(5) = \frac{7\pi - 60}{4}$

134. $G'(x) = -3 + g(x)$, $G'(-1) = -3$, $G''(-1) = 3$

135. $G'(x) = 0$ when $g(x) = 3$. This occurs at $x = 0$. We also need to check the endpoints, $x = -5$ and $x = 5$. $G(-5) = 18$, $G(0) = 0$, $G(5) = \frac{7\pi - 60}{4}$. So G has an absolute maximum at $x = -5$.

136. The graph of G has a point of inflection at $x = 0$ and $x = 4$ because $G'' = g'$ changes sign at each of these values.

137. G is concave up when $G'' = g' > 0$, ie. when g is increasing. This occurs on the intervals $(-2, 0)$ and $(4, 5)$.

138. Average rate of change is -2. The statement does not contradict the Mean value Theorem because g is not differentiable at $x = -3$.

139. $\frac{7\pi - 132}{4}$

140. $y = 3ex - 3$

141. 63.881

142. 8.945

143. Yes. Since f is twice-differentiable, f' is differentiable. In particular, f' is continuous on $[1,3]$ and differentiable on $(1,3)$. The Mean Value Theorem guarantees that there is a value c, $1 < c < 3$ such that $f''(c) = \frac{f'(3)-f'(1)}{3-1} = -2$.

144. $-2 + k(k+2)e^k$

145. $\frac{dx}{dt}\Big|_{t=2} = \frac{\ln 2}{\sqrt{2}} > 0$. So the particle is moving right at time $t = 2$.

slope $= 1.686$ or 1.687

146. 2.596

147. 1.062 or 1.063

148. $\langle .393, 0 \rangle$

149. $.444$ or $.445$

150. $t = \pi$

Since $x'(\pi) = \frac{\ln \pi}{\sqrt{\pi}} > 0$, the particle is moving to the right at time $t = \pi$

151.

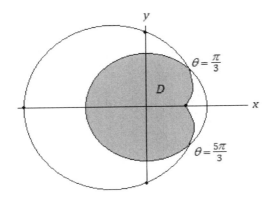

209

152. Area $= 24\pi + \int_0^{\frac{\pi}{3}}(8 - 4\cos\theta)^2 \, d\theta = 48\pi - 30\sqrt{3}$

153. $-2\sqrt{3}$

154. 2

155. 10

156. $y(t) = 3$ when $t = .693$

Position vector $= \langle x(t), y(t) \rangle =$
$\langle (8 - 4\cos(2t^3))\cos(2t^3), (8 - 4\cos(2t^3))\sin(2t^3) \rangle$

Velocity vector $= \langle x'(t), y'(t) \rangle =$
$\langle 48t^2\sin(2t^3)(\cos(2t^3) - 1), 24t^2(2\cos(2t^3) - \cos(4t^3)) \rangle$

157. $h(x) = 1 - \frac{4}{3}(x - 5) + \frac{2}{3}(x - 5)^2 - \frac{32}{81}(x - 5)^3 + \cdots +$
$\frac{(-1)^n(n+1)2^n}{n3^n}(x - 5)^n + \cdots$

158. $\lim_{n\to\infty} \left| \frac{\frac{(n+2)2^{n+1}}{(n+1)3^{n+1}}(x-5)^{n+1}}{\frac{(n+1)2^n}{n3^n}(x-5)^n} \right| = \frac{2}{3}|x - 5|$ which is less than 1 when

$|x - 5| < \frac{3}{2}$. So $R = \frac{3}{2}$.

159. $|x - 5| < \frac{3}{2}$ is equivalent to $\frac{7}{2} < x < \frac{13}{2}$.

When $x = \frac{7}{2}$, the series is $\sum_{n=0}^{\infty} \frac{n+1}{n}$ which diverges by the divergence test.

When $x = \frac{13}{2}$, the series is $\sum_{n=0}^{\infty}(-1)^n \frac{n+1}{n}$ which also diverges by the divergence test.

So $I = (\frac{7}{2}, \frac{13}{2})$.

160. $H(x) = -6 + (x - 5) - \frac{2}{3}(x - 5)^2 + \frac{2}{9}(x - 5)^3$

$+ \cdots + \frac{(-1)^{n-1}2^{n-1}}{(n-1)3^{n-1}}(x - 5)^n + \cdots$

This Taylor series does not converge at $x = 3$.

ACTIONS TO COMPLETE AFTER YOU HAVE READ THIS BOOK

1. **Continue to practice AP Calculus problems for 20 to 30 minutes each day**

   Keep practicing problems of the appropriate levels until two days before the exam.

2. **Use my Forum page for additional help**

   If you feel you need extra help that you cannot get from this book, please feel free to post your questions in the AP Calculus section of my forum at

   # www.satprepget800.com/forum

3. **Review this book**

   If this book helped you, please post your positive feedback on the site you purchased it from; e.g. Amazon, Barnes and Noble, etc.

4. **Sign up for free updates**

   If you have not done so yet, visit the following webpage and enter your email address to receive updates and supplementary materials for free including additional AP Calculus AB problems with solutions.

   # www.thesatmathprep.com/320APCalSup.html

About the Author

Steve Warner, a New York native, earned his Ph.D. at Rutgers University in Pure Mathematics in May, 2001. While a graduate student, Dr. Warner won the TA Teaching Excellence Award.

After Rutgers, Dr. Warner joined the Penn State Mathematics Department as an Assistant Professor. In September, 2002, Dr. Warner returned to New York to accept an Assistant Professor position at Hofstra University. By September 2007, Dr. Warner had received tenure and was promoted to Associate Professor. He has taught undergraduate and graduate courses in Precalculus, Calculus, Linear Algebra, Differential Equations, Mathematical Logic, Set Theory and Abstract Algebra.

Over that time, Dr. Warner participated in a five year NSF grant, "The MSTP Project," to study and improve mathematics and science curriculum in poorly performing junior high schools. He also published several articles in scholarly journals, specifically on Mathematical Logic.

Dr. Warner has over 15 years of experience in general math tutoring and over 10 years of experience in AP Calculus tutoring. He has tutored students both individually and in group settings.

In February, 2010 Dr. Warner released his first SAT prep book "The 32 Most Effective SAT Math Strategies." The second edition of this book was released in January, 2011. In February, 2012 Dr. Warner released his second SAT prep book "320 SAT Math Problems arranged by Topic and Difficulty Level." Between September 2012 and January 2013 Dr. Warner released his three book series "28 SAT Math Lessons to Improve Your Score in One Month." In June, 2013 Dr. Warner released the "SAT Prep Official Study Guide Math Companion." In November, 2013 Dr. Warner released the "ACT Prep Red Book – 320 Math Problems With Solutions." Between May 2014 and July 2014 Dr. Warner released "320 SAT Math Subject Test Problems arranged by Topic and Difficulty Level." for the Level 1 and Level 2 tests. In November, 2014 Dr. Warner released "320 AP Calculus AB Problems arranged by Topic and Difficulty Level."

BOOKS BY DR. STEVE WARNER

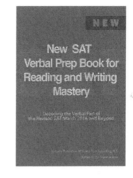
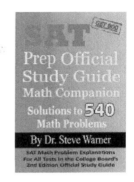

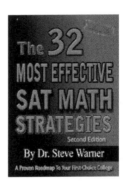

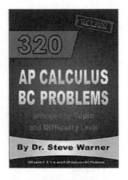

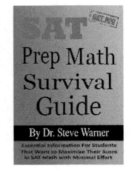

Made in the USA
Lexington, KY
11 August 2016